Catholic Scholars Dialogue with Luther

Jared Wicks, S.J., Editor

Joseph Lortz
Erwin Iserloh
Otto H. Pesch, O.P.
Paul Hacker
Harry J. McSorley, C.S.P.
Peter Manns

Warren A. Quanbeck, Afterword

LOYOLA UNIVERSITY PRESS
Chicago 60657

© 1970 Loyola University Press

Library of Congress Catalog Card Number: 78-105429
SBN 8294-0181-4

Cover photograph,
"Ghent, Belgium,"
from
Photographs / Algimantas Kezys, S.J.
Loyola University Press, 1966.

INTRODUCTION BY THE EDITOR

This collection of essays on Luther's theology hopes to be a substantial though economical introduction to a theological and ecumenical venture of great promise. In the words of George Lindbeck, "Catholic Luther scholarship has come of age." The authors of our six studies are committed Roman Catholics who share the distinction of being full-fledged members of the international band of Luther scholars. Each of them has written on Luther at greater length in works published in Germany. Our present collection seeks to introduce them to the English-speaking world and to draw attention to the conclusions they have reached through their immersion in Luther's works.

Each essay offers in its own way an evaluation of Luther's theology from a Catholic standpoint. In face of the complexity of Luther--so well described in Joseph Lortz' essay--our contributors vary considerably in their judgments. Their positive evalu-

ations often lead to more nuanced criticisms. This is the way of any serious work in the field of religious and theological history. Luther presents special problems by reason of his vastness and the long tradition of apologetic treatments of his work by both Protestants and Roman Catholics. What our contributors seek is not a simplistic rehabilitation of Luther among Catholics, but rather a more sensitive treatment freed from pseudo-problems and alert to the deeper intention and peculiar style of his work.

Of equal importance with this evaluative work is the contribution these essays make toward clarifying Luther's theological method and toward further elucidating his doctrine of sin and salvation. Thus we hope that this volume will be the occasion for Lutheran readers to come to a deeper understanding of the man they honor as the prophetic renewer of Christianity.

The essays center around two foci of interest. Joseph Lortz begins by setting forth Luther's thoroughly original style of doing theology. Erwin Iserloh develops this more methodological theme by pointing out the mystical strain in Luther's work. Paul Hacker draws attention to Luther's overriding concern to relate salvation to the Ego or self. Peter Manns shows how Luther's deep involvement in polemics inhibited his development of important Catholic themes he had nonetheless affirmed. Otto Pesch unfolds his thesis that Luther was an "existential," not a "sapiential," theologian-- an analysis that sums up well this first concern of our book.

A second focus of interest is Luther's vision of man under God's judgment and justifying grace. Joseph Lortz singles out Luther's intense interest in the paradoxes of this situation of the Christian man. Erwin Iserloh amasses texts attesting to Luther's rich conception of Christ's vital, operative presence in the life of the Christian. Harry McSorley brings needed clarity on Luther's often misunderstood polemic against "free will" in sinful man. Otto Pesch points to the themes dominating the prayer of the justified sinner. Paul Hacker's critical contribution submits Luther's idea of saving faith to the acid test of comparison with the New Testament. Finally, Peter Manns' careful reading of Luther's magisterial Commentary on Galatians (1531-1535) shows the unmistakably Catholic thesis at the center of Luther's theology of grace.

The concentration of our six essays brings with it the advantage that they complement, enrich, and even criticize each other. Their attention to the doctrines of sin, freedom, faith, and saving grace accords well with Luther's own description of theology: "The proper subject of theology is man guilty of sin and condemned, and

viii

God the Justifyer and Savior of man the sinner" (<u>Exposition</u> of <u>Psalm</u> <u>51</u>). Admittedly, we leave important areas of Luther's work, such as sacramental doctrine and ecclesiology, untouched. Studies in these areas would surely lead to thornier problems of evaluation. Let us hope that in five years there will be enough intensive studies of Luther's work on these topics to warrant a second Catholic collection.

One of our contributors, Otto H. Pesch, O.P., has surveyed the work done by Catholics on Luther since the Second World War. The reader is referred to his article, "Twenty Years of Catholic Luther Research," in <u>Lutheran</u> <u>World</u>, Vol. XIII (1966), pages 303-316, for an overview of all the books, articles and dissertations that make up this Catholic reassessment of the person and work of Martin Luther. We prefer not to extend our Introduction by going over this ground again. In our introductions to the studies in this collection, we have reported on the respective roles our contributors have played in the first stages of this scholarly project

I speak for the contributors and for myself in thanking Warren Quanbeck for the thoughtful "Afterword" in which he has made this book a true dialogue. I am grateful to Mr. Calvin Schmidt and his associates at the McGaw Memorial Library of McCormick Theological Seminary for their help as I prepared these essays for English publication. I also want to thank Paul Hacker for translating his contribution into English, and William Seidensticker for collaborating on the translation of the essays by Joseph Lortz and Peter Manns. I have myself translated the contributions of Erwin Iserloh and Otto Pesch.

May these studies lead all our readers, whether Catholic or Protestant, into the center of the encounter with Luther and thus serve to enrich them by bringing their life and thought under the stirring influence of his Christian witness.

Jared Wicks, S.J.
Bellarmine School of Theology
North Aurora, Illinois 60542

October 1, 1969

Introduction to Joseph Lortz

Joseph Lortz, born in Luxemburg in 1887, has contributed decisively to the Catholic understanding of the Reformation and to the reassessment of the towering figure of Martin Luther. The story of the Catholic
portrayal of Luther through the past four centuries has been told often--
recently, for instance, by Leonard Swidler in Chapter 2 of The Ecumenical Vanguard (Duquesne, 1966). In this story, the critical turning
point is always the appearance in 1939 of the first volume of Joseph
Lortz' history of the Reformation in Germany. With Lortz' great 300-
page essay on Luther, Catholics left behind the unscrupulous hatred of
Cochlaeus (whose legends of 1549 turned up monotonously in Catholic
works on Luther for over 350 years), the charges of immorality and
ignorance leveled by Denifle, and the cold and onesided reading of Grisar.
Where stormy polemic had blurred our vision, Lortz' sensitive portrayal of Luther's deeply religious intentions created a new atmosphere where
understanding--and even some significant agreement--was possible. In
late 1968 Herder and Herder released the long awaited English translation of Lortz' The Reformation in Germany.

Joseph Lortz pursued his theological studies at the Gregorian University and at Fribourg in Switzerland, leading to ordination in 1913. After
further work in Church History at the University of Bonn he received the
doctorate in 1919. Lortz first taught at Würzburg and Braunsberg, and
in 1935 he took over the chair of Church History in the Catholic theology
faculty in Münster. In 1950 Lortz accepted the invitation to become co-
director of the Institute for European History in Mainz, where he has
since exercised wide influence in promoting research and publications
on late medieval and Reformation topics.

Especially in the years immediately after the Second World War,
Lortz gave himself untiringly to popular lecturing in connection with
ecumenical activities, once being dubbed "the wandering preacher of
the Una Sancta movement." In recent years his own research has concentrated on Luther and led most recently to articles on Luther's theology of the Church and of the sacraments in the transition years 1518-
1519 even as Lortz' eighty-third birthday approached.

As a historian Joseph Lortz' primary interest has been the history of
ideas, whereby he sought to sketch the overriding thematic and wider
context within which investigations of detailed questions can lead to
genuine understanding of epochs and great figures. Lortz has never immersed himself in the past for its own sake, but has seen it as the heritage that can burden us, fructify our lives, and pose us ever new challenges. Many will recognize these characteristics of his historical interest and method from his smaller works, How the Reformation Came
(Herder and Herder, 1966) and The Reformation: A Problem for Today
(Newman, 1964).

The following essay was first given as a lecture in 1964 inaugurating a new phase of concentration on Luther studies at the Catholic Ecumenical Institute in Münster. Here we present a translation of the printed version that appeared in the Festschrift for Hubert Jedin, Reformata Reformanda (Münster: Aschendorff, 1965). Lortz asks about the characteristics of Luther's thinking and writing that must be singled out to make up the framework of any successful study in detail. He asks about Luther's geistige Eigenart, the original, utterly personal, all-pervasive spiritual-intellectual stamp that Luther left on everything he said or wrote. Lortz' answer comes as a valuable reformulation of his earlier theses: Luther's central, overriding concern was the affirmation of a Catholic doctrine; much of the Church of Luther's day was corrupt enough to fail to see this; but Luther's polemical and one-sided formulation of his concern made division inevitable--but not irreparable.

Notes begin on page 167.

The Basic Elements of
Luther's Intellectual Style

Joseph Lortz

THE PROBLEMS IN APPROACHING LUTHER

It is a difficult undertaking to attempt a valid and comprehensive interpretation of even the most basic elements of Luther's
thought within the scope of one article. With Luther as with no
one else it is easy to sketch distortedly, a fact that found formulation in Heinrich Boehmer's well-known statement, "There are
as many Luthers as there are books about Luther."[1] This judgment received corroboration in Wilhelm Link's survey of contemporary scholarship twenty years ago.[2] Such a situation opens up
a number of questions.

Should we accept this condition as fixed and unchangeable?
Should we subscribe to A. Brandenburg's judgment that one can
prove anything and everything out of Luther?[3] But this would be
to declare bankruptcy for historical research in the study of the
towering figure of Luther.[4]

Or should we accept the thesis that Luther can be understood with exactitude only with respect to isolated details? The determination of details is certainly the indispensable first step in the study of Luther, and we will see the reason for this shortly. But investigations of detail are satisfactory only to the extent that we approach a scientifically valid, comprehensive interpretation. The study of Luther's early lectures on the Psalms (1513-1515) and on the Epistle to the Romans (1515-1516) is essential, but this does not afford an adequate conception of the whole Luther. Actually, one can show that in many ways these lectures bear the stamp of uniqueness.

Or, following Rudolph Hermann, should we limit ourselves to Luther's "solemn" statements?[5] Rather, should we not probe beneath and behind the theological formulations to grasp Luther's own specific concerns? The formulae, we shall see, are not a perfectly consistent unity. It is startling, but we actually do not have detailed investigations of Luther's major theological concepts that would trace these concepts (such as justification, faith, faith and works, faith and love, the Church) continuously through all of his vast writings. This makes it difficult for the researcher, but it hardly justifies a false modesty that would limit our study to the early works.

We should rather make a virtue of necessity and try to view the young and the mature Luther together in as balanced a manner as possible. It is certainly possible to locate decisive patterns of his Reformation thinking, certain central ideas and theses, both in the early Luther as well as in the later, more mature Reformer. But then again, what a difference there is between the early lectures and, say, the 1531 Lectures on Galatians. The mature Luther is no longer the genial attacker of the Lectures on Romans. From this mature Luther it would be difficult to extract an existentialist theologian.

The problems of an adequate treatment of Luther are obvious from several points of view. First, Luther is an intellectual giant, or, to use a word from Paul Althaus, an "ocean."[6] The danger of drowning in him, of not being able to come to grips with him satisfactorily, arises from his tremendous output, but no less from his own original style, which we are going to take up. It sounds banal, but cannot be left unsaid: Luther belongs in the first rank of men with extraordinary intellectual creativity. He is in the full sense a genius, a man of massive power in things religious and a giant as well in theological interpretation. Because of this, he has in many respects shaped the history of the world--even of our world

4

today. For Luther is the Reformation. Consequently, we cannot speak of him with detachment and from a distance. With him we do not have mere data, but truly history; for he works on us and makes demands of us today.

Second, it is a fact that Luther often returns to the same few fundamental theses. He initiated an impressive movement aimed at simplifying the bewildering complexity of ideas and structures in Church, preaching, and theology. He takes us back to the Gospel and to its few fundamental themes, particularly that of justification.

In a certain sense, this reduction is a boon to analysis. But at the same time and in at least the same measure it makes the task more difficult. First, there is the variety of expressions Luther used to articulate the same idea, a variety conditioned profoundly and complexly by such factors as the struggle marking his inner development, his inspiring and wide-ranging polemic, the deep impress on him of particular situations, and the pervasive presence of paradox in his thought and expression. In short, the greatest difficulty in an adequate treatment of Luther is Luther himself. As a thinker, he is, above all else, a phenomenon of life-activity. But how does one go about depicting life-activity? It must speak for itself, and thus we are forced to turn to Luther's own words.

The huge literature on Luther presents many profound and valuable analyses, albeit with conflicts among them, which do bring us close to his thought. However, they see him almost exclusively as a theologian and give us ideas excerpted from him. But is this the authentic Luther?

One must spend a lifetime in intimate contact with Luther, ever working one's way into him anew, as did Paul Althaus, in order to write such a masterful book as his Theology of Martin Luther. This book not only deals correctly with the major issues but probes deeply into the more subtle ramifications of Luther's thinking. Significantly, Althaus' many citations and his own language keep his book close to Luther's own wording. It is a book which we do not intend--even ever so gently--to leave aside.

Still, even so rich a book as Althaus' work poses these same questions and difficulties, and in particular a problem which has long troubled me and which I brought up years ago. It is the fact that even the most conscientious and accurate presentation of the contents of a work of Luther's offers at best a pale reflection of Luther's own thinking. Wherever Luther is sketched, one feels the gulf between the man and what is said about him. One is tempted simply to quote him--his wonderful outpouring of self, his tireless thrust to discover and express, his massive power, the immeasurable height, breadth, and depth of the message, the as- tounding vitality and fullness present in this man so captivated by the spirit of Scripture. And all of this--in spite of the constant repetitions.

But Luther's power, on the other hand, is intimately connected with--and often disturbed by--an impulsive tendency to stray from his theme, to be uncritical, overbearing, and distortive. But then this occurs with his appealing and often sensitively phrased naiveté. In any case we must question just how much one can intellectually abstract and formulate of Luther's thought.

We have, of course, no other alternative than to set out in this direction and make an attempt. It is already a contribution to the study of Luther to have recognized the limited possibilities of anal- ysis, and it is a step toward a solution to be aware of such limits.

We add immediately that this style of Luther's we have just described stems primarily from the prophetic-religious style of biblical thought and language. Even here, however, we must add an important complementary reservation: Luther came from a long theological tradition, and despite his renunciation of this tradition he never ceased to speak as a theologian dealing with binding doctrine.

Finally, there is the question of a Catholic's approach to Luther. I wonder if one still needs a special effort to "get in tune" with Luther?

Actually, I speak no differently about Luther than do Protestant scholars, with scholarship of course entailing critical observa- tion. I do not speak polemically,[7] although naturally I cannot omit the eventual critical judgment. However, we are not impeded today by the particular difficulties Catholics had to overcome earlier with regard to Luther. Our situation makes it possible for us to deal justly even with him whom earlier writers saw exclusive- ly as the principal opponent of the late medieval, hierarchical church, as the enemy of the sacramental priesthood, the papacy, monasticism, and the mass.

I would not say that all Catholic historians and theologians wholly agree with this position. There are Catholics, and Protestants too, who relish the fixity of the past, but these have no direct influence on scholarship. In addition, this more "advanced" Catholic scholarship is gaining ground as well on more official levels in the Church.

Today I would even go so far as to ask whether the Catholic scholar might not be in a better position to understand Luther adequately than the Protestant researcher. First, we can take it for granted that we have abandoned the evaluative categories of a Cochlaeus, which dominated for over 400 years, and those of the great Denifle, and even those of Grisar (who was particularly well-versed in details). This assumption holds also for Italy, Spain, and Latin America. Gradually Catholics have come to recognize the Christian, and even Catholic, richness of Luther, and they are impressed. They now realize how great the Catholic guilt was that Luther was expelled from the Church to begin the division that burdens us so today--even in theology. Finally, we are anxious to draw Luther's richness back into the Church.

Whether the freedom of the Protestant scholar with regard to the hero of the Reformation is equally as great is by no means an idle question, but it is not one I will attempt to answer here. True, we must admit that it is only recently that Catholics have learned to take deep draughts from Luther's works and to gain an intimate acquaintance with them. With Protestant Christians and theologians the situation is quite different. Luther has been a source of life for them for generations. They have learned at home, so to speak, to live quite naturally inside Luther's skin. But we must somehow work our way inside in order to view from within things that, up to now, we have seen only from without. But even this entails a certain advantage for the Catholic. He finds himself both at a critical distance from Luther and at the same time has easier access to certain original, deep-set Catholic values of the Reformation.

Thirty years ago, in The Reformation in Germany, I put forth the thesis with regard to the central Reformation article, justification by faith alone, that Luther here rediscovered an old Catholic doctrine, which though was new for him and seen onesidedly.[8] In the meantime I have not abandoned this view. On the contrary, Luther is, in fact, more Catholic than I then realized.

If we were to start from here, we would then have to deal with the question of the "Catholic Luther."[9] But this would take us beyond the space available here.[10] I can only say that in affirming a "Catholic Luther" I do not mean that with the passage of time and with his growing animosity toward the papacy Luther became less and less Catholic.

The notion of a straight and single-purposed development from the young to the old Luther must be entirely rejected if one wants to give an exhaustive account of this phenomenon. For it can be shown that Luther's development resembles a series of irregular waves which come together from different directions and with different force to reach a peak then followed by a depression. The main stream has an undercurrent, or rather several such currents, so that Luther's whole life contains Catholic elements, which are found in, along with, or even opposed to, the Reformation elements. This complex situation explains the great difficulty in answering the disturbing question about the content of the specifically "Reformation element" in Luther.

Even after the decisive years of breakthrough and spiritual readjustment into what we call "Reformation," Luther continued in many ways to grow. And in this growth his Catholic reading exerted a positive influence. And here, what an amazing vitality! What a sensitivity to new situations and perspectives! What an untiring intellectual curiosity!

In Luther's development there occur also a number of shifts of accent confirming his table remarks about how he was later not as sure of himself as his usual robust tone suggests and more than suggests. He was not so thoroughly Protestant as to prevent several passages of Scripture apparently supporting the Catholic position, for example on good works and on charity, from posing themselves to him as fundamental and disturbing problems.

Today though it is no longer so much Luther's powerful personality, explosive development, and fullness of activity sending shock waves through his world that interests scholars in Luther. Most turn to the theology and piety of this towering man. But in this respect the Luther portrayal of contemporary scholarship can be shown to be inadequate. I should like to record here my own strong reservations against such narrow scholarship.

In his class lectures, sermons, books, and table remarks, Luther was an active personality. The works marking the major steps of his development--his early lectures on the Psalms and on Romans, the Disputations in Heidelberg and Leipzig, his reform writings of 1520, his works of liturgical renewal, the lectures and disputations of the 1530's and 1540's--have all formed human history. This was not merely because of their theological content, but also because of their power of expression and the personal strength that permeates them. Luther was not simply a theologian. In fact, he was very seldom and only briefly just a theologian, even in the classroom. He was more than all else a believer, a prophet, and a battler. To this day, Luther's works have retained much of his vitality. Thus they are not adequately understood when their abstract theological content is extracted and repeated. Successful interpretation must be tinged with prophecy. As we look back at Luther, we must bring out Luther's many instinctively sure resonances with historical developments in the world and in the Church. We must show the mutual influence between Luther and history.

8

All of this leads to an important conclusion: we should not demand too much from Luther as a theologian. We would be doing
him an injustice, and at the same time do a disservice to present
and future Christians. It seems to be necessary to inquire into
the peculiar style of Luther's thought. Basically, this is my purpose in what follows.

THE STYLE OF LUTHER'S THOUGHT

The dominance of will and feeling

Luther was a theologian of the highest rank. My previous posi-
tion--that Luther was not a theologian--was therefore misleading.[11]
But the decisive question is <u>how</u> one is a theologian. Luther cannot
be analyzed like Ockham, Duns Scotus, or even Thomas Aquinas,
who, in spite of everything, stands much closer to him.
Rudoph Hermann raised a fundamental problem when he asserted
that Luther was dominantly an intellectual type.[12] This I cannot
accept. Luther was rather a man of will and was influenced by
deeply felt emotions. He worked explosively and eruptively, and
this temperament stamped deeply his intellectual work.
If this aspect of Luther be brought into an analysis based on
sufficient factual material, then we have the basis for an adequate
interpretation not merely of a segment of Luther's work, but of
the bulk of his theological writings. We can thereby understand
his early development, including the Reformation breakthrough
in the so-called tower experience. Unfortunately, his breakthrough
does not lend itself to easy and precise explanation because, like
so many of the related spiritual events in Luther's life, it was not
only an act of receptive understanding, but a creative experience
that grew out of deep spiritual struggling. And then Luther's own
later remembrances of this event were not mere descriptions of
a past experience but were themselves basically testimony and
proclamation.
The thorny problems connected with Luther's remembrances
are well known. However, if we are to avoid turning Luther into
an insincere rhetorician, we cannot deny that what we may call
his "Reformation breakthrough" was bound up with a deep spiritual
experience of inner distress, spiritual struggle, and finally deliverance. This central point shows up quite clearly in Luther's
autobiographical preface to his Latin works in 1545, but is also
clear in 1518 in the letter to Staupitz accompanying the <u>Resolutiones</u>
of the theses on indulgences. We can also see this experiential fac-

tor in table remark No. 5518, where Luther captures the sense of triumph in the words, "There is where I broke through."

However the detailed contents of this event are to be assessed in detail, even after this experience Luther continued to grow. The circumstances of his growth were not only his powerful and complex internal struggle, but as well his many involvements both on the defensive and on the attack, whether against Rome, the radical enthusiasts, the peasants, Anabaptists, Jews, and time and time again in personal and often heated disputes with the legalistic papists.

Because of this engagement of Luther's will, our research should be careful to avoid demanding too much of him as a theologian. I believe scholars have sinned often in this regard up to now.

Let there be no misunderstanding. Luther was a man of rare intelligence, as his works reveal. Examples are endless, beginning with the numerous passages in his early lectures which even today give the mind such a bushel of nuts to crack. Think of the Heidelberg Disputation and of the peculiar, scholastically conceived explanations found in the lectures on Galatians in 1531. All of this stands without question.

But amid even the theses and disputations we also discern the powerful and even violent warrior who works from emotion. The theses on indulgences are a striking and familiar example of this phenomenon. We could examine this point more in detail, because its importance is deeper than has been recognized to date. I need only mention the term "experience" to indicate one aspect of what I mean and to focus attention on the complexity of the matter. For Luther, not only is the whole of being a Christian a matter of experience, but in particular theology is a sapientia experimentalis, non doctrinalis.[13] To indicate how deep a problem "experience" is in Luther studies, we need only recall that W. von Loewenich's book on Luther's "theology of the cross" devotes a chapter to faith as beyond experience, and another to faith as experienced. One does not exaggerate in terming this state of affairs disturbing.

It is instructive to note that in a table remark Luther once went so far as to say that his terrifying temptations and disputes with the devil over the Incarnation and the Trinity had brought him so far that he no longer "believed" these articles of faith, but rather, "I know by experience."[14]

One must also consider how Luther's strained and tormented conscience plays a dominant role, so much so that "temptation" was for him both the sign of the true theologian[15] and a key factor

10

in his own sense of vocation.[16] This is the tormented conscience that all too easily revealed itself in Luther's writings--not always in a manner harmonious with the New Testament--and that has thereby gained such a strange hold on the linguistic usage of Lutheranism.

A number of questions come to the fore here that can be grouped under such categories as "psychological introspection," "sense of responsibility," "defiance of responsibility," "crudity," "scrupulosity," "spiritual instability," etc. In this regard it is true that Luther suffered injustice from Grisar and Reiter, and more recently from the American psychologist, Erik H. Erikson, but the factual situation still exists and must be critically assessed.[17]

Luther's sense of responsibility coexists with daring defiance of responsibility. His crudity is an indicative factor, one that extends into his impulsive hatred for and rejection of the papacy. Nevertheless along with this trait we find an all-embracing, pastoral drive which--as with St. Paul--impels him to share the sufferings of all. And then again, the ever present scrupulosity and temptations!

All of this, taken together with Luther's realization of faith, which is also an experience of faith,[18] stamps Luther's huge life's work in manifold ways. It would, it seems to me, be false to gloss over these elements as intellectually irrelevant. It is critically inadmissable that they be omitted as basic elements of the style of Luther's thought.

Linguistic genius--paradox and exaggeration

What we have just discussed is particularly important for the Luther exegete, because these elements leave their mark on Luther's highly individual linguistic style.

Every great man rightfully demands that attention be paid to his uniqueness, including his uniqueness of language. In Luther's case, this claim takes on a special urgency. He emerged from a tradition that had developed a fixed technical language, the scholastic idiom, but he broke out of this tradition with great originality. He expressed new ideas partly under the guise of the old terminology, but in boldly novel formulations which can be exactly interpreted only with great difficulty even by those used to the old modes of expression.

The difficulties posed by Luther's mode of thought and style of expression are so great that extensive efforts are still required to set the facts in order and to reveal possible regularities of Luther's usage of which we are not yet aware. One of the most demanding tasks for Luther scholars lies in deciding the question of Luther's consistency or inconsistency. This compact statement contains what is formally the most important problem of Luther scholarship. We will now investigate how far this insight takes us toward understanding Luther and his constant thinking in terms of opposites.

Luther's style of language is not only elegant--concrete, lively, engaging--but it is essential to what he has to say. In fact we shall never attain the desired scholarly opinio communis about Luther, unless we have many penetrating investigations into the formal structural elements of his thought and style that go beyond previous efforts.

We can begin with four specific points:

1 Luther was a genius with language. Spontaneously his thoughts found concrete expression in the most sensitive of linguistic phrasing. It would perhaps be more exact to say that his thoughts take form in words.[19] In any case, with Luther thought and word are to a great extent one. This fact goes far toward explaining their particular forcefulness and true power. At the same time, it accentuates the difficulties, noted above, of delineating their content with all its living and radiantly diversified reality.

2 Along with Luther's genius, however, we find an inclination toward amplification, a verbosity, which leads to repetitious and careless use of successive, inexact synonyms. We shall examine the scope of this trait more carefully later on. In 1535 this verbosity surprised Luther himself when he was shown the notes of his lectures on Galatians that had been prepared for publication. He came to admit this trait as one of his vices, when he once distinguished himself from Melanchthon: "I am a prattler, much more the orator."[20] Luther can be clear and penetrating, but to a greater extent he is complicated.

3 Luther's strictly theological lectures and disputations constitute a special group among his writings. Although among them abundant passages are marked by verbosity and complexity, there are also passages written with outstanding technical mastery of scholastic method. We often think we are back in the milieu of the late medieval disputation. Luther was aware of this ability and boasted of it before his Catholic opponents.[21]

This scholastic terminology was in part the expression of theological points of view which Luther attacked vigorously. He rejected them sharply, but, in the last analysis, not with complete success. The opponent of the scholastics remained himself a scholastic.

4 Difficulties arise in any critical reading of Luther because of his frequent lack of logical clarity, particularly in his numerous forced overstatements. The early polemical term, Doctor Hyperbolicus, is unfortunately to a surprising extent correct.[22] There

is in Luther a high degree of superlativism.

Luther's frequent use of unrestrained exaggeration, especially in his polemics against papists, enthusiasts, and even against his former follower Agricola in the Antinomian controversy,[23] presents us with serious theological and more basically human problems. I see it as a state of emergency that scholarship has not thought it worthwhile to investigate this question more in detail. Of course, the superlatives should not always be pressed from a theological point of view. We must be somewhat lenient with Luther, taking account of the religious and pastoral situation, understanding Luther's great vitality in different polemical and threatened situations. His overriding aim of saving the Gospel and justification by faith from sub-Christian reduction to commercialism absorbed his attention with such urgency and totality that overstatements become understandable.

But there are other works of Luther that cannot be so saved from criticism, for instance his 1533 tract on the Mass and priestly ordination. He went so far as to contend that in the Roman Mass there is nothing but mere bread and wine. He burdens his treatment with quite intolerable and superficially grounded overstatements. This significant trait, which stamps the whole work, also appears in the form of an extraordinary unevenness of emotional tone. Luther can follow a very profound statement with a bewildering overstatement with apparently the same degree of seriousness.[24]

This set of questions gains its full historical significance in view of Luther's extensive authority in his lifetime, and the fact that through 400 years it was not seldom that precisely these exaggerations exerted significant influence.

One can only make this wholly clear by going into details. The material is inexhaustible for him whose eyes are open. Those well acquainted with Luther are perhaps too used to neglecting this aspect of his work. For Luther's works are filled with inexactitude and fluctuation both in terminology and in the emotionally accented style of expression. For instance, Luther intensifies the promise of forgiveness of sin to the extent that no sins of any kind need disturb the conscience except unbelief.[25] He can say that after the bestowal of forgiveness no harm can come, "no matter how gravely, how intensely, or how often one may sin."[26] Wilfried Joest rightly pointed out that if it were not the case that other passages express the possibility that we, the children of the Heavenly Father, may become His enemies, we should be deeply shocked at the seductive power of such words, which, taken in themselves, seem to be identical with the position St. Paul sharply rejects in Romans 6:15. Joest then asks if one can really take comfort in Luther's guarantee of the harmlessness of sin. Although we know that this is not what Luther intends, Joest can only judge Luther's wording as a theological blunder.[27]

The most important aspect of Luther's linguistic style, from a theological point of view, is its addiction to paradox. This trait stems basically from the Bible, and more precisely from St. Paul's letters to the Romans, Galatians, and Corinthians. This poses the problem of Luther's terminology in a narrower perspective.

It is the opinion of Ihmels and Bizer that Luther was too little concerned about terminology to place any value on refined distinctions.[28] Unfortunately, this is true, but the problem is thereby intensified, not eliminated.

In the Heidelberg Disputation (1518) Luther referred to his theses as paradoxes.[29] Paradoxical formulation, in his mind, represents the search for the denial within the affirmation, for the affirmation within the denial, and for the revelation of contradiction as the mirror of truth. Luther pursues this search by means of constant accumulation of pairs of opposites.

The pattern of hiddenness (absconditas) was of fundamental importance for Luther. This is his doctrine of the hidden God-- the God who veils himself in the midst of his self-revealing actions. This is revelation in and through God's hiddenness. Here we have Luther's penchant for thinking in opposites and his well-known category of God being hidden beneath contrary appearances. In 1515-1516, this involuted thought caused Luther to present the message of the Epistle to the Romans in a manner much more complex than we find even in the depths of Paul's original text.

Luther did not simply devise the paradoxes he used in describing revelation. It came in part from Paul, and even more so from the cross. Luther saw the kenosis manifest in Christ crucified, where the divinity is emptied in humiliation even to the real experience of being forsaken by God. Thus absconditas is the cognitive form in which Luther formulates and expresses the mystery presented to us in revelation, particularly in the cross.

Luther's starting points are Galatians 3:13 ("Christ became a curse for us") and Second Corinthians 5:21 (Christ "made sin" on our behalf). Luther accepts these texts with complete seriousness and not only as pious figures of speech. Thus Christ becomes "the sin of our sin," the "sin" in which our sins die, as they change from holding reign to being under dominance (from peccatum regnans to peccatum dominatum).

14

The further unfolding of this insight brings in endless cumulation the paradoxical identification of pairs of opposites, love-hate, free man-servant, heaven-hell, life-death, flesh-spirit, letter-spirit, law-gospel, action-passion, and most frequently sinner-just. All these are contained in, and supported by, a fundamental eschatological vision, which itself bears its own paradoxical traits. For revelation and salvation are guaranteed, but not absolutely guaranteed for specific individuals. Revelation and salvation are present, but not entirely so. We sinners are not healed, but being cured (non sani, sed sanandi), but nevertheless already cured (sani). We are justified but not perfectly so; salvation is suspended in hope and is given not in re but in spe.[30]

Here the decisive question is whether the contradictory tension denies the positive, as appears to be the case, or actually affirms it in a more intense manner. Luther's paradoxical thought is most clearly present in his "at once just and a sinner" (simul iustus et peccator). Here our question about the denial of the positive side poses itself most intensely. This is especially true when Luther speaks of two totalities: totus iustus, totus peccator.[31]

The importance of explaining this paradoxical simul can hardly be overstated. Its function in Luther's thought can be made ultimately clear by comparison with scholastic thought. Ever since Abelard's Sic et non and Gratian's De concordantia discordantium canonum, the scholastics had sought to harmonize apparent or actual contradictions. But not Luther! On the contrary, he forced the apparently or actually contradictory concepts together as tightly and sharply as possible, in order to derive from their opposition the proof of their truth, including the truth of both.[32] Luther did not intend the credo quia absurdum but he was not far from it.

Immediately a danger crops up. There is a tendency to become too deeply enthralled with such a profound and clever use of language. As a fact Luther no more circumvented this danger than do our contemporary existentialists, who offer thought-binding tautologies to explain already unintelligible formulations by a yet more mystifying dialectical tension.

There is another danger that has been costly in the history of Lutheranism. One can incline to regard real tensions of opposites as not really serious so long as one holds fast to Christ, the one basis supporting all things.

It is a fact that Luther never saw an antinomy in his paradoxical simul,[33] and correctly so, for what Luther intends to proclaim is none other than the Christian paradox of the Incarnation and the cross, where God has so abased himself that he signifies his abandonment in what Luther calls those great words, "Eli, Eli" (Matthew 27:46).

Luther's paradoxes also aim to give expression to the revelation of God under cover of what is opposite to divine power, that is, in weakness, ignominy, and distance from God. Nowhere in the history of Christian theology has anyone accomplished this aim so effectively as did the Reformer, Martin Luther.

The simul iustus et peccator applies to man the mystery of concealed Redemption through the saving defeat on the cross. Man is sinful and he must acknowledge this fact. In the acknowledgment he is admitting that God is right. God's judgment becomes the justice that justifies us. It appears to be defeat and weakness, but it is in fact the conquest of sin, death, hell, and the devil.

This, though, does not yet explain the simul. Luther's point is that since we cannot fulfill God's law in this life with all our strength and with complete joy, we remain sinners. Luther sees the same spontaneous willingness with which we sin as precisely what is asked of us in doing good. Thus, according to Luther, Paul's sorrow in Romans 7 is not that he does not do the good that he wills, but that he does not do it as freely, joyfully, and completely as demanded by love, that is ex omnibus viribus.[34]

Here the insight arises that Luther's thought is in a comprehensive manner dialectical thought. It is no dialectical game,[35] but a deadly serious struggle with two facts found in revelation and presenting themselves to our minds as sharply opposed to one another.

Since one pole of this tensional unity is negative (sin), and since Luther places the greater emphasis here, it is decisive in interpretation and evaluation whether one has discerned the limit of the given negation. In other words it is clear that the dialectical tension in no way denies objective being, but rather presupposes it. More concretely, the assertion of remaining sinfulness must not deny a true, somehow ontological, justification. We do not do justice to Luther's thought with the idea of purely imputative justification in a wholly external, forensic or nominalist sense.

Thus Luther's dialectical thought goes beyond conceptualist theology. He respects the mystery, and even seeks it out. He rediscovered the method of monastic theology found in St. Bernard. In any case, we should not overlook the fact that the pattern of Luther's ideas was essentially complete quite early and then underwent development in connection first with the attack on the theology and practice of the Church and then in confrontation with the reaction it caused. Luther's final development was in terms of self-defense and was marked by a resulting obduracy and tendency to overstate his position.

The theological evaluation will in the end depend decisively on the mode and degree of that reality which is not just forensic but ontological as well. From this alone we can determine Luther's relationships to the biblical witness and to the uniquely Catholic sacramental conception.

The basic question still remains whether for Luther justification by faith alone, which he said was the same in the Old and the New Testament,[36] is only a relation, a pure declaration, or whether faith in Christ really eradicates my sin while leaving a remaining sinfulness. Does justification truly grant me a new life, the life of Christ, so that I live no longer, but Christ lives in me?

It is important to note that when Luther was justly opposing the excessively material sacramentalism of the Middle Ages and of his own time, he frequently made use of spiritualistic or nominalistic formulations. The nature of the opposition explains why he spoke so. But then there are statements from Luther openly denying that the result of God's work of salvation is something ontological in the creature, in the believer, and in the Church. Y. Congar finds this view well summarized in the sentence, "The Church lives not from what it is in itself, but from that which God is for it in Jesus Christ."[37] It must be said further that the general movement of Luther's thought is away from ontological concretization toward personal relations, which are only realized in faith.

There are, however, other statements, for instance, dealing with transformation in Christ, that can be understood ontologically. These are analogous to texts in which Luther complements the exclusive efficiency of God with the cooperation of man empowered by God. Thus we must question whether Congar is correct when he indicates that Protestant religious realism contains nothing that approaches an ontology and that the order of personal relations excludes the ontological aspect of justification.[38]

Of course justification does mean that the "alien justice" of Christ is given to me by God through faith. According to Luther God makes it become my justice. Its origin and essence are external to me, but to the degree that God can become man, it becomes man's inner possession, which though in no way negates its nature as a pure gift. The Church is Christ present now, but present within man.[39] God does not merely make promises, but He communicates Himself.

Looking at Luther's whole work, we find that in his later years he applied and developed his paradoxical style in a much less complicated manner than in the early lectures on the Psalms and on Romans. But this style always remained an essential part of Luther's theology, as in the simul iustus et peccator and the doctrine of the hidden God. Here we see also how tightly Luther's use of language is connected with the content of his theology and with what critical exactness his language should be examined and tested. This must be made clear: much of the depth and richness of Luther's theological position is to be classified under the heading "overstatement." His theology of the cross is filled with this. When God wills to save man, He kills him. Before God gives man peace through absolution, He plunges him into doubt and dread. In his 1536 Disputation on Justification Luther returns to the involuted language and thought patterns of the early exegetical lectures. He says:

> Contrition is by derivation a grinding down, that is, a mortification and unbearable terror, because God, through the manifestation of sin in the Holy Spirit, slays man. Whoever feels remorse is filled with dread before God, fears him, and flees from Him because he cannot bear His judgment and wrath. . . . Therefore I ask what a man can merit who flees in such a manner from God, who hates God and cannot listen to Him, and even repulses Him?[40]

Here we have one of those excesses typical of Luther, in this case on contrition. It is far from being pure rhetoric, for it expresses a deep Christian seriousness about the decision regarding the salvation of our souls. Nonetheless, one cannot miss the annoying flavor of immoderate exaggeration. We cannot avoid ascertaining that this passage does not correspond with the general portrait of authentic Christian living as we know it from the synoptic Gospels, from John, and even from Paul outside Romans--and yes even there. Nor does Luther's description correspond with what we learn from many examples taken from the earliest history of the Church.

Luther attempts to give his thesis the greatest possible linguistic force and impact, and thus he tries to exclude every possibility of qualification. In terms of content, he expresses his fundamental convictions with utter earnestness, showing a resolute tenacity amidst qualms of conscience. But he speaks of an extreme borderline case, where faith is a total emptying of self. Faith arises in the terror of separation from God, in dread of God Himself, and in the readiness to accept one's own damnation. The conditions

18

therefore are such that, of necessity, there can be very few real
Christians. Luther's saying, "The Christian is a rare bird,"[41]
not only points to human failures but also expresses the fact that
the Christian message, as Luther interprets it, is suited only for
an elite. Far too much is demanded of ordinary men. This is an
austere theology of the cross in which the message of the Gospel
becomes "a hard saying" (John 6:60).

Scholarship cannot simply accept these overstatements as expressing an uncompromising seriousness about the cross. Man is
not permitted to make the requirements of salvation higher and
greater than has God Himself in his biblical revelation. In Scripture
the demand for perfection is admittedly addressed to all: "Become
perfect even as your heavenly Father is perfect" (Matthew 5:48).
But Scripture also shows that God wills to make place in His kingdom for souls of lesser spirituality. Examples are numerous, such
as the hemorrhaging woman of Matthew 9:20 ff. The life-ideal presented in the synoptic Gospels points this way, for the just man is
the one who performs the works which are to be normative in the
Last Judgment.[42] In fact one may--and even must--ask whether
Luther has not hindered advance in the Christian life of faith because of his method of overstatement and because of his polemic
against the visible elements such as good works.

Admittedly, this stress on the difficulty of faith is accompanied
by a powerful second line of thought conforming more to God's universal saving will and focusing on a simple, joyful faith. The young
Luther developed this side attractively in his explanations of the
Our Father, the Ten Commandments, and the Magnificat and in
numerous sermons. The older Luther does this even more so,
without however wholly eliminating the paradoxes and overstatements
with their accompanying fluctuations and disharmonies.

Luther's sola's (faith alone, grace alone, Scripture alone) are the
supreme--and here deeply grounded--expression of his theological
seeking after the essentials of the Gospel. The great question, which
we will have to consider in turn, is whether these exclusively phrased
formulas are intended as strictly exclusive. The importance of this
question is growing today. Can it be that these apparent exclusions
permit and even call for complementary statements from the deposit
of revelation? Do we find such complementary statements in Luther?
For instance, is there anything even complementary to "faith alone"
in Luther? Alone the later lectures on Galatians show that the question was posed by the Bible and not just by theological controversy.
Luther's exegesis presents a highly illustrative, affirmative answer,

especially but not exclusively in his treatment of faith and hope.
We will return to this below.

Dynamism

Another characteristic of Luther's thinking and of his whole
work--its dynamic character--emerges from the threatened situation caused by the remaining presence of sin even in believers
and from the need for constant repetition of our confession of sin.
Also the biblical conception of the Christian life as a spiritual
struggle was basic for this aspect of Luther.[43] This overall
dynamic character appears in Luther's consistent opposition to
a static conception of salvation, to a spirituality definitely "in
possession," to the feeling of self-confidence, or to an already
complete existence. The exception posed by Luther's insistence
on the eucharistic Real Presence serves to highlight his stress
on the dynamic element all through his work.

Luther's furious struggle against what he called the "accursed
word formatum" in the formula "faith formed by charity" was part
of this insistence on the dynamic aspect, i.e. of faith. Thereby,
however, Luther made it unnecessarily difficult to determine the
relation between faith and charity.

We have already seen that Luther's thought was from its basic
point of departure eschatological.[44] Redemption already took
place, but is not yet completely dispensed. The whole of life is
essentially a process of growing justification. Throughout our
lives, ever anew and tirelessly, we must seek God. The characteristic designations are motus, apprehendere, quaerere, vincere,
pugnare, fieri, de bono in melius. It would be helpful to know
precisely whether this terminology is used to the same degree
through all of Luther's works, or whether there are important
differences with respect to time and theme.

Luther's own long life presents an illustration of this process.
Of course, the heroic heights of the struggle for personal growth
in the cloister and during the early stages of his university years
did not persist in a simple manner throughout his life. The creative
theological breakthrough of 1513 to 1522 (or perhaps to 1525), which
was so full of anguish in the beginning, neither could have nor should
have been extended indefinitely. This is also true of the intense constructive efforts of the 1520's. Luther did gain a position and it suf-
ficed to preserve it. In fact, a certain bourgeois complacency was not
entirely lacking in the mature Luther.

But with regard to matters of faith, Luther never became one who had fully "arrived." This fact does not conflict with him being the preacher of personal certitude of salvation, because for him this certitude remained essentially bound theologically with the holy fear of uncertainty of salvation. The fact that this holy fear overlapped the awareness of being a definitely saved--but sinful-- child of God corresponds to Scripture and thus does not disprove this thesis.

We find particular illustrations of this condition in Luther's engaging admissions of his own lack of progress in faith, of his sense of failure, of always learning something anew, even from his children. There are more than a dozen such texts, some even applying this to his grasp of the Our Father and the Ten Commandments.

1 Luther spoke of Law and Gospel being as different as earth and heaven and of how easy it is to talk about the difference. "But in the conflict of conscience and in practice it is difficult even for those who have had a lot of experience to hold to this for certain."[45]

2 Luther opposed nothing so intensely, yes so crudely and aggressively, as the confidence the papists placed on good works. But then he can say, "I myself am still immersed in this up to the ears. There is no one of us who lacks this vice. I cannot get rid of it."[46]

3 One could say that Luther's whole message is grounded in the idea of the free bestowal of grace. However, in a sermon on Luke 7:11 in 1529 he confessed, "Only with great difficulty does one grasp that a gift is given gratis. It's like learning the ABC's and I cannot get to B and C."[47]

4 In several remembrances Luther has described how he was delivered from his long struggle to understand Romans 1:17 by the Habacuc quotation and how this insight set him on the right path. Especially in table remark No. 5518 he indicated how decisive was the distinction between the righteousness of law and of the Gospel, which he grasped from this text: "This is where I broke through."[48] However, in another table remark he said, "I have preached for twenty-five years and still do not yet understand this text."[49]

5 Luther stressed frequently how one must put reason aside if he is to come to faith. But then he could add, "That is a difficult art, and I am still a student and learner in it."[50]

6 In the lectures on Genesis he said, "And even now it is difficult for me to strip off and cast aside the doctrine of the pope."[51]

And then, "I indeed, whenever I make a comparison of these things, am angry with myself and am ashamed of my life and full of regrets, because after Christ has been revealed, we have such a cold attitude toward our gifts and believe the Word so weakly."[52]

"Subjectivism"

In my <u>Reformation in Germany</u> I put strong emphasis on Luther's subjectivism, and this thesis has been the main point of criticism of my book. This criticism has consistently overlooked the limits I think I drew quite clearly. For I said that Luther felt himself completely bound to the objective Word of God and that this bond was marked by the thorough seriousness we associate with him. Indeed, he encumbered this earnest concern for God's Word with the emotional and theological exaggerations we discussed above, but it is not thereby diminished or eliminated. His overstatements by no means give grounds for the reproach of dishonest subjectivism.

Still I am quite amazed that my thesis has met such extensive criticism. For Protestant scholars have themselves underscored Luther's highly self-willed personality. We all know Luther's supreme independence of every normative source except the Bible, which, nonetheless, he interprets in terms of <u>his</u> Gospel. We are aware of Luther's intransigence regarding those not sharing his articles of faith, whether papists, enthusiasts, Zwinglians, or Anabaptists. Somewhat inconsistently, Luther consigned all of these to hell. We know too Luther's strong personal vacillations, which even Protestant scholars have not failed to criticize. They themselves even stress the strong influence of Luther's personal opinions in the theses he put forth. Why then is the term "subjectivism" so unacceptable?

The term may well be uncongenial. It could be replaced or softened, for instance by "subjective tendency," "individualism," or perhaps "personalism." However, I believe, as before, that the thing itself must be asserted. I do not see how it can be glossed over.

To take the most important point first, the Bible was not entrusted to one individual, but to the Church. It was the Church which, in an eternally memorable life-process and without single authoritative direction, determined the canon of binding apostolic writings and thus made herself the normative interpreter. In contrast, Luther puts aside the Church and the papal teaching authority as it has been understood up to that time. In spite of the Creed he confesses, he no longer believes because of the Church, but because of the Word of God, which however he interprets. Adhered to strictly, this position leads to only one conclusion--free interpretation. "Sola scriptura" entails a complete denial of normative dogmatic determination. Every position is accepted as fundamentally open to scrutiny. I must concur with W. von Loewenich in saying that Luther was the father of Liberal Protestantism. This was clearly counter to his intention, but it was the logical consequence of his appeal to Scripture.[53]

It is of great importance, both for Luther's style and content of thought as well as for much that he bequeathed to Lutheranism, that he did not intend to engender an autonomous conscience. Without a doubt he would have strongly condemned such a doctrine. But that does not alter the basic point I have made, namely that the personal judgment Luther himself came to working on Scripture became normative for preaching and doctrine. Von Loewenich is undoubtedly right in calling this a subjective starting point.

We have already considered the wide-ranging significance for Luther of the notion and fact of experience. The entire Christian life is experimentalis vita. The illustrative material in Luther's works for this point is immense. The manner of Luther's internal development is significant in this connection. With the Bible he is alone sitting with Mary at the feet of Jesus. "No one," he says, "no one taught me until I was taken away from the crowd to listen only to Christ. As I listened and heard him alone, sitting with Mary at His feet, then I learned what Christ and faith mean."[54]

Personal experience of faith does lead to corresponding growth in inwardness. There emerges the fundamental idea which within the Church is thoroughly legitimate, namely, that God and His revelation in deed and doctrine have but one value, a value for me. This is Luther's pro me: "Ut credunt, ita habent."

We need no elaborate discussion of the need and significance of this attitude. In Luther's time it was in fact needed with a certain exaggeration. It would have meant rescue from death in the face of the reifying objectivism and sacramentalism of late scholasticism and the tendency to quantification in the Church of Luther's time.

When Luther sought ecclesiastical justification for his activity as a condemning prophet he pointed to his position as Doctor of Theology and emphatically asserted the rights--apostolic rights-- and duties this gave him. Naturally, his Catholic opponents insisted that such authority was bound within the limits of Church doctrine. Subjectively, Luther would be justified, in view of the theological confusion of the late Middle Ages, that confusio opinionum for which Luther later reproached the Church and which was even mentioned as an evil at the Council of Trent. This confusion is part of the spiritual enervation of the Church on the eve of the Reformation. Added to this was the pluralism fostered by the theory of conciliarism. In the midst of this situation the conciliarist canonist Panormitanus (Cardinal Nicholas of Tudeschi, O.S.B., who died in 1455) gave Luther the principle he then used for his own justification, namely that even an individual can be right over against all others in the Church, provided only that he has better arguments for his position.[55]

Luther took full advantage of this principle, of course going beyond Panormitanus who still held fast to the hierarchy and Magisterium. For his argumentation, Luther quoted Scripture with a vengeance. Here we face the phenomenon that shaped the course of history. Luther encountered Scripture and reacted to it in painful interior wrestling until he broke through. The massive power and fullness of this new birth is seldom matched in history. From it emerged the extraordinary and towering force which was his conscience, the conscience to which he tirelessly appealed and which truly shaped history as he appealed to it before the Diet of Worms in 1521 in a scene that still excites us today.

But because of this Luther is thoroughly ego-oriented, as he repeatedly speaks of "my Gospel and my Bible." Although he only wants to be God's evangelist, he does not admit the Epistle of James and the Apocalypse to "his" Bible. "Because I am certain of my teaching, with it I will be judge over the angels, so that whoever does not accept my teaching cannot attain heaven, because it is God's, not mine."[56]

Luther's subjectivism is also quite massively perceptible in his terrifying prophetic anger against the rebelling peasants in 1525. We need not go into his impulsive hatred of the papacy which led into twisted caricaturing, but never caused him a scruple.

Finally, I would like to touch on a problem that generally finds little sympathy among Lutherans. What about Luther's holiness? Was Luther a saint? Many of my Lutheran friends have answered, "No, thank God." I would consider that a questionable attitude and an indirect contraction of the scale of Christian values. The Protestant Reformation seems to me to be undergoing self-correction in the recent return of the category of personal holiness to a central function again, through the positive evaluation of a cloistered life under vows, as with the brothers of Taizé.

24

In any case, Luther did not summon up the heroic humility and patience which could have prevented the division of the Church. I freely admit that this point leads us into the area of the charismatic. Critical intelligence cannot formulate an explanation of how Luther might have mustered such heroism without affecting insincerity. Here we are dealing with a mystery.

Therefore, the ego-orientation is a powerful, almost overwhelming aspect in Luther the Reformer and in his message. This orientation, as bearer of his word, was the great force behind its spread. However, in light of the Gospel's call for meekness and self-renunciation, this orientation is an awful burden, particularly for a reformer.

Can we also discern pride in Luther? We spoke earlier of a defiance of responsibility. Nothing has to be taken away from this. We need only take note of Luther's fundamental doctrine that man is nothing. And his final words remain the moving statement, "We are beggars--this is true."[57]

The influence of situations

Luther spoke or thought comparatively seldom on theological or pastoral subjects in a strictly objective fashion. His most direct treatments of topics are found in sermons and in individual books, such as the Small Catechism, in which the biblical riches flow out through his works without any polemic being directed against an adversary. Most of the time, however, Luther thinks and speaks within the scope of a particular situation in order to reach a definite goal or to overpower an opponent's errors.

This is not a secondary or insignificant matter. It touches an essential point, because Luther was extraordinarily influenced by situations. His partners and opponents in dialogue decisively affected the tone of his statements, and sometimes the influence went beyond the tone even to the content itself.

The recognition that Luther's style of thought was essentially situation-bound seems to be a basic question in the emergence of a valid opinio communis in Luther interpretation. This point has broad consequences and could have a surprising effect on the ecumenical discussion. H. Bornkamm formulated this recently, saying how "Luther grew through his adversaries," and that "His opponents drew from him the most extreme ideas and most daring statements."[58] This leaves us the question whether the extreme conclusions necessarily belong to the fundamental concern of the unsystematic teacher, Martin Luther. Could not the basic concerns have stood independently of the exaggerated consequences? If this is so, one would have at times to give a differentiated answer regarding the essential Reformation element in the midst of Luther's fluctuating thought.

Examples of this state of affairs are many. The clearest instance is Luther's much stronger emphasis on the objective and static elements of doctrine and the Church from the time he began defending the absolute sense of the Real Presence against Zwingli and the practice of infant baptism against the Anabaptists. Similarly, in De servo arbitrio in 1525 Luther was the captive of his own antagonism against Erasmus, which led him to do his opponent a grave injustice and led him to speak of an arbitrary God not revealed in Scripture--a doctrine that otherwise has no place in his teaching.

The major commentary on Galatians of 1531-1535 offers us striking examples of Luther being influenced by the situation. In treating the theological virtues, he investigated the relationship between faith taken by itself (nuda or abstracta) and good works (which he terms fides incarnata). Of course Luther is familiar with the passages in Scripture which demand activity and good works from man. He even remarks that these passages are innumerable. However, he is incapable of integrating these passages dispassionately into his theological analysis. Ever since his struggles in the cloister he suffered from the very real trauma of works-righteousness. The biblical passages dealing with good works make him unsure of himself, because he almost automatically connects good works with justification by works.

Luther knew and preached assiduously that faith is genuine only when good works flow from it, just as the good fruit comes from a good tree. Still at times the biblical passages on good works distressed him to such an extent that he appealed against them to Christ the Lord and King over Scripture.

> Even if the sophists are more clever than I and so over-whelm and entangle me with their arguments in favor of works and against faith that I simply cannot untangle myself--although they cannot actually do this--yet I would rather have the honor of believing in Christ alone than of being persuaded by all the passages that they could produce against me in support of the righteousness of works . . . . I am not put off at all by passages of Scripture, even if you were to produce six hundred in support of the righteousness of works and against the righteousness of faith, and if you

were to scream that Scripture contradicts itself. I have the
Author and Lord of Scripture, and I want to stand on His
side rather than believe you. . . . Therefore see to it how
you can reconcile Scripture, which, as you say, contradicts
itself. I for my part shall stay with the Author of Scripture.[59]

In attempting to determine the relation between faith and good works
Luther comes to formulations like the following, which point striking-
ly to his occasionally desperate attempt to integrate good works with
Christian faith:

Therefore we, too, say that faith without works is worthless
and useless. The papists and the fanatics take this to mean
that faith without works does not justify, or that if faith does
not have works, it is of no avail, no matter how true it is.
That is false. But faith without works--that is a fantastic idea
and mere vanity and a dream of the heart--is a false faith
and does not justify.[60]

When we turn to Luther's words on the relation between faith
and hope, we find this surprising statement: "Without hope faith
is nothing."[61] Here the absolutely sovereign sola fides is de-
throned by hope, since hope shares in the vital growth of justification, of which faith only secures the beginning.

Or again, when Luther speaks of charity in distinction to
faith he makes it a simple transitory virtue, a mere instrument,[62] whereas for St. Paul charity is the bond of perfection
and alone abides when all else passes away. But then this formulation of Luther's stands in stark contrast to other statements
where he calls charity the supreme virtue which does all things.

Only if we look beneath the words and beneath Luther's programmatic polemical utterances can we come to understand
Luther's extreme statements as the results of situations that
modify his thinking. It is true that he was not always able to
formulate this concern adequately and consistently. But still
recognition of the influence of the situation will serve to
relieve some of the theological burden stemming from Luther's
polemical exaggerations. We must recognize that Luther's
theological statements often give unclear, inexact, and easily
misunderstood expression to what he really wanted to say.

Luther's negative thesis, on the other hand, is crystal clear
--in no sense is there justification by works. But his attempt
to give theological expression to "faith incarnate in good works"

does not succeed. This negative thesis, however, is Catholic. But was Luther really trying to say something un-Catholic in the unclarity of his positive statements which were conditioned by a change of polemical direction in which the situation was a hindrance to Luther? The un-Catholic element would have to be proven. The texts do not indicate it. On the contrary, it can be shown that the bugbear of "faith formed by charity" led Luther to obscure statements, while his true concern leads directly to the central Catholic assertion of a "charity which does all things."

As discussed earlier, the manner in which Luther dealt with hope is entirely different. Here, where he was not struggling with an opponent, one senses how he develops a clear teaching with a calm sureness of touch. He sees hope as essential to the vitally important growth of righteousness, which faith began by receiving the beginning.

In his treatment of charity, Luther falls under the force of his polemic against "the accursed word 'formed'" since he sees the idea of faith being further formed by charity as a sublime distortion of justification by faith. Here his tone is excited. But we must note that his concern is not that faith should exclude charity, but rather that faith joined with hope be the support of charity. Thus charity grows toward the fulfillment of righteousness only in faith and hope.

These reflections lead to the important conclusion that it is arbitrary to take Luther's onesided and sharply drawn statements as alone constituting what is properly Protestant.

ON LUTHER'S THEOLOGY

Within the framework of our sketch of Luther's intellectual style we must now say something about his theology. In such brief compass, I can only point to a few central ideas.

As a theologian Luther was basically a "homo religiosus"--a man of a religious character that, in view of his office, took on a pronounced pastoral character. This great believer, who led a constant and rich life of prayer, belongs as well among the great pastors. Occasionally, the term "homo religiosus" has met criticism as being too vague and general. This is incorrect. The term indicates that Luther, in his thought and very being, was totally bound (according to the root sense of religio) to a single value--God. This term is truly the most comprehensive description of the Reformer because Luther suffered

through all his struggles and all his prayer <u>before</u> <u>God</u>, because
he carried out the varied aspects of his work <u>before</u> <u>God</u>, and
<u>before</u> <u>God</u> he gained answers and strength. The term is valid,
because with it we do not refer to some general God of the universe, but to the Father of the crucified Lord Jesus, and to
Christ himself.

The decisive background of Holy Scripture and Luther's encounter with it, that process of extraordinary fruitfulness, we
mentioned before. On many occasions it became a struggle--
like Jacob's struggle with the angel. The theme "Luther and the
Bible" is immense. Scripture first flooded over him quickly and
entered into his bloodstream during the early years of his growth
as the Reformer. But Luther never ceased to drink from the
biblical fountain. For many years he read the entire Bible twice
in every twelve month period.[63] Scripture was always close to
him, throughout the days, the weeks, the months, in his sermons
and lectures, in his table talk, in the instruction of his children,
even as he was falling asleep. He meditated its message, and
spread its seed abundantly.

The topic takes on a controversial character because of the
way Luther turned chiefly to Paul, and more specifically to Romans, Galatians, and I and II Corinthians, while concerning himself much less with the Synoptic Gospels and not at all with the
Epistle of James and the Apocalypse. This is obviously a decisive
point. As Luther thankfully acknowledged, he received Scripture
from the Church. But he was deeply convinced that the word of
Scripture forced him to interpret it differently than had the Church
up to that time.

The question thus arises whether Luther's message of faith corresponds to what is found in the Bible. Was Luther a total hearer
of Scripture? This question, and especially my subsequent negative answer to it, must be taken together with what I have just
said, namely that listening to the Bible was the heart of Luther's
life, and that he reaped from it during a lifetime with marvelous
zeal and epochmaking success. In considering this question, then,
we cannot attribute to him superficiality or subjective egoism.

What does it mean to be a "total hearer"? This cannot mean
mere addition, as if every part of Scripture was on the same level
of importance and possessed the same value for the Christian message. Rather, it has to do with the essence, with the central point,
as Luther occasionally said himself. But who determines this essence?

Luther pursued with great success just this isolation of the central message. He had a good sense of the specific character of revelation, for instance how it is compactly expressed in the two great commandments of love of God and neighbor. He expressed this central message with a number of different formulations very similar in content. On this score we must in fact attribute to him an extraordinary power for intellectual systematization (if we may use such a word in Luther's case). But at the same time we must point to a fault. Although the ideal of fully hearing the Bible cannot be attained by mere summation of the various parts of Scripture, yet every comprehensive statement of Scripture, such as those Luther strove for and then presented in a binding sense, must be so formulated that all the important elements of the Bible can be integrated into it. Conversely, none of the important biblical doctrines may be excluded. There is but one possible way to affirm the whole of the Bible, or even the whole of St. Paul. The authentic Paul is the whole of Paul; the authentic Bible is the whole of the Bible. It is impossible to isolate the "whole" positively in an abstract formula. That is the task and the art of a comprehensive message that embraces all parts. But when something important is missing from such a message, we must speak of an objective fault and of a subjectively or individually conditioned selection.

Luther was familiar with and "knew" the whole of Sacred Scripture to a truly amazing extent. But he did not preach it evenly. Neither the Synoptic Gospels nor Johannine Christianity are given just representation by Luther, even though he praised John's Gospel as the finest of the four.[64] Luther followed Paul. No one in the history of Christianity has listened to Paul's voice as intensely as Luther. That, however, does not mean that the whole of Paul entered evenly into Luther's work. Luther received from Paul the message of justification. From this he lived and preached, and in its terms he read the entire Bible.

Luther was aware that in the Synoptic Gospels doing good works and having a good intention play a positive role, to the extent that in Matthew 25:34 the Last Judgment is announced in terms of good works. Luther knew this, but he did not even begin to bring it to full realization.

And John's Gospel? There are some Protestant scholars who hold that Luther has given an authentic interpretation of John. I believe that the majority is correct in the idea that the Johannine Gospel plays an insufficient role in Luther's theology. This fact means that a powerful segment of the Christian Gospel did not gain adequate representation in Luther.

If I were to add to this Luther's not wholly uniform rejection of the Epistle of James and his equivalent elimination of the Apocalypse, [65] then I do not see how anyone can deny that Martin Luther, the great hearer of the Word, was not a total hearer of Scripture.

In discussion of this assertion the objection has been raised that Luther did not at all need to be a total hearer of Scripture. But this is only an evasion. Against this is the fact that Luther undertook his gradation of value in Scripture by eliminating particular books. In specific parts of Scripture, for instance, he looks rightfully for the main point and basic intention, as in the parables. [66] Still, he never viewed Scripture as a unity, nor as containing a single binding meaning. I should underscore that the critique I have developed stands even if the Epistle of James and the Apocalypse are somehow excluded from the central Gospel message.

Luther's message centers on justification by faith alone. This is a good Catholic formula. Like the other formula, "Scripture alone," it is found in Bernard and Thomas. [67] The decisive point is the meaning of the formula.

Here we must take very seriously the fact that today--in distinction to the past four hundred years--the doctrine of justification is hardly anywhere considered to divide Protestants and Catholics. This is a correct assumption. For although Luther tends to exaggerate the invisible and interior factors according to his spiritualistic tendency, we must recall that he never lapsed into a merely imputed, forensic or nominalist, theory of justification. God's word of acquittal is creative. The alien righteousness of God and of Christ is given to me, becomes mine, transforms me, so that "No longer do I live, but Christ lives in me." For this thesis the textual proofs in Luther's works are innumerable. Certainly, we must not overlook the difference from the Catholic sacramental and ontological idea of justification, as we discussed earlier. Luther's manner of expression stems from fear of teaching only a reified, objective change. Consequently one can argue that the transformation through justification, as Luther conceives it, does not fully reach the deepest, most interior level of the creature. Similarly, one might say that in Luther's Christology the humanity joined to divinity is strictly speaking not elevated and therefore strictly speaking not really co-redeemed. Also Christ and His life are never viewed as so tightly or centrally joined to the Church, as the very Body of

Christ, that the Church could lose its sinfulness. However one would want to stress these reservations on behalf of a strictly ontological righteousness, still Luther's moderate spiritual realism does signify a true transformation of the old man into the new man in Christ. One could say that Luther here stands essentially within the classic Catholic tradition.

Thus we have returned to the question about "the Catholic Luther," which we only touched on briefly above. It is understandable that Protestant Christians, both in theology and in the Churches, are put on the defensive and even shocked by the notion that Luther, the enemy of the Pope, the man who "championed the free Gospel against Roman tyranny," could be integrated into Catholicism. There are similar reservations on the Catholic side.

Meanwhile, the Second Vatican Council has taught us to see, or to sense, that the deplorable onesidedness of many Catholic formulations can be legitimately complemented so that the Catholic element expands so as to include a previously ignored, or insufficiently viewed, biblical fullness. If, then, the central article of justification, the articulus stantis et cadentis ecclesiae, is today no longer divisive, and if we agree with Luther on this central point, could we not attain to agreement in other areas? Perhaps a conception of the Church could be developed, naturally in strict fidelity to the Word of the Bible, which could be accepted by both sides. Does Luther really exclude a teaching authority? Does he really exclude ecclesial office which is of divine right? We must remember how situation-bound his statements were. Can we rightly say that he would have rejected an apostolically valid and sacramental hierarchy living and teaching out of faith in Christ?

In any case, the Augsburg Confession subscribes to an episcopal magisterium in the Catholic sense. And Luther has assured us in a serious theological context of his major Commentary on Galatians, "Once this has been established, namely that God alone justifies us solely by His grace through Christ, we are willing not only to bear the pope aloft on our hands but also kiss his feet."[68] I know this is not a recognition of papal teaching authority, much less of his infallibility. But it is a powerful, wide-ranging statement that gains more weight if one recalls the idea of the young Luther that there must be a teaching authority in order to prevent a dangerous confusion amid God's people.[69] Admittedly, he gave up this idea, but he did not refute it. One should also take into account Luther's idea of a true dogmatic unity in the Church of Jesus Christ.

Luther's "No" to the papal Church is both in content and inten-sity such that one could hardly imagine it more radical. But this "No" needs sober reexamination. For it was directed against a Church whose sub-Christian reality would deserve the strongest condemnation, if one took the sub-Christian elements as the es-sence of the Church. This is precisely what Luther did. His reli-gious and pastoral zeal seemed to leave him no other way. Here we have a special case of the influence of situations on Luther, as we elaborated above, and this should enter into our analysis.

The most important condition for Protestant Christians coming to a correct judgment on the thesis asserting "the Catholic Luther" is that they free themselves from the false notion that Catholicism is simply a brand of semipelagianism. Much could be said here, but I will make just a brief indication. Our Protestant friends should read through the prayers that the Catholic priest is given to pray before and after the mass. Before mass the idea of merit is changed in a striking manner to "receiving" and "being made worthy"; <u>mereri</u> becomes <u>accipere</u>. And after the mass there is a supplication stemming from Peter Damian and revised by Thomas Aquinas in which one speaks of oneself as "a sinner, your unworthy servant, who by no merits of my own, but only by the gift of your mercy . . ."

In order to remain as objective as possible I shall quote the words of Roger Schutz, the Protestant prior of the community of brothers of Taizé, spoken at the second session of the Council. He remarked, ". . . I could not avoid thinking of Martin Luther in the years before his excommunication. I often said to myself that he would have thanked the Lord on his knees if he had heard such courageous declarations and such stirring cries of repentance as we hear at this Council."[70]

This strikes me as a pronouncement that illuminates both the Reformation and the figure of Martin Luther as well as our con-temporary situation and tasks. It echoes in full agreement with Luther's programmatic first thesis on indulgences, which itself describes the course of action all Christian groups must follow as the supposition for realizing the potentialities presented to us today: "When our Lord Jesus Christ said, 'Do penance,' he meant that the whole life of a Christian must be penance."

Introduction to Erwin Iserloh

Erwin Iserloh was born in the Rhein city of Duisburg in 1915. He studied theology in the Catholic faculty in Münster and, after ordination to the priesthood in 1940, he received his doctorate in 1942. Under Joseph Lortz, Iserloh had concentrated on the theology of the pre-Tridentine Catholic controversialists. His dissertation presented the Eucharistic doctrine of Johann Eck, Luther's principal Catholic opponent. After years as a soldier and prisoner of war, Iserloh did research in Rome on Eucharistic doctrine in the late Middle Ages. Here he sought to uncover the roots of the mentality that led in the sixteenth century both to bitter rejection of the Mass and to lamentable ineptitude in its defense. After surveying the initial Reformation controversy on the Mass in Der Kampf um die Messe (Münster: Aschendorff, 1952), Iserloh submitted his second dissertation, a study of grace and the Eucharist in William Ockham's theology, under Hubert Jedin in Bonn.

From 1954 to 1964 Iserloh taught medieval and modern Church History in Trier, where his interests turned to the life and doctrine of Luther himself. In a lecture in Mainz on November 8, 1961, Iserloh first presented his startling conclusion that the event traditionally marking the beginning of the Reformation, Luther's public posting of the 95 Theses on indulgences on the door of the Wittenberg Castle Church on October 31, 1517, was in fact a legend that first arose after Luther's death. The arguments for and against Iserloh's position have been heatedly discussed in Germany for seven years and have led to the joint publication of his book The Theses Were Not Posted by Beacon Press of Boston and Geoffrey Chapman of London in 1968.

The public argument over the event or non-event of October 31, 1517, was only one part of Iserloh's work. Especially after returning to Münster in 1964 to direct the Catholic Ecumenical Institute, he pursued his study of all aspects of Luther's theology. Early 1968 saw the publication of Volume IV of Handbuch der Kirchengeschichte (Freiburg: Herder), in which Iserloh collaborated with Hubert Jedin in presenting a full-scale history of the Reformation era. In 1966 Iserloh was invited to speak on Luther and mysticism at the Third International Congress on Luther Research at Järvenpää, Finland. Iserloh was thus the first Catholic scholar to address this group of predominantly Lutheran theologians and historians. The German original of his paper appeared in the congress volume, The Church, Mysticism, Sanctification and the Natural in Luther's Thought, published by Fortress Press of Philadelphia in 1967.

We present here a slightly revised version of this paper in English translation (with some reduction of footnote material). Iserloh argues implicitly that the traditional Lutheran stress on God's extrinsic imputation to the justified of Christ's merits and justice has led to neglect of a mystical strain running through many parts of Luther's theology.

The paper thus points to an important area of agreement between Luther's thought and Catholic doctrine. It presents a challenge to contemporary Catholics to recognize the richness of Luther's conception of Christ's vital union with the Christian. It also challenges Lutherans to a deeper assimilation of a forgotten dimension of Luther's thought.

Notes begin on page 173.

Luther's Christ-Mysticism

Erwin Iserloh

Mysticism in Luther?

Generally, Luther has been thought to have had a negative relation to mysticism, both by scholars of the last century and of
our own day. This was inevitable, since Albrecht Ritschl and his
influential school saw "mysticism" as a typically medieval, Catholic form of piety, which Luther overcame. Up to a few decades
ago, no one thought to investigate the Catholic roots of Luther's
theology and the Catholic heritage which the Reformer never
gave up. Such an independent thinker as Adolf von Harnack indeed stressed, "Mysticism is always the same: above all there
are no national or confessional distinctions to it."[1] But Harnack
went on to define mysticism in a manner that contradicts this;
for "mysticism is Catholic piety in general, . . . mysticism is
the Catholic expression of individual piety in general."[2] In fact,
Harnack added a page later, "A mystic that does not become a
Catholic is a dilettante."[3]

Therefore, we are not surprised to find an extensive and influential tradition in Protestant scholarship which treats our topic according to the following oversimplified and erroneous model:

> Mysticism is Catholic. Whatever is Catholic is dominated by an idea of God or a basic idea of religion which is alien to Lutheranism. Therefore, there could not have been a truly positive relation between Luther and mysticism.[4]

But it is certain that we must take into account Luther's intensive encounter with Johann Tauler and with the booklet Eyn theologia deutsch. As evidence for this we have Luther's marginal notes of 1516 to Tauler's sermons and his editing of Eyn theologia deutsch for publication both in 1516 and 1518. In 1518 Luther wrote of Tauler in the Resolutiones of his theses on indulgences:

> Indeed I know that this teacher is unknown in the schools of the theologians and is probably despised by them; but even though he has written entirely in the German vernacular, I have found in him more solid and sincere theology than is found in all the scholastic teachers of all the universities or than can be found in their propositions.[5]

And in the preface of his second (1518) edition of Eyn theologia deutsch, Luther attested, "No book except the Bible and St. Augustine has come to my attention from which I have learned more about God, Christ, man, and all things."[6]

Historians and theologians who like Heinrich Bornkamm assert apodictically that Luther was no mystic[7] are inclined to see in these passages of 1516-1518 a Luther still the prisoner of his Catholic past. They say that Luther was for a while impressed by mysticism, but not truly influenced by it. Kurt Aland sees these references to and echoes of mysticism as indications that Luther had not yet travelled the "road to Reformation" to the end. But when Aland finds mystical terminology in Luther's 1525 revision of his exposition of the penitential psalms, then that is a proof that Luther did not take the time required for a thorough revision of his earlier work. The echoes of mysticism are for Aland hardly compatible with Luther's polemic against Carlstadt in 1525.[8] Basic to this reasoning is the conception that the specific "Reformation element" in Luther's thought is incompatible with his mystical element and that therefore at least when Luther turned against the fanatic spiritualists he had definitely broken

with mysticism. However, this is immediately contradicted by
the tone of Luther's references to Tauler in the 1530's.[9]

The purpose of this essay is not to trace out once more Luther's
relationship to German mysticism or to mystical theologians like
Dionysius Aeropagite, Bernard of Clairvaux, or John Gerson. Rather, we want to present the basic mystical element in Luther's
theology and spiritual teaching.

For this task, however, there must be some agreement about the
nature of mysticism. We cannot presuppose this agreement. In
fact, more recent research has pointed to the ethical emphasis
in Tauler and thereupon questioned the propriety of calling even
him a mystic.[10] But we do not need to enter into this argument
over the essence of mysticism. Instead, we understand "mysticism" in this essay in the general manner that corresponds to
the "Christ-mysticism" of St. Paul.[11] Accordingly, mysticism
is a form of spirituality which seeks a direct union or contact
of man with God. This takes place in the depths of the soul, that
is, at a level of the human person that is prior to the powers of
knowing, willing, and feeling. In Christian mysticism this union
is granted in Christ; here the Christian is in Christ and Christ is
in him. This is, as Luther stressed against the Spiritualists,
a real phenomenon, a pneumatic (spiritual)--not just a psychic
and conscious--presence of the crucified and risen Christ in the
Christian.[12] This is a communion in life and destiny, not merely in attitudes. Certainly this shared life with Christ should be
actualized in attitudes and deeds, in self-giving on the level of
knowing, feeling, and willing. Therefore we speak of a mystic
when we find an especially strong and living sense of being rooted,
grounded, and governed by the "Christ in us." This union with
Christ is strictly speaking only given in faith and is not experienced, but it can be perceived in its effects. Thus St. Paul urged,
"Examine yourselves, to see whether you are holding to your
faith. Test yourselves. Do you not realize that Jesus Christ is
in you?" (II Corinthians 13:5).

In contrast to the ordinary view, but in agreement with Heiko
Oberman,[13] I would stress from the beginning that there was no
basic change in Luther's attitude to mysticism, neither through
his acquaintance with the mysticism of Tauler and Eyn theologia
deutsch, nor through his defense against the Spiritualists, nor
even through his own reformation breakthrough--whether we date
this in 1513-1515 or in 1518. We find a notable degree of continuity
all through Luther's work. He rates mysticism positively as a
sapientia experimentalis in which a man does not speculate on and

theorize about religious realities, but rather lives within these realities and from their power.[14] Ultimately, there is but one reality: Christ, the incarnate, crucified, and risen Lord, with whom the Christian enters a mysterious communion of life and destiny. Since Christ in his saving deeds is contemporaneous with the Christian, scripture can and must be interpreted tropologically, and what is true for Christ and what happens to Christ can also be affirmed of the Christian.

Luther's theology has this mystical dimension because of the deep influence of St. Augustine on him.[15] Even more important is the fact that Luther stood in the rich stream of what is weakly termed "monastic theology," the unbroken tradition that did not experience the early medieval divorce between spirituality and scientific theology.

The mysticism in Luther is a Christ-mysticism, which makes him from the outset sceptical and hostile toward a Logos-mysticism. Luther rejects any speculation which seeks union with God independently of the incarnate Christ.[16] Such a mysticism runs the danger of disregarding the concrete way of salvation that God has determined by his potentia ordinata in the events of the birth, death, and resurrection of Christ, events into which we are assumed by the mediation of word and sacraments.

But when Luther rejected mystical speculation because of his exclusive concentration on Jesus Christ and him crucified (I Corinthians 2:2), this does not mean that he was at one with the thoroughly unmystical spirituality of the late middle ages which centered on contemplating Christ's passion, as Martin Elze recently maintained.[17] We are grateful to Elze for showing how closely related Luther was to late medieval spirituality, but still there are decisive differences to be noted. Luther was critical of such a piety, since for him it was not enough to immerse oneself only meditatively in the Passion of Christ and then to live out the Passion in an ethical-moral imitation of Christ. In fact, Luther forcefully denied any possibility of such a following of Christ, unless a man is first one with Christ in the depths of his person in a union which is prior to all deeds and which is usually not consciously experienced.

We wish to show, therefore, that Luther took a stand on two fronts: on the one side, against a speculative mysticism that disregarded the incarnate Word; and on the other side, against a late medieval spirituality centered on the passion of Christ which, however, remained psychological and moralistic by seeking an imitatio before attaining to a conformatio, and striving after Christ

40

as exemplum before He becomes sacramentum. -- We will present four themes of Luther's theology to illuminate his position.

Critique of speculative mysticism -- Christ-mysticism and union with God sub contrario

On occasion, Luther referred approvingly to Dionysius the Areopagite in the Dictata super Psalterium (1513-1515), since his negative theology expressly urged the hiddenness and incomprehensibility of God.[18] Since God transcends all thought and understanding, the negative theology is more appropriate than the affirmative. Negative theology is not carried on with disputing and excessive talk, but in repose and silence, and even in rapture and ecstasy.[19]

But in the Dictata Luther sees the hiddenness of God even more strikingly in the Incarnation, in the Church, and in the Eucharist.[20] One can therefore conclude that for Luther a theology centered on the incarnate Christ is even nearer to the mystery of God. In the Lectures on Romans (1515-1516) this conviction occasioned his attack on a mysticism that disregards the Incarnation and avoids the way of salvation through the death and resurrection of Christ. Luther saw in Romans 5:2 a criticism of those who "want to come to God by faith alone, not through Christ but past Christ, as if they no longer needed Christ after having received the grace of justification."[21]

Luther concluded on the same verse:

> This affects also those who, following the mystical theology, exert themselves in the inner darkness and, leaving aside all pictures of the suffering of Christ, desire to hear and contemplate the uncreated Word itself without having had the eyes of their heart justified and cleansed by the Word incarnate. For the heart must first be rendered pure by the incarnate Word. Only one who is thus purified can then in rapture ascend through the incarnate to the uncreated Word.[22]

Here the issue is not between devout meditation on the Passion and mystical theology,[23] but between a Christ-mysticism and a speculative Logos-mysticism. Just as Bernard[24] and Bonaventure[25] before him, Luther stressed that we can only approach the eternal and incomprehensible God through the incarnate and crucified God, that we can only know the hidden God through the revealed God.

Further, Luther's often cited marginal note (probably from 1516) to Tauler's Christmas sermon shows both respect for mysticism and criticism of it. It also indicates the starting point for Luther's own mystical way.[26] On the one side, Luther places the contemplative life and the spiritual birth; on the other, the exercise of virtue and the moral birth. The latter, shown in Martha, is the easier and more frequented way; the former, shown in Mary, is rare and only for people with experience. Tauler's sermon is based wholly on mystical theology, that is, sapientia experimentalis et non doctrinalis." This kind of theology deals with the spiritual birth of the uncreated Word. But theology properly so-called deals with the spiritual birth of the incarnate Word. The latter has the one thing necessary and the better part; it is not worried about many things and thereby confused, but is concerned only for virtue and its victory over vice, and because of this striving does not yet enjoy perfect peace.

This latter theologia propria, according to the terminology Luther took over from Dionysius,[27] is discursive, rational, and scientific. It concerns itself with describing the given plan of salvation according to God's ordinate power. This theology Luther distinguished on the one side from a theology based on images grasped by sense perception and on the other from mystical theology. In his Lectures on Hebrews Luther interpreted the outer tent and the two tabernacles (Hebrews 9:1-5) according to the threefold theology, "namely, the symbolic, pertaining to the senses; the proper, pertaining to reason; and the mystical, pertaining to yet higher understanding."[28]

In the continuation of the note to Tauler, it is noteworthy that Luther did not carry through the distinction between spiritual and moral birth, but spoke instead of a spiritual birth of the uncreated Word and of a spiritual birth also of the incarnate Word. Thus it is true of the theologia propria that although technically unmystical it is concerned like Mary with the one thing necessary and has chosen the better part. Like Bernard and Bonaventure, Luther warns mystics against seeking mystical contemplation directly, since one who storms heaven like Lucifer runs the risk of being toppled like him.[29]

With Luther, however, it becomes clear that the encounter with the incarnate Word is not merely pedagogically necessary as a preliminary step which is eventually left behind when one attains to the uncreated Word or to the Deus nudus. In the encounter with the crucified Christ we have the one union with God that we can never surpass. But this union is not realized in meditation only and in moralistic imitation of Christ, but in an ontological communion of life in the depths of the human person, a union which is prior to knowing and willing and not open to our conscious awareness. The issue is not ascetical or pious, but is seriously mystical, although of a somewhat different kind of mysticism.

Both before and during his battle against the Spiritualists, Luther warned against the mysticism of mere speculation that disregards the crucified Christ. This mysticism is vain, conceited, and self-satisfied, truly a snare of the devil. It is not merely useless, leaving the heart void, but it is a dangerous occasion for men to think that on their own they can by immersion into the depths of their own soul or by mystical ascent come to union with God.[30] Thus, in the margin of a Tauler sermon Luther suggested that "syntheresis" (moral instinct) be dropped, and that "fides" be put in its place.[31]

All through his life Luther opposed sharply the platonic conception of grades of ascent that he found in the Areopagite with its image of a ladder to heaven. This conception suggests that a man can ascend on his own to God.[32] Our one ladder is the humanity of him who first descended to us. Our ascent must start with his lowliness.[33]

Still, as I have said, this rejection of a speculative mysticism tending to disregard the way of salvation determined by God's ordinate power does not imply that Luther was content, as was the devotio moderna, with what Martin Elze called a "psychological realism devoid of all exuberance, which was intent on prudent moderation and a solid devotion, while being suspicious of the often ephemeral flares of pious feeling."[34] Such an all too correct spirituality was simply beneath Luther's religious greatness, and it could not offer answers to the questions that forced themselves on him. Moreover, he saw here the danger of reliance on the psychological and moral powers of man. Therefore he stressed while commenting on the Epistle to the Hebrews that one who wants to imitate Christ's example must first grasp in faith that Christ suffered and died for him as a sacramentum. "Consequently, those people make a huge mistake who first try to blot out their sins by good works and penitential practices, for they try to begin with Christ as example when they ought to begin with him as sacrament."[35]

Luther demanded a practical or "existential" theology centered on the cross, not a mysticism of the negative way but by way of the contrary:

> For our good is hidden and that so deeply that it is hidden under its opposite. Thus our life is hidden under death, self-love under self-hatred, glory under shame, salvation under perdition, the kingdom under banishment, heaven under hell, wisdom under foolishness, righteousness under

sin, strength under weakness. And generally, every yes
we say to any good is under a no, in order that our faith
may be anchored in God, who is the negative essence and
goodness and wisdom and righteousness and whom we cannot possess or attain to except by the negation of all our
affirmations.[36]

Luther's denial entails, therefore, not an ascent by way of
negation, but by way of the contrary:

Therefore, just as the wisdom of God is hidden under the
disguise of foolishness and truth under the form of a lie, so
also the word of God comes, whenever it comes, in a form
that is contrary to our own thinking in so far as it pretends
to have the truth by and from itself.[37]

On the will of God:

It is so hidden under the disguise of evil, unacceptableness,
and hopelessness that it seems to our will . . . in no way
the will of God but rather that of the devil.[38]

According to this thought pattern of ever new contrasts:

Faith is a sort of knowledge or darkness that nothing can
see. Yet the Christ of whom faith takes hold is sitting in
this darkness as God sat in the midst of darkness on Sinai
and in the temple.[39]

Luther's negative theology, therefore, is a theology of the cross,
for on the cross God hid himself beneath the contrary, beneath
the appearance of him who was a worm and no man.[40]
    The trials we endure are ultimately not temptations to sin
caused by the devil, nor are they the dark night of the soul in
which God departs from us, but in them God presents Himself to
us under a contrary form. The issue here is the contradiction
between the God who commands and the same God who promises.[41]
"All other trials are only hints and preliminaries for the trials in
which we must learn to flee from God to God." [42] "Against God,
we must learn to force our way to God." [43] "From God the Judge
to God the Father."[44] Unless one accepts God the tyrant, he will
never find Him as friend and Father.[45] "For since we are liars,
the truth can in no other way come upon us than in a form that
contradicts our thoughts."[46]

In the bridal embrace of Christ, the soul grasps the cross, that is, death and hell, and thereby receives life.[47] "For as Christ, by his union with the immortal divinity, overcame death by dying, so the Christian, through his union with the immortal Christ, arising through faith in Him, also overcomes death by dying. And thus God destroys the devil himself, and carries out his own work by means of his alien work."[48]

I will now make this mystical element in Luther's theology yet clearer by considering in turn his understanding of faith, his conception of the "happy exchange" between Christ and the Christian, and his use of the formula sacramentum et exemplum.

The mystical element in Luther's notion of faith

The assertion of justification "by faith alone" has often led people to conclude that Luther rejected all mysticism. But Luther's idea of faith has mystical aspects, and is furthermore described as raptus, one of the central concepts of mysticism. In the Dictata Luther described ecstasy as the "sensus fidei" and as the mind's rapture which carries it into the clear understanding of faith.[49] The previous text from the course on Hebrews says that in faith we are one with Christ, so that his death and resurrection in his humanity is also our destiny. Repeatedly in these latter lectures Luther spoke of faith as raptus:

> Faith in Christ is . . . being torn away (raptus) and removed (translatio) from all things which can be inwardly or outwardly experienced, and being carried into those things which can neither be inwardly or outwardly experienced, into the invisible, exalted, and incomprehensible God.[50]

> Faith makes the heart hold fast to heavenly things, and be wholly enraptured so as to dwell in the invisible. . . . The man of faith hangs between heaven and earth and 'in medios cleros.' as the Psalm says, 'he sleeps,' that is, he is crucified and hangs with Christ between heaven and earth.[51]

> On the one hand Christ through faith is called our 'substance,' that is, our riches, and on the other, through the same faith, we are made his 'substance,' that is a new creation.[52]

Faith means putting on Christ, becoming one with Him, and having all things in common with Him.[53] In faith, the Christian

becomes one with the Word made flesh,[54] "quasi una persona."[55]
"He who believes in Christ is joined to Christ, is one with Christ,
and shares the same justice with Him."[56] Faith is not just holding to Christ, but being seized and transformed in Christ.[57] "Be-
hold, through Christ into Christ Himself."[58]

Faith is springing across to Christ's righteousness,[59] being
thrown over to Him,[60] snatching Christ for ourselves,[61] being
torn away from ourselves and glued to Christ.[62] The sinner
crawls into Christ and hangs onto his neck.[63] "A man who relies on Christ by faith is carried on Christ's shoulders. He will
cross over happily with the bride, 'who comes up through the
desert leaning upon her beloved.'"[64]

On this basis Luther opposes the conception that grace is a
static possession. It is rather a constant activity through which
the Spirit of God seizes us and draws us along.[65] But Luther
opposes no less forcefully a spiritualization of the presence of
Christ in us:

> I believe in the Son of God, who suffered for me; I see my
> death in his wounds and I see and hear nothing else but Him.
> This is faith of Christ and in Christ. The fanatics say that
> he is in us spiritually, that is, speculatively, while being
> realiter in heaven. But no, Christ and faith must be joined
> together, and we must dwell in heaven while Christ is in
> our hearts. This does not happen speculatively, but
> realiter.[66]

This is what I would call a mystical conception of justification,
understood as the communion of life and love with Christ, which
we are then to constantly make more intimate. This does not fit
into the framework of merely imputed justification, and thus is
a source of no little difficulty for Lutheran theologians.[67]

Once more, toward the end of his life, Luther interpreted
faith as "knowledge" in the sense of a mystical communion in
love. It is an "agnitio experimentalis," a way of knowing akin
to sexual love ("Adam knew his wife"), not a speculative or
historical, but an experiential knowledge. Historical faith knows
of Christ's passion for us and even "for me," but it does not add
the "for me" as a sensation or experience. "True faith firmly
posits this, 'my beloved is mine and I embrace him in joy.'"[68]

In speaking of this experiential aspect of faith, Luther is not
indicating the natural powers of sensation and feeling. To rely
on feeling, or on one's conscience and works, is to build on the

"sensus peccati." This gives no certitude. But when we take our stand outside of ourselves through faith, relying on Christ and his promises, then we have certitude of salvation.[69] One must not rely on the experience of the old man, but after justification there is a certain--yes, mystical--experience of salvation. "Once I am justified and know that by grace my sins are forgiven independently of my merits, then I must begin to feel this, so that I somehow come to comprehend."[70]

Over against the cry of the law, of sin, and of the devil, which we endure in trials, there is the experience of faith, the cry of the Spirit, which, however, is but a slight sighing.[71] There is therefore for Luther a sigh (gemitus) which is a sign of the gift of the Spirit (Romans 8:26), and not of a sinful weakness.

The "happy exchange"

The central mystical motif in Luther's thought is the "happy exchange" between Christ and the Christian.[72] A man exchanges his sin for Christ's righteousness. This conception can only be understood within the context of the patristic idea of the redemption, as opposed to scholasticism's stress on a moralistic and juridically conceived satisfaction theory. According to the Fathers-- including Augustine--man broke himself off from the God of life through disobedience and delivered himself to death. But Christ took upon himself this flesh doomed to death and on the cross submitted to death. But death could not hold fast its prey, since it was exhausted by the fullness of life in Christ. The humanity of Christ was the bait on the hook of the divinity, and death collapsed in death after grasping this bait. In his kenosis of obedience unto death on the cross Christ not only atoned for human hubris but also divested death of its power. In his resurrection Christ not only healed human nature but also granted it divine life.

Luther treated this "happy exchange" at length in "On the Freedom of a Christian Man" (1520), and explicitly connected it with the mystical idea of faith as the marital embrace between the soul and Christ:

> Faith not only gives the soul enough for her to become, like the divine word, gracious, free, and blessed. It also unites the soul with Christ, like a bride with the bridegroom, and, from this marriage, Christ and the soul become one body, as St. Paul says. Then the possessions of both are in common, whether fortune, misfortune, or anything else; so that what

Christ has, also belongs to the believing soul, and what the
soul has, will belong to Christ. If Christ has all good things,
including blessedness, these will also belong to the soul. If
the soul is full of tresspasses and sin, these will belong to
Christ. At this point a contest of happy exchanges takes place.
Because Christ is God and man, and has never sinned, and
because his sanctity is unconquerable, eternal, and almighty,
He takes possession of the sins of the believing soul by virtue
of her wedding-ring, namely faith, and acts just as if he had
committed those sins Himself. They are, of course, swallowed
up and drowned in Him for His unconquerable righteousness
is stronger than any sin whatever. Thus the soul is cleansed
from all her sins by virtue of her dowry, i.e., for the sake of
her faith. She is made free and unfettered, and endowed with
the eternal righteousness of Christ, her bridegroom. Is that
not a happy household, when Christ, the rich, noble, and good
bridegroom, takes the poor, despised, wicked little harlot in
marriage, sets her free from all evil, and decks her with all
good things? It is not possible for her sins to damn her, for
now they rest on Christ, and are swallowed up in Him. In this
way she has such a rich righteousness in her bridegroom that
she can always withstand sins, although they indeed lie in wait
for her. Paul speaks of this in 1 Corinthians 15: "Praise and
thanks be to God, who has given us that victory in Christ Jesus,
in which death is swallowed up together with sin."[73]

Luther understands this union of the Christian with Christ so
realistically that he can apply the communication of idioms to its
exchange of natures. In Christ the two natures are so united that
we can predicate of the humanity what is properly only true of the
divinity. Similarly, we can predicate of the Adam-nature of a Christian that which is true of his Christ-nature, saying that the carnal
man is spiritual. In his Lectures on Romans, Luther explained this
sharing of proper qualities:

One and the same man is spiritual and carnal, righteous and
sinful, good and evil. Just so the one person of Christ is
at the same time both dead and alive, both suffering and
blessed, both active and passive, etc., because of the com-
municatio idiomatum, even though there belongs to neither of
his two natures what is characteristic of the other, for, as
everyone knows, they differ absolutely from each other.[74]

The "happy exchange" means that Christ bears all our sins. And so we can endure the sin from which we are only gradually healed, as we live the simul iustus et peccator:

> It is enough that our sin displeases us, even though it does not entirely disappear. Christ bears all sins, if only they displease us, for they are no longer our sins but his, and his righteousness is ours in turn.[75]

In Luther's idea of the "happy exchange" Philippians 2, 5 ff. was a key text, as was also true in the view of the Fathers. According to Luther's Sermo de duplici iustitia (1518),[76] which is based on this text, Christ emptied himself of the "form of God," but not of the "substance of God." That is, He put off wisdom, honor, power, righteousness, goodness, and freedom, and he took on the form of a servant, namely our sins, and granted us instead his righteousness. This righteousness ("iustitia essentialis") must then become fruitful in a second righteousness, which because of our cooperation is called our own righteousness. The latter flows from the first and is its fulfillment. The flowing, cooperating, and perfecting is carried out in an exchange of love between husband and wife.[77] "Through the first righteousness arises the voice of the bridegroom who says to the soul, 'I am yours,' but through the second comes the voice of the bride who answers, 'I am yours.' Then the marriage is consummated."[78]

We do not need to follow this motif of the "happy exchange" through Luther's whole work, but it seems good to indicate its important place in the commentary on Galatians of 1531 (published 1535), so it might be made clear that this is more than just a relic of Luther's Catholic period that occasionally slips from his pen.

In this lecture-commentary faith and righteousness are also elements of a mystical union with Christ in the depths of the person. In fact, in faith the Christian receives a new personal depth in Christ:

> But faith must be taught correctly, namely, that by it you are so cemented to Christ (conglutineris Christo) that He and you are one person, which cannot be separated but remains attached to Him forever and declares: "I am as Christ." And Christ, in turn, says: "I am as that sinner who is attached to me, and I to him."[79]

By this fortunate exchange with us He took upon Himself our sinful person and granted us his innocent and victorious Person. . . . [Christ:] "I shall empty myself; I shall assume your clothing and mask; and in this I shall walk about and suffer death, in order to set you free."[80]

Thus Christ has become sin (II Corinthians 5:21). He has the guilt of all our sins and thus we are freed through him and not through ourselves.[81] Christ took on the person of all sinners and thus became guilty of sin. He took on himself not just the punishment, but the very nature that was captive to sin. "He came as a sinner under the wrath of God in my person taking me on his shoulders."[82] In Christ sin was wrestled to the ground and absorbed (Colossians 2:15). Thereby sin exists no more:

But because he was a divine and eternal Person, it was impossible for death to hold Him. Therefore he arose from death on the third day, and now lives eternally; nor can sin, death, and our mask be found in Him any longer; but there is sheer righteousness, life, and eternal blessing.[83]

The righteousness imparted to human nature in Christ comes to us in faith:

Because He lives in me, whatever grace, righteousness, life, peace, and salvation there is in me is all Christ's; nevertheless, it is mine as well, by the cementing and attachment (per conglutinationem et inhaesionem) that are through faith, by which we become as one body in the Spirit.[84]

Luther applies the relation between the divine and human nature in Christ and their cooperation in the redemption to the relation between faith and works in man. The communion with Christ grounded in faith must become fruitful in good works. The fides absoluta must as it were take on flesh and blood and become fides incarnata. But just as it was not the humanity of Christ that conquered sin and death, but the hidden divinity, and just as it is not the bait on which the devil bit but the hidden fishhook that brought him to death, so it is not works that justify, but the faith of which the works are the fruit. Faith is thus the divinity of the works, and is poured out into them just as the divinity is poured out into the humanity. The communication of idioms can be applied again, so that--because the divinity is joined to the humanity--just as one predicates of

50

the humanity what belongs to the divinity, so--because of faith--
one can predicate of the works what properly belongs to faith.[85]

   This is not the place to investigate whether polemic prejudiced
Luther here, or--more positively formulated--whether his concern to save at all costs justification by faith alone[86] led him to
a somewhat monophysitic suppression of the cooperation of the
human nature of Christ in the redemption. Luther missed here
an opportunity to ground with yet greater theological precision
his fides incarnata, this is, the "incarnation" of faith in works
on the analogy of God become man.[87]

   We can also omit posing the critical question of who precisely
is the subject of this quasi-hypostatic union between a sinful nature
and a Christ-nature in the Christian. This same question about
the subject arises as well when we consider the self-annihilation
leading to mystical union, and even when we seek to understand
Romans 6:3-11 and Galatians 2:20. The relevance of this question
for Luther's thought is itself further proof of the mystical element of his conception of the "happy exchange."

Sacramentum et exemplum

   Luther used the formula "sacramentum et exemplum" in order
to exclude a superficially moralistic understanding of Galatians
2:20 ("With Christ I have been crucified") or First Peter 2:21
("Christ suffered for you, leaving you an example").[88] Thereby
Luther emphasized that works do not make the Christian, but the
Christian does works. Christ must first become a sacrament for
me as his death is carried out in my death to sin, and only then
can he be an example for me.

   Luther took over this formula from St. Augustine's De Trinitate, Book IV, Chapter 3. There Augustine explains how Christ
was without sin and so in no need of inner renewal. But Christ
had taken on our mortal flesh and thereby death as the punishment decreed for this flesh because of sin. Christ died therefore
only according to the flesh and needed only a bodily resurrection.
Thus it is that his single death and single resurrection are put
before us with double significance, as both sacrament and example. We must die a double death and we need a double resurrection.
We must die to sin and rise to new life and we must endure suffering and death as punishment for our sin until we rise bodily.
Christ, therefore, endured a single death for our double death,
and rose once to bring about our double resurrection, since he
placed his single resurrection before us both as sacrament and
as example.[89]

In the margin of this text Luther made (in 1509-1510) a sche-
matic outline of its wide-ranging and complicated train of thought.
Accordingly, the crucifixion of Christ is a sacrament by signifying
the cross of penance on which the soul dies to sin. The crucifixion
is an example by exhorting us to truly deliver our bodies to death
or to the cross.[90]

The crucifixion of Christ is a sacrament because it is an event
that is not closed and ended, but is a sign that points toward an
event in the life of the man moved by it. The crucifixion, though,
does not point merely to a conscious process in this man, as
when he understands its meaning for salvation or comes thereby
to a change of attitude. Rather, the crucifixion effects something
in this man, something essentially hidden: "The death of Christ
make the soul die to sin, so that we are thus crucified to the
world and the world to us."[91]

Ernst Bizer's interpretation of this text goes directly against
Luther's intention by seeing the sacramental significance of
Christ's death as only a matter of knowledge and moral conduct.
He explained, "We can simply say that the death of Jesus on the
cross shows us humility as the way to salvation, for humility is
the attitude of the penitent. . . . The sacrament does not primarily give something, but mediates an insight into the cross of
Christ on the basis of a particular interpretation of the cross."[92]
But Luther said explicitly, "ut mors Christi faciat animam
mori."[93] If Bizer had understood Luther rightly, then it would
have been nonsense for Luther to stress so strongly the essential
difference between sacrament and example. It would be the example that stirs me more to penance and that points to humility as
the way to salvation. But Luther wants to exclude just this mistake
of late medieval passion piety, which strove to imitate Christ's
humility in suffering before His death and resurrection became a
sacrament for us by being accomplished in us in mysterio.

It is not true that Luther simply brushes aside the traditional
idea of sacrament, as Bizer contends.[94] On the contrary, by
recurring to the more ancient tradition of Christ as the primal
sacrament, Luther overcame the Nominalists' attenuated idea
of a sacrament. Further, he restored the normative patristic
conception of the redemption to primacy over the heavily juridical
emphasis on satisfaction.[95] According to the Fathers, Christ
took upon himself our sin-infected nature and bore this nature
through death home again into the glory of God. We come to share
in this divine life by union with Christ crucified, by coalescence
with his death and resurrection. In his life is our life, and then

52

we share in his sonship, righteousness, wisdom, and love, so that these can be predicated of us. Death and resurrection are not just events that happened once to Christ historically, but are as well sacraments, that is, signs that both signify and effect our salvation.

What happened to Christ tends to expand like the root into the tree, or is like a cause tending toward its effect. This interpretation admittedly goes beyond Luther's 1509-1510 marginal to Augustine, but his early lectures on Scripture do warrant this line of thought. In the Dictata super Psalterium Luther explained that the "marvelous works" of Psalm 110:4 ("Memoriam fecit mirabilium suorum") are not the miracles of Christ, but rather the marvel that in dying Christ brought death down to death, that his suffering demolished punish-ment, his passion ended suffering, and his ignominy killed ignominy.[96] In Christ death became "precious in the eyes of the Lord," so as to signify eternal life. In him suffering means joy, passion pleasure, ignominy glory. Here God and man view these events differently. God has done marvels to his holy one (Vulgate of Psalm 4:4).

But these marvelous events have further significance and fur-ther effect. For they took place radicaliter and causaliter in the pas-sion of Christ.[97] That is, there were events which are only ful-filled in us as they work further, like the root in the tree and the cause in the effect. For we must all be formed according to the example of Christ. This can be said because the passion is contem-poraneous with us in the sacrament of the Eucharist and becomes there an effective sign for us. The Eucharist is the "memorial of God's saving events" through which those who fear the Lord are fed and refreshed. This feeding and recalling are twofold, the sacrament and the word of the Gospel proclaiming Christ.

The Christ-event tends to impress its form on us, and, as it were, to gain its full reality in the believer. As Luther said on another occasion in the Dictata, Christ is our abstractum, we are his concretum.[98]

Here we have the ground for the possibility of the tropological interpretation of the Psalms, a basis that makes this something more than artificial allegory. Because the Christ-event is con-temporaneous with our dying and rising in and with Christ, and because we then share in the Christ-life, the Psalms which speak literally of Christ can as well be applied tropologically to the life of the Christian. Further, the works done in faith must correspond to this life in and with Christ that is given by faith alone. But the sacrament is the supposition for the example, and existence in Christ tends to the imitation of Christ.

Even though Luther does not refer to the text of Augustine's De Trinitate explicitly, nor to the concepts sacramentum et exemplum, still he intends precisely this, that is, that Christ's death both exemplifies and mediates salvation for us and is to be carried out in our bodily and historical existence. Christ's death and resurrection find a twofold correspondence in the Christian: first, as he dies spiritually--in faith--to sin and constantly rises in the victory over his death-dealing flesh; and finally, in meeting his fate outwardly in bodily death so as to come to share in the victory of Christ.[99]

Whereas in us there is the twofold evil of sin and punishment, there is in Christ only the punishment that he took on for us. His prayer that he be freed from punishment is a prayer that we be freed from sin and punishment. The correspondence in outward destiny (example) presupposes that Christ's death become for us an effective sign (sacrament) of our death to sin.[100]

This pair of concepts and the underlying idea turn up not just in Luther's early works, where they might be written off as results of his study of Augustine, but as well through the whole work of the Reformer. The formula is especially amazing, when one's idea of Luther's doctrine has been too much influenced by the systematizations of Lutheran orthodoxy and by the textbooks stemming from that tradition.

In his Lectures on Romans Luther used sacramentum et exemplum (or simply, sacramentaliter) five times in his effort to bring out the pro nobis significance of the death and resurrection of Christ. For instance, Luther glossed Romans 6:19 by explaining that Christ rose from the dead, "sibi corporaliter, nobis sacramentaliter."[101] This shows how wrong it is to theorize that Luther replaced the mystical "in nobis" with the "pro nobis." The marginal gloss of Romans 5:10 shows clearly that Luther applies sacramentum to Christ's death and resurrection in the technical sense of an effective sign that brings the believer to a resurrection and new life.[102]

In his scholion on Romans 4:25 Luther emphasizes that faith is the required condition if the death and resurrection of Christ are to become effective signs of our death and resurrection:

> Christ's death is the death of sin, and his resurrection is the life of righteousness. For by his death he has offered satisfaction for our sins, and, by his resurrection, he has affirmed righteousness for us. And so his death does not merely signify but it effects the remission of

our sins as a most sufficient satisfaction. And his resurrection is not only the sign of our righteousness, but, because it effects it in us if we believe it, also its cause.[103]

Luther does not speak explicitly of baptism as the way in which the death of Christ becomes for us an effective sign in faith of our death and resurrection. However, the context of Romans 6 indicates that baptism is presupposed as part of the background of Luther's argumentation.[104] The total context of the <u>Lectures</u> <u>on</u> <u>Romans</u> enables us to conclude that the Christ-event comes to bear on our lives in word and sacrament, although it is properly ours only in faith.

Luther worked out the idea of the death of Christ as sacrament and example in greater detail in the <u>Lectures</u> <u>on</u> <u>Hebrews</u> of 1517-1518, where he made a yet closer connection between the Christ-event and justification. Luther's idea of justification is here remarkably christocentric.

Luther calls the passion of Christ a divine sign (<u>sacramentum</u>) of death and the forgiveness of sins.[105] A man must die with Christ in faith so that Christ comes to live in him, yes, to work and reign in him:

> In this way works issue spontaneously from faith. Thus our patience comes from Christ's patience, our humility from his humility, and his other gifts in the same way. . . . Therefore if any man wants to imitate Christ as an example, he must first firmly believe that Christ suffered and died for him as a sacrament. Therefore they make a huge mistake who try first to blot out their sins by penitential works, beginning with Christ's example, when they ought to begin with [his passion as] the sacrament.[106]

On Hebrews 10:19 Luther interpreted Christ's death and entry into the glory of the Father as a sign and sacrament of the imitation of Christ.[107] The death of Christ is God's sign of the mortification of concupiscence, indeed of its death. His entry into heaven is a sacrament of "the new life and the way in which we love and seek after heavenly goods."[108] Christ is correspondingly not only the example of our passage into new life, but is our helper and ferryman. "One who relies on Christ in faith will be carried across on Christ's shoulders."[109]

This conception of the death of Christ as sacrament and example is closely connected with the "happy exchange" and like this cannot be understood on the basis of the Anselmian theology of redemption through satisfaction, but only on the basis of the patristic, "mystical" view of the redemption. In order to give some idea of the importance of this return to the patristic tradition, we would have to present here the Christology of Nominalism with all its aridity and shortcomings, for which there is not enough space or time at our disposal.[110]

Luther never tired of underscoring the point that our conversion to this sacramental and spiritual dying and rising with Christ must come before all moral and external imitation of the suffering Christ. We can indicate only a few of the relevant texts.

According to the "Asterisci" in which Luther countered the "Obelisci" of John Eck against his indulgence theses, the passion of Christ is a sacrament in as much as it justifies us in the spirit without our help, and it is an example working with us in exhorting us to go and do likewise.[111]

In the Galatians Commentary of 1519 Luther explained the words, "I have been crucified with Christ" (2:20) thus:

> St. Augustine teaches that the suffering of Christ is both a sacrament and an example--a sacrament because it signifies the death of sin in us and grants it to those who believe, an example because it also behooves us to imitate Him in bodily suffering and dying.[112]

In connection with Galatians 3:14 Luther explains that Christ must first work in us and fulfill his promises before we can follow his example: "It is not imitation that makes sons; it is sonship that makes imitators."[113] Mere imitation makes monkeys out of us, by solely outward imitation in conduct that does not touch what we really are.

Luther's Christmas sermon in 1519 stressed that Chirst is more than just an example. Otherwise, he would be no more than any saint. Instead, Christ works in us and grants that of which he is the example. This is what Luther means by the word, "sacramentaliter": "All words, and all narratives of the Gospel, are sacraments of a sort (sacramenta quaedam), that is, holy signs through which God brings about in believers what the narratives signify."[114]

Luther does not restrict the idea of a sacrament as effective sign of salvation to the sacraments of the Church. When he calls the Word a sacrament, he does not give up the traditional conception of a sacrament. In fact, he explains how the Word is a

56

sacrament by referring to Baptism and Penance.[115] It is also incorrect to say that only in 1519 Luther understood sacramentum as an efficacious sign in line with the traditional doctrine of the sacraments.[116] As we saw, the Lectures on Romans of 1515-1516 showed clearly that the scholastic definition of a sacrament served as the background of Luther's argumentation.[117]

Luther's treatment of Galatians 3:27 in his 1522 Christmas sermons urges again and again that interior communion with Christ must precede outward moral imitation of Christ. Before he becomes my example and presents me with a task, I must put Christ on. He must first be a gift to me. Here Luther speaks of Christ as donum in place of sacramentum, which is a substitution of the effect for the cause.[118]

In his later works, Luther used the idea of sacrament and example especially in the Disputations against the Antinomians. Thesis 50 of the fifth disputation (1538) reads: "We know, and they have learned from us, that Christ became both sacrament and example for us."[119] In the second disputation, Luther explained:

> You know that Paul usually joins two things, just as Peter did in First Peter 2:21: first that Christ died for us and redeemed us through his blood to purify for himself a holy people. Thus he shows us Christ as gift and sacrament. Then, they show us Christ as an example we should imitate in his good works.[120]

In the Galatians commentary of 1531 Luther stressed that the text "I have been crucified with Christ" (2:20) should not be referred to being crucified with Christ by imitating his example, but "he is speaking here about that sublime crucifixion by which sin, the devil, and death are crucified in Christ, not in me." Christ does all this alone, and then by believing in him I am crucified with Christ so that also for me sin, the devil, and death, etc., are crucified and dead.[121]

It is impressive to see how Luther continued to apply the Augustinian theme of sacramentum et exemplum. He emphasized against a moralistic misunderstanding of the following of Christ that something must take place in us sacramentally, that is, spiritually, in grace and hiddenly, before we can imitate the example of Christ in our actions. Christ must be at work in us before we can go to work with him.

Conclusion

I have shown some examples of how Luther thought of the Christian's union with Christ as a spiritual reality. This takes place at a deep level of the person, which mysticism called "the ground of the soul" (Seelengrund), where union with Christ can determine the whole of a man. This is not merely an event in consciousness, nor does it only transform the affections. If we understand clearly that "ontological" does not denote something reified, material, and static, then we should not hesitate to speak of an ontological transformation.

Further, it has become clear that for Luther the righteousness of Christ is not just imputed extraneously, but is given to be one's own, as the bridal gifts are given to the bride. This righteousness is "alien" in its origin, for it does not come from man, nor is it gained or merited by his effort. Christ's merit comes from without and is given out of pure grace, but this does not mean that it remains without and continues to be extraneous.[122]

This matter we have presented makes it clear what pleased Luther in Tauler's sermons and in Eyn theologia deutsch. In opposition to the scholasticism of his day, Luther felt a real kinship with these theologians. If we speak of these works as "mystical," then we must speak all the more of the same in Luther. If this still needs proving, one need only compare Luther's sermon on the Assumption of the Blessed Virgin with Sermon 46 on the same subject by Johann Tauler.[123]

Introduction to Otto H. Pesch, O.P.

Otto H. Pesch was born in Cologne in 1931. After entering the Do-
minican order he made philosophical and theological studies at the
Albertus Magnus Academy in Walberberg near Bonn. After ordination
to the priesthood, he was a doctoral student from 1960 to 1965 under
Heinrich Fries in the Munich faculty of Catholic theology, where he
wrote a mammoth dissertation on the theology of justification in Luther
and St. Thomas Aquinas.

During his graduate studies Father Pesch wrote numerous articles
on Thomism, Luther research, and systematic questions for the new
edition of Lexikon für Theologie und Kirche, for Catholica, and for
other periodicals. One of his most valuable Catholica articles was a
two-part study in 1966 of Ernst Bizer's widely discussed attempt to
rechart the stages in Luther's early development in Fides ex auditu.
In preparation for the 1966 Congress for Luther Research, Father Pesch
surveyed "Twenty Years of Catholic Luther Research" for Lutheran
World (Vol. XIII). At the Congress, he made important interventions in
favor of a profitable systematic dialogue between Luther and Aquinas.

Father Pesch is now teaching systematic theology and ecumenism at
Walberberg and is working on a commentary on St. Thomas' treatise on
the Old Law for the Latin-German edition of the Summa Theologiae. He
has also begun his second major comparative study of Luther and Thomas,
this time dealing with their respective understanding of the Eucharist.

Father Pesch is emphatic in styling his own work as a systematic comparative study of the two theologians. He disavows the aim of primary
research on Luther, and is instead interested in proceding from the
results gained by reputable Luther scholars to inquire of St. Thomas what
of Luther's teaching is a common conviction of the two, what has been
added in Luther's thought, and how Thomas would judge Luther's additions.
The principal result of Father Pesch's work is the discovery of large areas
of significant agreement and a further openness on Thomas' part to many
of Luther's "additions." The present essay will demonstrate both of
these points, and will further indicate Father Pesch's approach toward
an intelligible correlation of the remaining divergences between the two
theologians.

We are fortunate in having this essay, since it presents the main
thesis of the concluding section (pp. 935-948) of the published version
of Father Pesch's dissertation, Theologie der Rechtfertigung bei Martin
Luther und Thomas von Aquin (Mainz: Matthias Grünewald, 1967). This
essay originally appeared in the October, 1967, issue of Theologische
Literaturzeitung, but has been considerably expanded for the present
collection.

Father Pesch's purpose is to present the central "hermeneutical consideration" that must control methodology in this work of comparing

Luther and Aquinas. We note that his "existential" theology (existentielle) has no direct connection with the investigation in contemporary metaphysics of the Existentialien of human existence.

Notes begin on page 182.

Existential and Sapiential Theology--the Theological Confrontation between Luther and Thomas Aquinas

Otto H. Pesch, O.P.

Why Luther and Aquinas?

A systematic theological confrontation seeking to bring Luther and Thomas Aquinas into dialogue with each other is by no means an obvious task. Why should we set precisely these two in dialogue? They did not meet to dispute in life, as did Luther and Cajetan or Luther and Johann Eck. Centuries--very eventful ones--separated them. There is not even a direct historical line of intellectual influence by which Luther would be dependent on the great scholastic. Luther did not come out of the Thomistic tradition, but from the via moderna that began with William of Ockham. When one investigates the medieval roots of Luther's theology, especially of his doctrine of justification, one finds connections with German mysticism and with the Franciscan school of theology.[1] Researchers are sharply divided over the significance of these influences on Luther, but it is certain that Luther himself read almost nothing of Thomas.[2] Thus Thomas Aquinas is not to be counted among the sources of Luther's thought, not even as an underground source. Nor is Thomas in any way preferred by Luther as the addressee of his polemic. Ordinarily Luther sees him as just another of the hated "Sophists" of scholastic theology whom he fundamentally rejects. Luther gives Thomas no special place or rank.

Thus the historian finds the idea of a theological encounter between Luther and Thomas unfruitful, since historically no such encounter took place. Only the systematic theologian can bring about this encounter as he reflects on the respective positions of the two theologians and tries to bring them into relation with each other.[3]

But still why should we be interested in this confrontation? Fortunately, the Lutheran theologian, Ulrich Kühn, has recently given us an enlightening answer to this question in his study of Thomas' theology of law.[4] A Catholic theologian and especially an admirer of St. Thomas can agree wholeheartedly with the ideas Kühn develops. He points out that for learning to understand one's dialogue-partner it is not enough to deal with his official dogmatic or confessional statements, nor with his contemporary theology. One must also deal with those comprehensive products of theological thinking which are commonly termed "classic" and which serve as part of the native soil of all theology in a given confession. Such comprehensive positions give one a basis for understanding the characteristic dogmatic statements of the confession one is dealing with, and often enough the classic theology is an actual source of the dogma.[5] Frequently theologians study their own tradition in this manner, but rarely does one present such an idea as the reason for calling upon Lutherans to turn to the study of Thomas Aquinas, as does Kühn.[6] Nonetheless, this approach is repeatedly although implicitly used in the discussions of controversial theology, where in spite of clear knowledge of the tenuous historical connection between our two theologians still they are very often key witnesses in setting off Catholic and Reformation theology from each other.[7] Accordingly, it ought to make sense in our contemporary ecumenical discussion to carry out an extensive comparison of Luther and Thomas on the questions dividing Lutheran and Catholic theology. Since they give classic comprehensive statements of Protestant and Catholic thinking, it would furthermore be a real service to our ecumenical search for agreement, if we can show that both on the whole and in detailed questions a profitable dialogue can be begun between Luther and Thomas.

Ulrich Kühn goes even further in listing the reasons for Protestants to study St. Thomas, thus implicitly calling for the confrontation of Luther and Thomas. This study can clearly promote mutual understanding and thereby possibly contribute to the ecumenical discussion. Kühn poses the further question whether Thomas as the high point of the medieval synthesis belongs only to the Catholic Church and to her theology, or whether there is not also an evangelical Thomas who should be discovered, or at least a Thomas who has important words for Protestant theology.[8] Kühn reviews some striking examples from recent research, where a different Thomas is emerging than the one we know from the grace controversies or from modern neo-scholasticism. Kühn looks upon Thomas Aquinas as part of the heritage of Protestant theology.[9] These are extraordinarily courageous words which indicate a significant task. In principle, they can be referred to the whole of that scholasticism which Luther so abhorred. Kühn affirms programmatically something which up to now has seemed allowable both in theory and practice only to biblical scholars: namely, that in a certain sense there is a pre-confessional theology which cannot be claimed exclusively by one or the other confession. In any case, the ecumenically active theologian must be ready to admit that in studying St. Thomas he is dealing not only with a classic presentation of Catholic theology but as well with part of the heritage of Reformation theology -- at least according to the opinion of one Protestant theologian. If this latter view be true, which sees Thomas' classic Catholic theology as more than just a discussion partner, in fact as somehow part of the Lutheran heritage, then we have another weighty reason for thinking that it makes good sense and may be very promising to carry out dialogue between Luther and Thomas.

We can be thankful that today all this is no longer merely something to be desired or recommended, but that Protestants have produced a series of historical and systematic studies of the theology of St. Thomas. On both sides different topics have been investigated with a view to asking whether and to what extent Luther and Thomas are in basic agreement, so as to make some of the traditional controversies superfluous.[10] The increasing number of affirmative judgments do not stem from ecumenical euphoria, but from careful and thorough examination of the texts and their background of conception and thought.[11]

Still, the agreement found in these investigations is always qualified as being "basic" or "in principle." It is often depressing to observe the peculiar helplessness with which scholars find themselves forced to admit that Luther and Thomas are very close to each other, with only the last--but most decisive--step toward full agreement still impossible. In fact, it can happen that an investigation ascertains complete agreement between the two regarding theological content in spite of different terminology, but then it is said further that precisely this difference in terms and concepts is of such objective importance that in their very agreement an abyss still separates Luther and Thomas. In what follows we will abstract from the question whether the opposition which remains in such a situation is ecclesially divisive, preferring to ask instead about the precise nature and character of this opposition.

Much is already achieved when one clearly admits that different words often refer to the same content and, more important, that behind the same words there can be different concepts and even whole systems of categories. In our case these differences come down to the basic point that while Luther thinks in the category of relationship, [12] Thomas thinks in ontological categories of nature. We do not want to debate here the respective justification of the two approaches. Rather let us move on to the further important realization of the different orientations toward understanding that separate Luther and Thomas. [13] At this level there is a difference in basic concern and interest which is prior to all theological reflection, which may not even be conscious, but which produces the diverse structure of the questions each ask.

In spite of the contemporary efforts to elaborate Luther's theology of creation, [14] it is still right to state this basic difference in brief form by opposing Luther's concentration on human salvation to Aquinas' concentration on God as creator and on the world as his creation. This difference received classic formulation in the texts in which the two theologians stated the task and object of theology. Luther writes:

> The proper subject of theology is man guilty of sin and condemned, and God the Justifier and Savior of man the sinner. Whatever is asked or discussed in theology outside this subject, is error and poison. [15]

St. Thomas states:

> Christian theology should be pronounced to be a science. Yet bear in mind that sciences are of two kinds: some work from premises recognized in the innate light of in-

telligence, . . . while others work from premises recognized in the light of a higher science. . . . In this second manner is Christian theology a science, for it flows from founts recognized in the light of a higher science, namely God's very own which he shares with the blessed.

Christian theology . . . is like an imprint on us of God's own knowledge . . .[16]

We can take yet a further step and go beyond the question of the different content and themes of the two theologies to ask about the respective patterns of thought. The contrast here would be between Luther's well-known use of antithesis and opposition all through his work and Thomas' apparently orderly derivation of one idea from the other.[17]

But with all that we have ascertained we have not yet reached the ultimate level of opposition. One can still ask further about the source of this diversity in categorical systems, basic interest, and patterns of thought. This question does not lead us to an opposition in the area of thought content, but to the difference between two ways of doing theology. More precisely it is not an opposition of two forms of thought (Denkformen), but of two intellectual styles of performance (Denkvollzugsformen). We will refer to this difference with the concepts, "existential theology" and "sapiential theology."

In this context we wish to develop a two-part thesis. 1) These two intellectual styles of performance, which we will further explain, necessarily produce diverse and even opposing dogmatic formulations about one and the same given reality. 2) All the differences between Luther and Thomas which we have mentioned, even those coexisting with agreement as to content, stem from the fact that Luther does existential and Thomas sapiential theology. This latter situation gives rise to the question whether the other oppositions which have not yet been thoroughly studied do not in fact stem from this basic difference of style in performing theology.

Neither Luther nor Thomas refer to our distinction in their explicit considerations of methodology. However, we shall see that in both there are some texts pointing in this direction. From the nature of the question we could hardly expect it to be otherwise, since we are dealing with the deepest, pre-rational orientations and fundamental options of thought. These are most commonly recognized only by a third party.

We can and must observe the results of this basic difference in positions that are typical of each theologian. We find two classic and easily intelligible examples of this difference of two ways of doing theology in the respective answers of Thomas and Luther to the questions about certitude of salvation and about the "co-operation" or freedom of man under God's influence. Before we turn to three other more difficult problems, it will be helpful to at least briefly sketch out these first two examples.[18]

Certitude of salvation

Regarding the question "certitude of salvation" we can presuppose as a result of other research that the Lutheran-Catholic controversy on this point has been burdened by serious terminological misunderstanding. The certitude of grace, which Thomas and the Council of Trent speak of as impossible,[19] and the certitude of salvation preached by Luther are not the same thing. When Luther affirms certainty regarding salvation and when Thomas and Trent affirm uncertainty, this is not a Yes and a No to the same question. In addition, the reality which Luther indicates by the term "certainty of salvation" is at least implicit in St. Thomas' "certainty of hope," a fact which Trent has somehow overlooked.[20] But still the posthumous clarification of this controversy does not bring an exhaustive solution of the problem. For Luther is at one with Catholic teaching in denying that the salvation of the Christian is safe beyond any threat and in excluding the idea that the Christian can objectively make sure of his salvation in a way that frees him henceforth from all anguish. Nonetheless, Luther attacks the Catholic thesis affirming the ultimate uncertainty of the state of grace. Here we must seek a further reason, and we come eventually to the distinction between sapiential and existential theology.

A person can respond to this question about the conditions of our salvation and our certitude with a distinction. Accordingly, with a view to God's fidelity our salvation is irrevocably certain, but in view of human weakness and instability we cannot speak of certitude of final salvation, since a man can at any moment refuse to rely on God's fidelity. In giving such an answer, a person is viewing the problem from the outside, from outside one's concrete existence in faith. This reminds us of Thomas' words about God's own knowledge which he shares with the blessed. The answer based on this distinction is indeed true, but it is not the whole truth and it becomes false if one constantly omits the rest of the truth--as Luther charged was the case in Catholic teaching.

It is also necessary that the Christian be able to live with this "objective" state of affairs in his personal existence in faith. And from within the act of faith itself one can no longer apply the distinction from the objective description of his situation. Faith is by definition the trusting acceptance of God's gift of salvation. To speak of uncertainty of salvation within the act of faith is to cancel out faith. Thus certainty of salvation is no longer a given condition that one ascertains, but is so to say the decisive existential product of the very act of faith itself. In other words, "certainty of salvation" does not belong in the category of knowledge, but is rather a way of existing.[21] Thus we come to see that we are dealing with two ways of speaking of one and the same state of affairs as a man stands under God's grace. These two ways of speaking need not exclude each other, although they are signs of a deep difference in the manner of approaching a theological question.

Cooperation

On the question of human "cooperation" with God we can similarly presuppose that recent studies have considerably diminished the intensity of the older controversies.[22] Still, a deep difference remains. If one examines, as Thomas does, the ontological and theological structures of the event of justification and of the existence of the Christian in grace, then he will never want to say that man remains a lifeless and subpersonal object of God's working and so is purely passive. Even Luther does not say this. Rather God lays claim to man in his freedom and ability to respond. But from within the act of faith the issue is no longer the structural interrelation of divine and human action. The believer asks instead, to whom here and now do I owe my salvation? In this context, let us say in prayer, if I am to speak of "cooperation," then that will certainly not be in the unthinkable form, "O God I owe my salvation both to you and to myself." It is no accident that Luther attacked the doctrine of "cooperation" precisely with reference to the consequences it had in prayer.[23] Again we see Luther's completely different way of doing theology from that of Thomas. Conversely, the affirmation of human freedom and cooperation under grace by Thomas and in Catholic theology has never been so meant that it promotes the kind of prayer indicated here which Luther caricatured. -- All this will become yet clearer as we turn to three more difficult examples and take them up in greater detail.

67 / Pesch

Christology

A first, quite simple example that does not force us into the ultimate subtleties of our question is that of the respective viewpoints from which Luther and Aquinas saw the person of Christ. Recent research has made secure the thesis that the older Thomas developed from the so-called Neochalcedonian position of his early works toward a more original Chalcedonian Christology. In part this was due to his study of the primary sources, the acta of the council, as this was afforded him in the papal curia from 1259 to 1268.[24] This meant that in his later works it was precisely the undiminished humanity of Christ that was of ever increasing importance especially with reference to its significance in the work of salvation. In fact, in the Summa Theologiae the accentuation of the questions and the statements is such that one can easily show that Thomas' "special Christology" (Part III, Questions 1-26) is merely the dogmatic prologomenon to his treatment of the life and redemptive work of the God-man (Questions 27-59).[25]

Luther too had great interest in the humanity of Christ, also for soteriological reasons.[26] One could therefore say that Luther agrees with Thomas in this area. But still one cannot miss seeing the diversity present in materially identical affirmations. St. Thomas sees the primary task set before him by the human nature of Christ to be the metaphysical problem of how the one person subsists and exists in two natures. This he must think out in every possible direction in all its consequences, in order to set forth with the greatest possible clarity the mystery of the Redeemer and so make secure the salvific meaning of his work from its objective basis. Outside of faith this whole intellectual effort would obviously be meaningless, but faith is not itself thematic within the undertaking. Faith is present in the manner of the mathematical sign before the bracket.

Luther as well holds fast to the doctrine of the two natures of Christ, but he is also capable of sharply critical remarks about the speculative Christology of scholasticism.[27] Luther's insight is that true faith in Christ is each day a new task that needs support. It is not simply realized in Christological orthodoxy alone, but only comes to full term when a person sees and grasps in Jesus Christ "the reflection of the Father's heart" in this incarnate presence of God's saving will.[28] For Luther the great theme treated in scholastic Christology is reduced to the function of a presupposition.[29] The explicit theme of saving faith is the Lordship of Christ and the main interest of the theologian is the living presentation of Jesus as man so as to continually nourish faith.[30] Thus we have two different ways to express the same reality of the soteriological significance of the humanity of Christ.

Sin and grace

A second example is considerably more difficult, but especially characteristic of the difference between Luther and Thomas. This is the question of the relation between sin and grace, which Luther has expressed in the formula, simul iustus et peccator. We know the formulations with which Luther again and again causes consternation among Catholic theologians. Some examples would be these:

> . . . he is at the same time both a sinner and righteous, a sinner in fact (re vera) but righteous by reason of the reckoning and certain promise of God.[31]

> Those justified in Christ are not sinners, and yet they are still sinners.[32]

> No Christian has any sin, but then every Christian has sin.[33]

> You know that we are indeed righteous, pure, and holy, but then that we are also sinners, unrighteous, and condemned.[34]

> By the divine imputation we are in truth wholly righteous. . . . But we are also truly sinners through and through, but only in so far as we regard ourselves (sed ad nos respiciendo).[35]

> This corresponds to the situation of one who is baptized or is doing penance and yet remains in the weakness of concupiscence. Though his weakness violates the law "You shall not covet" and certainly is a mortal sin, God in his mercy does not reckon it as such. . . .[36]

St. Thomas' clear rejection of any idea of grace and sin coexisting in the same person is equally well known. He took this up in the famous question whether the justification of a sinner occurs in a single instant or in successive phases. Here he treated the simul quite precisely and rejected it.[37] For if the gift of justifying grace were not given in a single undivided instant, but in temporal succession, then it would either be the case that the soul was at least for a moment both in sin and grace, or that sin could be cancelled out at a moment before grace had taken hold of the soul. The first result is as impossible as the second. Therefore it appears that Luther and Thomas are in fact not at all near to each other, for they seem to be saying Yes and No respectively to the same question. About a decade ago, the most a Catholic theologian could grant here was that Luther's formula was an emphatic expression of his own personal religious life and so could be accepted much in the way the saints see themselves as the greatest sinners. But the simul could not be taken seriously as a theological or dogmatic statement.

Now, however, a significant modification of this opposition has taken place as Catholics have in more recent years begun to understand Luther's simul more exactly.[38] We can point to three aspects of this advance:

a) The state of the simul iustus et peccator is itself the result of God's new creation in man. An abyss separates the sinner who is also righteous from one who is only a sinner. Catholics have taken account of Luther's distinctions between peccatum regnans prior to the simul and peccatum regnatum in the simul. Similarly Luther distinguishes the simul peccator from the iniquus. Catholics have also seen how Luther speaks of sin being "treated differently" in the justified.[39] The peccator of Thomas belongs wholly on the side of Luther's iniquus with peccatum regnans. But these are precisely what Luther does not set in coexistence with the righteous man. The only way one can work out a legitimate comparison is by asking whether Thomas' righteous man can coexist with a "sinner" who is totally removed from the sinfulness that according to Thomas cancels justification itself. The creative deed of God must be seen to intervene.

b) This latter question will only be answered negatively when one thinks of sin and grace in terms of the category of quality. This is the one condition that excludes an agreement between Luther and Thomas from the very outset. As a fact Thomas does think of them as qualities that further characterize and determine a subject. He conceives of the sinner and the righteous man according to the model of a subject with attributes. In this context Luther's thesis is absurd. Just as the same body cannot be both hot and cold at the same time, so the same man cannot be at once both sinner and righteous.[40] But, as we already hinted, Luther does not think in terms of qualities (especially here), but in terms of personal relationships. For him sin and grace are opposing relations in which a person is involved. Sin is the relation-

ship he himself began by his enmity toward God. It is his relation
to God that man has broken. But grace and righteousness are the
relationship of friendship, communion, and benevolence which
God has established with man in spite of and against his sin. Since
these same words--sin, grace, and righteousness--mean something different for Thomas and Luther, it is not the case that the
two theologians come into immediate conflict with each other.
Also the favorite objection against accepting Luther's thesis is
excluded, that is, that his position entails a logical and metaphysical absurdity. For it is not impossible to conceive of the
coexistence of Luther's two relationships.

   c) The reflex question that the Catholic can then pose is
whether in fact the believing Christian is also in the relation of
enmity to God. However, this must be made more precise. The
opposed relationships of sin and righteousness are not factual
situations which one can ascertain by something like a medical
diagnosis. They are rather occurrences in the life of the Christian
that are brought about ever anew by divine and human action. According to Luther the Christian is in fact continually sinning by
failing in that which God wants of him. He is opposed to God's
will and the depths of this opposition is clearly attested by the
effort he must muster to act in accord with God's will. Then
when he has once fulfilled God's will, he gloats over his achievement instead of giving God honor and praise. But just as man is
continually sinning, so God is continually showing him a forgiveness that prevents man from frustrating God's benevolence. God
does not impute the sin--a concept which cannot be qualified as
part of an unreal "theology of the as-if," in view of Luther's way
of thinking in terms of personal relationships. In the midst of
his continuing opposition against God, the sinner can be righteous
if he does not allow his sin to cancel out God's word of non-
imputation. He is righteous when he accepts this word, or more
simply, when he believes.

   In the light of these three clarifications of the meaning of
Luther's simul we see the original sharp opposition between
Luther and Thomas shrinking down to the proportions of a simple difference. Although St. Thomas does no more than approach
Luther's simul from a distance, [41] at any rate his position is not
such as to give rise to the objection that Luther does not take
seriously the radical division separating existence in sin and
existence in righteousness. One cannot appeal to Thomas in attributing to Luther the patent absurdity of qualifying one and the
same subject with mutually exclusive dispositions. In fact Thomas

is quite open to the third point about man continually sinning and thus living by reason of God's forgiveness. One can see this by careful examination of how Thomas distinguishes the original justice of Adam from the justice of the justified sinner.[42] What separates them is precisely the simul.

Here another opposition also collapses, which has not been modified by any of the advances made so far. Does the constant sinning of the Christian only mean that he continually performs discrete sinful deeds, between which however there can well be a more or less long period of no sin? Is it that these deeds do not exclude other deeds of pure obedience and perfect love which are performed under the influence of grace? Before such a question the explicit texts of St. Thomas will not carry us further. But Luther intends to affirm a good deal more. He not only thinks of the possibility of discrete sinful deeds even in quite close temporal succession, but concerns himself as well with the per-during radical evil of the heart, with the sin, evil, and opposition against God which continually stirs in this heart. This is the sin that poisons all the discrete deeds, even the good ones, at their root. Precisely with regard to this sin one must turn over anew in faith to God's non-imputation. Thus there persists a strict and quite radical coexistence of sin and faith-righteousness which is not broken for a moment. And this coexistence is the inner structure of righteous existence in this life. At this point we have nothing more to "clarify," since we have arrived at a single question to which is given an affirmative and negative answer respectively. After we exclude the misunderstandings, an ultimate opposition appears all the more forcefully between the two theologies we have found so near to each other.

The traditional explanations we used in the course of the three clarifications are not sufficient to account completely for this ultimate opposition. What then explains it? We believe that the difference between existential and sapiential theology is operative here, and in fact this problem brings out well what is peculiar to this difference. For here we have a case in which one and the same given aspect of Christian existence, the interrelation of righteousness and sin with the former constantly threatened by the latter, being affirmed in theological statements of an existential and sapiential character, thereby gives rise to opposing dogmatic positions. One must note that the "evil heart" in Luther's view is not the result of an analytical examination of existence, not even in the manner of depth psychology. When he speaks of man's "evil heart," of the root-sin that remains

72

after justification, this is a word of confession before God. Admittedly Luther sought to base this confession on the biblical text, "Thou shalt not covet,"[43] from which he concluded that concupiscence, which according to Thomas and Catholic doctrine remains after justification, is in fact sin and not just the fomes or tinder of sin.[44] If Luther's position really depended on the biblical commandment, then his simul would have been long since placed among the curiosities of history. Modern Old Testament exegesis would not allow this command to support the whole weight of Luther's idea of concupiscence.[45] However, Luther's confession does not rest on one text, but rather upon that experience of faith which condenses into unity the total message of Scripture about man's sin and salvation. As I stand before God in the living experience of faith, I can only confess, "Before you I am a sinner. I never measure up to your holiness." This is the experience of Christians of every age, and in the posture of confession a Catholic can say nothing different. To realize this, he need only attempt to pray something like, "God, I thank you that I am righteous in your sight." This prayer simply does not work, even if the one who mouths it has just been to confession and been absolved.[46]

Here we have reached the ultimate cause of Luther's simul. It has been well described as "a reality of prayer."[47] The sin that remains after justification emerges in one's own prayerful self-description before God, and only here. This means that the simul peccator occurs as one formulates his own existence in faith, where at the same time he is prayerfully accepting God's word of grace! The more theoretical and dogmatic formulation of the simul iustus et peccator is nothing more than a subsequent descriptive statement of an affirmation originating within an I-thou encounter with God. Thus Luther's simul is a classic example of existential theology, i.e., of the theology which seeks to make thematic our very existence in faith.

The theology of Thomas Aquinas is far removed from the I-thou situation. He speaks descriptively of God in the third person and views creation and man objectively. As we hinted above, his theology strives to recapture God's own thoughts about the world, man, and history. The power to do this is given "by the light of faith"--and what a sublime spirituality lies behind Thomas' frequent references to "light"! This is not theology done from a neutral position, as the common criticism contends,[48] but from a position at which the act of faith does not itself play an immediate thematic role. Faith is rather the quite obvious supposition for the awe-filled pondering of God's glorious works. This is the medieval meaning of "wisdom," the understanding of reality in terms of its ultimate causes, as we learn in faith the very thoughts of God himself.[49] This then is sapiential theology.

Where then does sin have its place in this vision? Clearly it is impossible in this sapiential theology that sin play the wide-ranging and dominant role it has in Luther's work. If one chose to portray sin primarily in terms of its power, then it would be impossible to make a truly convincing presentation of God's sovereign mastery over the whole history of salvation. Thus Thomas' first and last word regarding sin speaks of its impotence. In predestining Christ, God has from all eternity chosen man for salvation. Because of Christ, God can "permit" sin. Because of Christ, sin is from the beginning the felix culpa in spite of the devastation it produces.[50] Since Thomas is a sapiential thinker, he cannot arrive at Luther's simul. The deepest root of the opposition between Luther and Thomas on sin and righteousness is the difference in their way of doing theology. Luther does existential theology, Thomas sapiential theology.

Salvation by faith or by charity

We can sketch briefly a third example, the respective teaching of Luther and Aquinas on the essence of man's response within God's work of salvation. Omitting a detailed treatment of texts,[51] it can be presupposed as proven that Luther's polemic against the idea "faith formed by charity" rests on his misunderstanding of the position at least of St. Thomas. Admittedly, this misunderstanding was practically inevitable after late scholasticism had reformulated the high scholastic teaching on grace. It is no accident that post-reformation Catholic theologians have also frequently contributed to this misunderstanding as they imply that faith must be "formed" by charity because it needs the supplementation of good works to avoid being "dead faith." Many seem to think here of a "work" or "act" of love of God, which is separate from faith.

In the service of truth, we must note that what Thomas calls "faith" is only one moment, the intellectual assent, within Luther's comprehensive idea of faith. This is no place to dispute the legitimacy of Thomas' use of terms, but it is clear that when he says that faith must be "formed," or more exactly, that God's gift of saving faith is in fact formed by charity, then he is saying that actually the intellectual assent is integrated within the totality of a more comprehensive act of accepting salvation. Admittedly this is somewhat oversimplified, but if one wants to use Luther's

sharp alternative between faith and good works, then this charity
that "forms faith" is not on the side of good works, but on the
side of faith.[52] Caritas is for Thomas the essential designation
for the total acceptance of salvation. According to Thomas--as
with Luther--this is so given by God through Christ that even
the acceptance of the gift is an effect of God's grace within the
area of human volition. In other words, Thomas speaks of
charity precisely where Luther speaks of faith. Here we can
confidently speak of an objective agreement between them.

Still, we must ask ourselves why Luther attributes salvation
to "faith" and Thomas to "charity, " even though both made extensive studies of the same Pauline epistles. Again, it seems, we
must come back to the distinction between existential and sapiential theology. Luther is in the posture of confession, where he
addresses God and gives an account of himself before God. Thus
he must speak primarily of his own nothingness and sin and seek
a word of pardon. In accepting salvation, the accent must thus
be on the encounter with the God of redemption and forgiveness.
This is precisely what from the time of St. Paul is preeminent
in the idea of faith. Luther has thus freed this idea from a somewhat questionable scholastic reduction.[53]

In contrast, St. Thomas looks on the world from God's own
vantage point. He sees all creation in the divine perspective of
its movement out from God and its return to God under his
sovereign influence. This is the synthetic structure of his Summa
Theologiae.[54] Charity is the form in which a man makes his return to God. Thomas does not hesitate to speak of a universal
law of love operative in the whole of creation. He can attribute
to every creature a form of love proportionate to its ontological
status. This love is the law and motive force of creation's return to its origin in God.[55] Thus when Thomas wishes to sum
up in one word the whole of the salvation-act he cannot do this
more meaningfully than the word caritas. By this he refers to
the more decisive and comprehensive aspect of human existence.
And it is well known that this is not just man's love for God, but
that it is Thomas' unique contribution in the history of theology
to have spoken here of the love of mutual friendship between God
and man.[56] Thus we see again, in the alternative between faith
and charity, how in the midst of objective agreement the diver-
gence between existential and sapiential theology contains and
conditions the further differences separating Luther and Thomas.

Existential and sapiential theology

Our examples should make clear the difference between existential and sapiential theology as applied to Luther and St. Thomas. We can draw together the main elements under the following headings:

Existential theology	Sapiential theology
has as theme the act itself of faith as well as its theoretical implications.	has the act of faith (only) as the basis for its statements, without it becoming thematized.
is literally directed to one's own existential self-accounting before God.	is directed to "wisdom," in the medieval sense of understanding through ultimate causes.
looks from man toward God and then from God back upon man.	looks from God upon man.
speaks prototypically within an I-Thou situation and only consequently and derivatively in the third person.	speaks primarily in the third person.
speaks in the mode of confession.	speaks descriptively.
regarding salvation stresses faith, humility, and repentance.	stresses wonder, charity, and friendship with God.

By way of definition we might say the following. Existential theology is the way of doing theology from within the self-actuation of our existence in faith, as we submit to God in the obedience of faith. Its affirmations are so formulated that the actual faith and confession of the speaker are not merely necessary presuppositions but are reflexly thematized. Sapiential theology is the way of doing theology from outside one's self-actuation in the existence in faith, in the sense that in its doctrinal statements the faith and confession of the speaker is the enduring presupposition, but is not thematic within this theology. This theology strives to mirror and recapitulate God's own thoughts about the world, men, and history, insofar as God has disclosed them.

Before our concluding remarks, we wish to secure our conception against possible misunderstanding.

a) The existential theology we have described is not the same as the "theological existentialism" of exegetes and systematicians like Rudolf Bultmann, Friedrich Gogarten, Gerhard Ebeling, and others. The catchword "existential theology" has been used by the opponents of this contemporary school. We need not investigate here whether Bultmann and his followers have really maintained all that both Catholic and Protestant theologians have attacked under this heading. It may well be that theological broadsides have been fired against straw men. It is also important to note that in recent years there has arisen an effort to understand Luther which opponents have termed an "existential Luther-interpretation." The opposition has proposed a "historical interpretation" as being more correct and more reliable. I admit that I am myself among the Catholic Luther scholars who--albeit with reservations--sympathize with this "existential interpretation" and see it as a significant and stimulating way to gain access to Luther and make him speak to men of today. This has in turn called forth concerned warnings from Catholic Luther scholars of genuine ecumenical convictions like Joseph Lortz, Erwin Iserloh, and Peter Manns. This, however, is not the place to carry on this argument.[57]

However, the essential point to keep in mind is that this disputed mode of interpreting Luther is not to be identified with our thesis in this essay about Luther's "existential theology." An "existential theology" in the present sense is one that speaks directly from the self-actuation of existence in faith and addresses this same self-actuation by making the act of faith thematic in theology. Distinct from this is the "existential interpretation" which lays down the methodological prescription that texts and statements about life are to be investigated not for their objective content but for the understanding of existence that is implicit in them. This method could be just as well applied in interpreting a given existential theology as a particular sapiential theology.

Therefore the existential interpretation of Luther can first mean the investigation of his work with an eye to the understanding of existence entailed in his theology. This methodology could be used as well in investigating any other theology and perhaps be both instructive and stimulating. This, however, has nothing to do with the distinction we have used in this essay. Further, it is in no way opposed to a historical investigation of Luther, but is rather one of history's genuine questions. On the other hand the "existential interpretation" of Luther can mean that Luther was already a theological existentialist like Bultmann and his followers. This thesis not only has nothing to do with the concept we have used, but furthermore is quite clearly wrong.

b) One should not speak of the existential theology we have described as a theology given to psychologizing our relation to God, and thereby opposed to the more objective sapiential theology. When we speak of the simul iustus et peccator as a "reality of prayer," this does not mean that the simul has no reality outside the psychic act of prayer. Rather, it refers to a reality that only emerges in speaking with God, not in descriptive speech about God. It is not a theoretical, but a confessional affirmation. Similarly, a sapiential theology would only be thoroughly "objective" if we had access to God's thoughts from a neutral vantage point outside one's existence in faith. But the sapiential theologian in fact reflects and ponders from within the total human submission to God in faith and love. The objectivity of this theology lies in this alone, that the act of faith, the necessary and single basis of the theology, is not itself thematized in every statement.

c) It would also be misleading to set parallel with our distinction the alternative between anthropocentric and theocentric theology. The latter distinction deals with content and with the more formal horizon of understanding within which the content is grasped. Our distinction deals rather with the way or style in which the theology is actually carried out. Furthermore, it can easily be shown that Luther no less than Thomas has elaborated a theology that is at the same time both theocentric and anthropocentric. Here they are quite similar. The fact that we are dealing with two distinct sets of alternatives is made clear in the contemporary case of Karl Rahner. His anthropocentric orientation is beyond question, and his is at the same time a classic example of a sapiential theology using a modern conceptuality. The most striking indication of the sapiential character of Rahner's work is the difficulty he has in giving sin its proper place in his system.

d) Finally, it would be wrong to identify the distinction we use with the alternative between personalistic and metaphysical modes of theological discourse. This has to do with what categorical sets are to be applied, and so again pertains to questions of content. We often hear that Duns Scotus and his school developed a theological personalism, but this was no defense against Luther's protest, precisely because it was a personalism with a sapiential orientation.[58]

In conclusion, we will take up three points.

1 In the absence of explicit methodological expositions, we can ask if there are any direct statements by our two theologians which would serve to confirm the distinction we have used. For Thomas the answer is easily made in the affirmative, by reason of his definition of theology. The text we cited above,[59] in which St. Thomas gave the purpose of theology, is as well a programmatic formulation for a sapiential theology. St. Thomas knows no other kind of theology. In Luther's case we can begin with the connection we established between existential theology and prayer. Accordingly, every theological statement is in fact a variation on a word spoken in prayer and can be easily transformed into prayer by a simple change in its grammatical form. This means that prayer becomes the norm in judging the legitimacy of theological affirmations. Thus our distinction between the two kinds of theology is confirmed in Luther's work, when he has recourse to prayer as a norm for the proof or rejection of a theological affirmation. And this is what he does in some of his famous texts. For instance, there is the prayer that he attempts to show follows necessarily from the theology of his opponent Latomus:

> Lord God, behold this good work which I have done
> through the help of thy grace. There is in it neither
> fault nor any sin, nor does it need thy forgiving mercy.
> I do not ask for this, as I want thee to judge it with thy
> strictest and truest judgments.[60]

In De servo arbitrio there is a text in which Luther argues against the freedom of the will that even the saints who defended it in theory forgot this freedom in their prayer and denied it.[61] Even more striking are two bitter table remarks in which Luther makes a direct connection between specific words of prayer and different theological constructions he wants to reject:

> When I pray, "Hallowed be thy name," then I am cursing
> Erasmus and all the heretics who insult God and blaspheme
> against him.[62]

> The first three petitions [of the Lord's Prayer] go
> diametrically against him [the Pope]: Accursed be
> his name, may his kingdom be destroyed and crumble,
> may his will be dishonored and opposed. [63]

Thus our distinction between sapiential and existential theology does not rest alone on our analysis of thought structures, but is also confirmed by direct statements of our two theologians about their respective theologies.

2 Strictly speaking, our analysis has only shown that some of the opposed answers given by Luther and Thomas to the same question are due to the differences between existential and sapiential theology. Can we go on to say that this is true in all cases where the two are still opposed after clarification of mere misunderstandings? We cannot simply presuppose that this basic difference of approach explains all differences, but this must rather be proven in each case. Naturally we cannot attempt this in this brief essay, [64] but it is sufficient that we have here made it clear that no systematic confrontation between Luther and Thomas can avoid dealing with this basic difference we have treated. The distinction between existential and sapiential theology must be an essential hermeneutical element in the systematic comparison of the theologies of Martin Luther and Thomas Aquinas.

3 So far our reflections have brought about a more precise determination of the basic difference and basic opposition separating our two theologians. Does this also entail an immediate gain in the ecumenical aspect of our efforts? An adequate answer to this question would be complex and extended, and would eventually pose an ultimate question whether Scripture prescribes or excludes either one of the two ways of doing theology, or perhaps legitimates both ways. [65] Let us at least mention briefly two aspects of the answer to this question.

First, if we can presuppose an alteration in St. Thomas' way of thinking theologically, in none of our three main examples must we conclude that Thomas would exclude Luther's position. Thomas makes no statement in his Christology that would exclude Luther's way of preaching about Christ. It is true that Thomas could not come to the point of affirming Luther's simul. But to exclude the simul, his theology would have to lead to the kind of prayer that we ourselves found to be impossible. This, however, is not the meaning of the Thomistic position. And one can ask how Thomas would have explained the "through my most grevious fault" of the <u>Confiteor</u> in his daily celebration of Mass. On the question of faith and charity, Ulrich Kühn has recently shown us how St. Thomas' teaching on charity is fully open to all aspects of Luther's idea of faith.[66]

Secondly, Thomas' sapiential theology is itself another form of existential theology, provided we do not simply identify this kind of theology with Luther's highly personal way of working. In a somewhat wider sense, it is "existential" in being the expression and incarnation of a heartfelt commitment to God, and of an existence in faith that is no less genuine for having none of Luther's personal stamp upon it. To ground this assertion we can here refer to more recent scholarly studies of St. Thomas.[67]

If this turns out to be true, then it can well be confirmed that the terms "existential" and "sapiential" point to a difference which is not an opposition--as we have consciously formulated it from the beginning. Then if a person refrains from making Luther's kind of existential theology an absolute from the very outset, so as to exclude any other kind of theology, then the presumption would favor the possibility that the difference we have treated here, and all the further derivative differences, could in fact dwell together in the same home. It could be that each of the two ways of doing theology needs the critical services of the other in order to guard against slipping off into distortions. It could be that the Church needs both theologies in order to live out all the tensions entailed in Christianity.

Introduction to Paul Hacker

Paul Hacker was born in the Rheinland in 1913. After studies at Bonn, Heidelberg, and Frankfurt, he received his doctorate in Berlin in 1940 majoring in Slavonic Philology and Indian Studies. During the war he served in the German navy as a language expert at Supreme Headquarters. His research after the war was in Indian philosophy and he established his competence as a student of the Advaita-Vendanta system with his second dissertation, which he submitted at Bonn in 1949. After lecturing at Münster and Bonn, and spending a year at the Mithila Institute in Bihar, India, Hacker took the newly established chair of Indian Studies in the University of Münster in 1963. He contributes regularly the results of his research on Hinduism to international journals devoted to his field.

Hacker speaks of himself "as a layman whose interest in theology was roused by the problems he faced as a Christian intellectual." He has always felt that his research was in the service of the Church, a purpose that led him to study the Church Fathers in their encounter with the ancient paganism of Greece and Rome. Hacker took an early interest in ecumenical work, attending the 1952 Faith and Order conference in Lund. In 1960 he joined with Pastor Max Lackmann and others in founding the League for Protestant-Catholic Reunion. Two years later, he became resigned to the impossibility of early corporate reunion and so was received into the Catholic Church as an individual in September 1962. Hacker's study of Luther had been intensive ever since his university days. After many discussions with friends he became convinced that he should publish the results of his discovery of a central point of dissonance between Luther and the New Testament. This resulted in the book, Das Ich im Glauben bei Martin Luther, published by Styria Verlag of Graz, Austria, in 1966.

Joseph Ratzinger wrote in the foreword of Hacker's book that--appearances to the contrary--it was in the best sense an "ecumenical" book, because of its decisive and passionate concern for the truth of the Christian Gospel. Hacker does not claim to present the whole of Luther. The other contributions to the present volume make this clear. But Hacker's intense search introduces a note without which this collection would be incomplete. He forces us back to the New Testament text which must be the eventual scene of our encounter and union.

Besides Hacker's provocative ecumenical contribution, his work has special significance in the narrower area of Luther research. His independent study of Luther invites comparison with Ernst Bizer's Fides ex auditu, a book that has all but dominated discussion among Luther scholars in the past decade. Hacker corroborates Bizer's finding that Luther's thought was significantly modified in early 1518. Where Bizer speaks of Luther rejecting a Catholic stress on humility as he discovered the Word of God as the exclusive means of salvation, Hacker points to the emergence of the "ego in faith." Both attribute great importance to Luther's Lectures on Hebrews (April 1517 to March 1518) and to his Acta Augustana (October-November 1518). The fact that the two scholars are diametrically opposed in evaluating Luther's decisive shift makes the comparison all the more intriguing.

The present article is taken in the main from Chapter II of Das Ich im Glauben. Only a small selection has been included from the abundant documentation of Hacker's book. Both author and editor are indebted to Styria Verlag for permission to reproduce parts of the book in translation.

Notes begin on page 194.

Martin Luther's Notion of Faith

Paul Hacker

The ego in faith

M artin Luther presented an exercise in the practice of what he conceived to be justifying faith in the exposition of the Apostles' Creed he gave in his Small Catechism of 1529. The English version of this exposition reads as follows:

> I believe that God has made me and all creatures; that He has given me my body and soul, eyes, ears, and all my limbs, my reason, and all my senses, and still preserves them; in addition thereto, clothing and shoes, meat and drink, house and homestead, wife and children, fields, cattle, and all my goods; that He provides me richly and daily with all that I need to support this body and life, protects me from all danger, and guards me and preserves me from all evil; and all this out of pure, fatherly, divine goodness and mercy, without any merit or worthiness in

me; for all which I owe it to Him to thank, praise, serve, and obey Him. This is most certainly true.

I believe that Jesus Christ, true God, begotten of the Father from eternity, and also true man, born of the Virgin Mary, is my Lord, who has redeemed me, a lost and condemned creature, purchased and won . . . me from all sins, from death, and from the power of the devil, not with gold and silver, but with His holy, precious blood and with his innocent suffering and death, in order that I may be wholly his own, and live under Him in His kingdom, and serve Him in everlasting righteousness, innocence, and blessedness, even as He is risen from the dead, lives and reigns to all eternity. This is most certainly true.

I believe that I cannot by my own reason or strength believe in Jesus Christ, my Lord, or come to Him; but the Holy Ghost has called me by the Gospel, enlightened me with His gifts, sanctified and kept me in the true faith; even as he calls, gathers, enlightens, and sanctifies the whole Christian Church on earth, and keeps it with Jesus Christ in the one true faith; in which Christian Church He forgives daily and richly all sins to me and all believers, and at the last day will raise up me and all the dead, and will give to me and to all believers in Christ everlasting life. This is most certainly true.[1]

A significant stylistic feature of this text is the predominance of pronouns of the first person singular and the corresponding possessive adjectives. If we leave aside statements not strictly belonging to the content of faith, such as the expression of the act of faith ("I believe") and the believer's acknowledgment both of his unworthiness and of the obligation resulting from his profession, the personal pronoun of the first person singular or the corresponding adjective ("I," "me," "my") occurs twenty-five times in the text of the English version (eleven times in the German original). In contrast, there is not one such occurrence in the text of the Creed Luther was commenting upon. In his exposition all the statements of the Creed are primarily and with rigorous consistency related to the self of the person professing the faith. The doctrine of God the Father means first and above all that God has created me and everything that belongs to me. The salvation wrought by Christ means that the Savior has redeemed me. The third article means that the Holy Spirit has called me. In the first and third articles, the rest of creation and the Church are mentioned briefly and summarily after the person professing the faith, while the second article is referred exclusively to the professing individual's self. One point of the Creed, the last judgment, is altogether omitted. Instead, one learns to profess that he is in a state of grace and will attain the final consummation with absolute certitude: Christ forgives all my sins daily and will give eternal life "to me and to all believers." Christ's resurrection and exaltation is represented as a guarantee of the believer's eternal beatitude.

This sort of faith bends back upon its own subject in its very act. We may fittingly describe it as "reflexive faith." From a passage in his Lectures on Hebrews (probably October 1517),[2] down to some of his last works,[3] Luther never tired of stating, sometimes with drastic emphasis,[4] that it was the reference to the believer's own self that constituted the justifying element in the act of faith.[5]

Luther himself described this faith as "fides apprehensiva."[6] The believer exercises the "seizure" of salvation denoted by this term in the practice of "stating with certitude"[7] God's favor toward himself, which implies that his sins have been forgiven and his good works are agreeable to God.[8] Certitude is virtually equated with faith[9] and with salvation.[10] In 1520, Luther spoke of this certitude as comparatively easy to attain.[11] But in some of his later works, especially in the commentaries on Isaiah[12] and Galatians,[13] Luther described the act of "stating with certitude" as very difficult and he emphasized that the believer must continually struggle in his mind to reach the consoling conviction of being in God's favor.

Reflexive faith is not equivalent to a believer's meditation on his being concerned and affected by the content of his faith. Such meditation has been practised by Christians at all times from antiquity.[14] This is a reflexion based on faith, and is not included in the act of faith itself. Luther differs from such a practice by making salvation dependent on the believer's reflex conviction of being saved.

Reflexive faith does not imply ethical individualism. On the contrary, Luther vigorously inculcates love of one's neighbor and he can explain the nature and necessity of fraternal charity in words of admirable profundity.[15] Nor is the sort of faith taught by Luther simply a kind of subjectivism. It has an objective basis, namely the word of Scripture and dogma as laid down in the Apostles' Creed and in the decrees of the first councils. But Scripture and dogma are interpreted in a peculiar way, as we shall see presently.

Luther's conception of faith did not result from an interpretation of Scripture. It first emerged in his exposition of Hebrews 5:1 in late 1517. But this text, which treats of the sacerdotal office, includes no idea from which the new conception might reasonably be deduced. Luther seems to have used his lecture simply as an opportunity to communicate to his students what seemed to him the discovery of a vital but forgotten truth. But of course he attempted very soon to substantiate his new doctrine from Bible texts. He drafted some relevant arguments in the Resolutiones of his ninety-five theses on indulgences in early 1518. He elaborated these some months later in the Acta Augustana, which include, among other subjects, Luther's defense against Cardinal Cajetan, who in October 1518 imputed to Luther "a new and erroneous doctrine."[16] The central issue here was Luther's thesis that faith justified only if a man believed with certitude that he was justified, without doubting about his receiving grace.[17]

Luther's argument for reflexive faith in the
    Acta Augustana

In his defense[18] Luther begins with a reference to Romans 1:17, "The just man shall live by faith," and to Romans 4:3, "Abraham believed God, and it was reckoned to him as righteousness." But these passages merely state that faith is the origin of justification, and Luther does not try to make them say more than this. He then quotes Hebrews 11:6: "Whoever would draw near to God must believe that he exists, and that he rewards those who seek him." In commenting on this verse, Luther does not go beyond stressing that the believer must have faith in God bestowing grace in general, even in this life. The believer's case is included but not singled out.[19]

Then Luther proceeds to demonstrate the gist of his thesis: "that a person going to the sacrament [of penance] must believe that he will receive grace,"[20] that is, grace is given if the recipient of the sacrament believes that it is given. He then receives grace through this very belief. Luther thinks this results from the sentence in Matthew 16:19, "Whatever you loose on earth shall be loosed in heaven." He comments, "Therefore if you come to the sacrament of penance and do not firmly believe that you will be absolved in heaven, you come to your judgment and damnation because you do not believe that Christ speaks the truth when he says, 'Whatever you loose,' etc. And with your doubt you make of Christ a liar, which is a horrible sin."[21]

This explanation is a remarkable application of the doctrine of reflexivity. The Scripture passage speaks only of him who

"looses," which Luther understands to refer to sacramental remission of sin. It speaks then of the effects produced by this act
in heaven, but not of the person to whom the act relates. Luther,
however, speaks of this person only. That the passage presupposes
faith, goes without saying. In the Church all Scripture words require faith, but faith of a different kind from that taught by Luther.
There is no hint in the text of this presupposed faith being the instrument of efficacy of the "loosing," whether this refers to the
remission of sin as Luther would have it, or to something more
comprehensive as is more probable. Rather, it is the apostle who
is the efficient cause of the loosing, for on him Christ confers the
power of "binding and loosing" in the passage quoted. In Luther's
interpretation, on the other hand, the function of the priest, who
in the post-apostolic times takes the place of the apostle, dwindles
to insignificance. Instead, the faith of the penitent, in particular
his conviction of receiving grace now, becomes the proximate instrument of his receiving the grace of forgiveness. Luther brushes
aside what the text says, namely that the apostle's loosing, in later
times represented by the priest's absolution, is as such effective
in heaven, that is, that God ratifies, or is operative through, the
agency of his minister. Instead, an idea not implied, namely the
dependence of the reception of grace on the belief in receiving it,
is inferred from the text.

Luther then adduces further texts from the synoptic gospels,
one from St. John's gospel, and one from the Epistle of James.
In addition, a few passages are briefly hinted at. The texts from
the synoptics were apparently regarded by Luther as especially
strong supports of his position. In discussing them he uses the
terms fides specialis[22] and fides particularis,[23] that is, faith
relating to a single case or to a present effect.[24] These terms
supply another characteristic of Luther's new conception of
faith. When this faith "seizes" salvation or grace (fides apprehensiva) by "stating" its subject's salvation or state of grace
(fides statuens) in a reflex movement (fides reflexa), it is referring to a special, single situation (fides specialis vel particularis). Theological existentialism, which rules out all religious realities except momentary events in which an individual's
existence is involved or engaged, is thus virtually pre-formed
in Luther's conception of reflexive faith, which strives to seize
salvation by stating it with reference to a particular, special
situation.

Let us look at the proofs Luther drew from the gospels for
his new idea, as he defended it in the Acta Augustana. A

"special" or "particular" faith was that of the Canaanite woman to whom Jesus said, "O woman, great is your faith! Be it done for you as you desire" (Matthew 15:28). Luther also found this faith in the centurion of Capernaum, who said to Jesus, "Only say the word, and my servant will be healed" (Matthew 8:8). Luther referred to the story of the two blind men whom Jesus asked, "Do you believe that I am able to do this?" and who replied, "Yes, Lord." Thereupon Jesus touched their eyes, saying, "According to your faith be it done to you" (Matthew 9:28 f). He pointed to the story of the officer in the royal service, to whom Jesus said, "Go, your son will live." The officer "believed the word that Jesus spoke to him" (John 4:50). Luther quotes Our Lord's words, "Therefore I tell you, whatever you ask in prayer, believe that you receive it, and you will" (Mark 11:24), and then again, "If you have faith as a grain of mustard seed, you will say to this mountain, 'Move hence to yonder place, ' and it will move; and nothing will be impossible to you" (Matthew 17:20). He adduced the words spoken by Elizabeth to Mary, "Blessed is she who believed that there would be a fulfillment of what was spoken to her from the Lord" (Luke 1:45). He cited St. James, 1:5-7, "If any of you lacks wisdom, let him ask of God. . . . But let him ask in faith, with no doubting, for he who doubts . . . must not suppose that a double-minded man . . . will receive anything from the Lord." Luther mentioned that Jesus frequently rebuked his disciples and St. Peter for their weakness of faith, and he pointed out that in all these cases a "special faith, " relating to a "present effect, " is meant. Finally, he hinted at some examples from the Old Testament, and cited St. Augustine and St. Bernard.

Luther argues that the same kind of faith which is meant in the texts quoted is required for effective reception of the sacrament of penance, namely faith regarding a present effect, which in the case of the sacrament is remission of sins. He contends that in addition to this faith no preparation or disposition must be required of the penitent,[25] and that this faith alone brings grace. He who is without this faith will forfeit grace.

Faith and forgiveness of sin in the Gospels

At first sight Luther's argumentation looks overwhelming. However, there is one objection at least which may presently emerge. The effect of the sacrament of penance is remission of sin; but none of the texts cited speaks of the remission of sin. Is it admissable, is it in accordance with Scripture, to treat remission of sin by way of analogy with those texts? To find an answer to this query, it is helpful to consider passages that do treat of remission of sin. The result of such study is plain: Nowhere in Holy Scripture, neither in the synoptics nor in the other writings of the New Testament can any instance be found of a person obtaining remission of sin because of his firm belief in the sin being forgiven.

The sins of the paralytic of Matthew 9:2 are forgiven, even though he and those who brought him to Jesus seek only his bodily recovery. It is in expectation of this recovery that they have faith in Jesus. Remission of sin is quite outside the range of their hopes. But the trust in Our Lord's person makes possible the gift that is infinitely more important than bodily recovery. The sinful woman of Luke 7 comes to Jesus and serves him silently in acts expressive of reverence, humility, love, and, probably, repentance. There is no word in the text to indicate that she is sure of receiving forgiveness. But Jesus does forgive her sins, "for she loved much," and the mental attitude expressed by her silent and humble service is interpreted by Our Lord as the faith that has saved her. Her faith (v. 50) and her love (v. 47) are one. The story of the centurion of Capernaum does not expressly speak of remission of sin. It is however relevant to our inquiry that the centurion does not consider himself worthy to ask Jesus to come to him, and according to St. Luke's version of the story he does not even presume to approach Our Lord in person (Luke 7:7). There is no trace of the cheerful audacity and bold confidence which, according to Luther's teaching,[26] should characterize true faith. Nevertheless, the centurion is praised by Jesus for his unparalleled faith--a faith full of humility and reverence and trust. The most important example is, of course, the tax-gatherer in the parable of Luke 18:9 ff, who however does ask for remission of sin. Overwhelmed by shame and fear, he keeps his distance and does not dare to raise his eyes up to heaven. It is inconceivable that he should have believed, as Luther's doctrine would have it, that his sins were forgiven in order that they might be forgiven. It is not even said that he was sure that God had heard his prayer: "God, be merciful to me a sinner!" According to Luther's teaching, lack of certitude would be equivalent to certain damnation. But Our Lord says, "I tell you, this man went down to his house justified rather than the other," namely the Pharisee.

The results of our inquiry so far seem devastating to Luther's position. It appears that the texts he adduced in the <u>Acta Augustana</u>

have to be interpreted in a different way. The question addressed
by Jesus to the blind men in Matthew 9:28 provides a clue: "Do you
believe that I am able to do this?" This means that what is required
of those who seek help of Our Lord is absolute trust in his divine
person and acknowledgment, at least implicitly, of what he really
is. Such trust involves self-abandonment and is therefore incompatible with reflexion on one's own self. Realization of one's helplessness disposes to such self-abandonment. People may even be
unaware of the real nature of their misery. That does not matter.
Our Lord accepts the offering of undeveloped faith, if only it be
informed with humility, trust, and love, and bestows on the
seeker a gift that he had never thought of, the forgiveness of his
sins. This gift establishes a personal relationship between God and
man. One can implore God for it and a man can receive it, but it
can never be attracted by an anticipating, "apprehensive," asserting act of consciousness which misinterprets itself as faith or
trust. God's gift must be sought in fear and trembling, as by the
tax-gatherer, and it is quite natural and by no means objectionable
that the justified man should not be certain of his being in God's
favor. Luther himself had vigorously emphasized this in his pre-
Protestant period, before he had conceived of his theory of reflexive
faith.[27]

But we must inquire further into the nature of the faith meant
in the passages cited. The story of the royal officer, John 4:46-53,
seems particularly instructive. For here faith is spoken of twice
(a fact Luther did not notice in his Acta Augustana). At first it is
said that Jesus answers to the officer's request to heal his son,
"Go, your son will live," and that the officer "believed the word
that Jesus had spoke to him." This much only was noted by Luther.
Then, after the officer returned home and saw that his son was already recovered, the Evangelist reports that he and all his household "believed," that is, became believers. Apparently the first
act of faith, which believed Jesus capable of performing the
miracle, is different from the second, which is more explicit
than the first and is grounded on the experience of the miracle.
This interpretation seems to be corroborated by Acts 14:9. Here
the lame man of Lystra "had faith to be made well," that is, he
trusted that Paul was capable of working the miracle. Thereupon
the Apostle cured him. This happened while he was listening to
St. Paul's preaching, that is, while he was only on the way to
becoming a Christian. The initial faith on which a person's being
healed depends in this and other pericopes is naturally a fides
specialis. It is not yet the whole of Christian existence, but

certainly is already a relationship to salvation. Theological existentialism is right in urging it, since the firm personal trust of this faith remains a quickening force even in mature faith, but it is wrong to represent it as the whole Christian faith, which is not a mere chain of momentary acts looking out toward the future, but also an abiding state.

But even the instances of initial faith reported in the New Testament do not justify Luther's doctrine. This is borne out, for example, by the story of the woman who was suffering from hemorrhages (Matthew 9:20-22). The initial faith, which is by nature and necessarily belief in the possibility of a miracle, appears in this woman in quite a rude form. She wants only to touch the edge of Our Lord's cloak, trusting to be healed by this touch. Rationalists tend to deride such primitive trust, which seems to rely on matter in a sub-Christian manner. But Jesus recognizes it as personal, salvific faith: "Take heart, daughter, your faith has made you well." Another case in point is the people's faith in the event recorded in Acts 5:15 ff: "They carried out the sick into the streets, and laid them on beds and pallets, that as Peter came by at least his shadow might fall on some of them." The faith meant in these two stories is personal trust, even though it leans on material symbols. The conviction of the medicinal operation of the sacraments, expressed in many liturgical prayers of the Church but disparaged today even by some Catholic rationalists, is a legitimate continuation of a sort of faith sanctioned by a number of New Textament passages. This is also found in the hope of being healed at places specially devoted to the veneration of saints. There is no trace in such faith of that bending back on the believer's own self, which according to Luther's theory, would be the salvific element in faith.

Luther has misinterpreted the faith meant in the passages he adduced in the Acta Augustana. He overstresses the instrumentality of trusting faith. He makes the faith which is the way to or the presupposition of salvation coincide with salvation itself. This becomes possible because he had first identified salvation with the consciousness of being saved or the certitude of salvation, and then certitude with this faith. He said in his later commentary on Galatians, "Therefore the freedom, forgiveness of sins, righteousness, and life that we have through him [that is, through Christ] are sure, firm, and eternal, provided that we believe this."[28] Obviously in his opinion the consciousness of salvation coincides with the existence of salvation, or even the consciousness creates the existence. Gerhard Ebeling, a modern Lutheran, has precisely grasped the intention of the founder of his denomination when he says, "Faith is not a pre-condition of salvation, but is the certainty of it; and as such it is itself the event of salvation."[29]

An examination of the arguments used by Luther to demonstrate his doctrine of reflexive faith from Scripture inclines us therefore to agree with Cardinal Cajetan, who said that the passages adduced by Luther "were not to the point and were misunderstood."[30]

The self and certitude in the New Testament Epistles

The points of view considered so far have allowed us to test the conformity of Luther's theory with Scripture passages taken chiefly from the canonical gospels. There are however other points of view. For instance, what is the function of the first person singular and the corresponding possessive adjective in statements of faith occurring in the New Testament? Are there statements in the New Testament which express a certitude of salvation, and if so, of what nature is this certitude? Such questions lead us primarily to the Epistles. Furthermore, it may be interesting to examine a few cases of Luther's exposition in his later work on passages he found favorable to his new doctrine.

There are many passages in the New Testament that have been interpreted ever since Luther's time as expressing individual certitude. The greatest of these passages is Romans 8:18 and 8:31-39.

> I consider that the sufferings of this present time are not worth comparing with the glory that is to be revealed to us. . . . If God is for us, who is against us? He who did not spare his own Son but gave him up for us all, will he not also give us all things with him? Who shall bring any charge against God's elect? It is God who justifies; who is to condemn? Is it Christ Jesus, who died, yes, who was raised from the dead, who is at the right hand of God, who indeed intercedes for us? Who shall separate us from the love of Christ? Shall tribulation, or distress, or persecution, or famine, or nakedness, or peril, or sword? As it is written, "For thy sake we are being killed all the day long; we are regarded as sheep to be slaughtered." No, in all these things we are more than conquerers through him who loved us. For I am sure that neither principalities, nor things present, nor things to come, nor powers, nor height, nor depth, nor anything else in all creation, will be able to separate us from the love of God in Christ Jesus

            our Lord. (Revised Standard Version--italics added)

   In this text the plurals we and us are used with the same consistency as the singulars I and me in Luther's works, and this
not only in his exposition of the Apostles' Creed in the Small
Catechism. Only in two statements of the act itself of profession
("I consider," "I am sure") is the singular used, which is quite
to the point since it is an individual who is speaking. The contents of the profession, however, are all referred to a plurality
("we," "us," "us all"), not to an individual ego.
   I have investigated whether elsewhere the New Testament
statements about salvation or communion with Christ are referred to an ego or to a we. The result I came to by this investigation was that Christ is called "Our Lord" about sixty or
more times, beside many cases where he is simply named
"the Lord" or "the Lord of all." On the other hand, the expression, "My Lord," so dear to Luther, occurs only four
times (John 20:13.16.28 and Philippians 3:8. These cases
are evidently reminiscences of a linguistic habit. In the Semitic
language of the first Christians it was usual to append to the
word "lord" a possessive suffix, which mostly denoted the
singular, "my lord." This implied that the speaker acknowledged
the person he addressed as a real master, as a person having
authority over him. Considering this, it appears the more remarkable that so few traces of this habit have remained in the
New Testament, where most of the authors had a Semitic language as their mother tongue. The fact that in most cases,
when speaking of Christ, the early Christians in their Greek
deviated from the usage familiar to them, must have a special
reason.
   The reason is, of course, the same which caused St. Paul to
use, in speaking of men enjoying communion with Christ, plural
pronouns exclusively in the hymn of Romans 8 quoted above.
The consciousness of salvation in the apostolic times, as well
as in later centuries, was universal and therefore entirely comprised within the consciousness of being the people of the Lord,
the people to whom the Lord has promised that no one shall
snatch them out of his hand (John 10:28). The individual's personal relationship to Christ has certainly been an integral and
vital constituent of the Christian religion from the very beginning, but in the mind of primitive Christianity as well as in
Catholicism it is inconceivable outside the primary, comprehensive relationship of the Lord to his Mystical Body or the com-

munity of his People. The individual Christian cannot think of his communion with Christ apart from his membership in that Body or community. This is reflected in the linguistic usage noted above.

The universal consciousness of salvation, as expressed in the New Testament, knows that the aim of redemption is the People of God, the Church, even the universe. God has ranged himself at the side of Israel "his servant," that is, he has elected his people (Luke 1:54, from Isaiah 41:8). Christ has "loved the Church, and gave himself up for her" (Ephesians 5:25). Jesus Christ "gave himself for us, to redeem us," that is, the whole of God's people (Titus 2:14). "He shall save his people from their sins" (Matthew 1:21). God "made him the head over all things for the Church, which is his body, the fulness of him who fills all in all" (Ephesians 1:22 f). "In him all the fulness of God was pleased to dwell, and through him to reconcile to himself all things" (Colossians 1:19). "In putting everything in subjection to him, he left nothing outside his control" (Hebrews 2:8).

Luther has reversed the spiritual order that had prevailed in the Church since the time of the Apostles. Consistently, though perhaps not deliberately, he transposed the biblical plural expressions into singular ones. Thus, under Luther's pen, St. Paul's words, "If God is for us, who is against us?" (Romans 8:31) become, "If God is for me, who is against me?"[31]

Crucial to Luther's religion and theology is his interpretation of the "for me" of Galatians 2:20, where St. Paul says that Christ "gave himself for me." Luther's commentary of 1531-1535 admonishes, "Therefore read these words 'me' and 'for me' with great emphasis, and accustom yourself to accepting this 'me' with a sure faith and applying it to yourself. Do not doubt that you belong to the number of those who speak this 'me.'"[32] This exegesis is questionable from two points of view. First, modern research has concluded that St. Paul often uses the pronoun of the first person singular not strictly with reference to his own self but in a general or typical sense. The fact that the Apostle turns without any perceptible reason from the plural "we" of Galatians 2:15-17 to the singular "I" in verses 18-21 makes it possible that this singular is to be understood in that sense.[33]

Secondly, a consideration of Galatians 2:20 is its context as well as in the context of the Apostle's theology definitely shows that Luther's exegesis is contrary to St. Paul's intentions. The text first speaks of a spiritual death. In saying, "I have been crucified with Christ," the Apostle professes to imitate the exam-

ple of Our Lord, an idea which Luther rejected in his Protestant
period as not pertinent to the center of Christian living, and admissable only for practical, ethical, or penitential efforts.[34]
So the words "for me" cannot be used as a legitimation for reflex
meditation to attain a salvation identified with the certitude of it.
On the contrary, it implies that the individual consciousness of
the Apostle has in faith been taken up into, and even replaced by,
the consciousness of Christ.

For the Apostle equivalently says, "The life I now live is not
my life, but the life which Christ lives in me, and my present
bodily life is lived by faith in the Son of God, who loved me and
sacrificed himself for me." Thus the use of "for me" in a typical
sense in Galatians 2:20 is not a mere habit of style, but has a
spiritual and theological basis. This basis has been convincingly
elucidated by Hans Urs von Balthasar.[35] The fact that the Apostle
has allowed himself to be taken up into the death and resurrection
of Christ is described by von Balthasar as an "expropriation."
In its positive aspect this is an "appropriation of man by God."
Therefore Paul here, for once, used the first person singular,
although elsewhere the "appropriation by God," which is the
acquisition of salvation (See I Thessalonians 5:9), is never
described in the singular, because it is always God's "acquisition
of the people" (See I Peter 2:9). Paul's ego has become, as von
Balthasar explains, "a paradigm of [a person] being sent out, a
paradigm of membership in the Body of Christ . . .; he is aware
of being thoroughly expropriated into the Communion of Saints."
Because the Apostle's self "carries the Church within itself and
has dilated into an anima ecclesiastica," his certitude of salvation is identical with that of the Church.

The predominance of the idea of a sacral community in the self-
awareness of primitive Christianity is reflected in the fact that
the "for me" of Galatians 2:20 is an isolated occurrence. Elsewhere,
whenever the New Testament specifies for whom Christ has acquired
salvation, the word after the preposition is in the plural: "for us,"
"for you," "for all," "for many," "for the Church." There are
more than twenty such cases.

Where Luther retains the biblical plural, he understands it as
a singular or he interprets it as denoting a plurality of individuals.
For instance, in expounding Galatians 1:4, a passage speaking of
Christ "who gave himself for our sins," the Reformer urges us to
note the word "our," but adds presently that a man should firmly
believe that he is one of those for whom the Savior sacrificed himself. Thus he uses the plural as a reminder for the individual to

realize that he is also meant. The individualization is at once turned to practice in exercises in certitude, of which the later commentary on Galatians gives copious examples in the exposition of the above mentioned passage.[36]

The statements of the New Testament on salvation are distorted in their meaning if they are used, as they are continually by Luther, as a basis or legitimation for exercises in asserting the ego's salvation. This practice inevitably dissolves the consciousness of a sacred community which is inseparably and essentially linked up with these New Testament statements.

That this assertive spirituality is quite alien to Scripture becomes clearer still if a passage is considered where it is really an individual who speaks of his salvation. In Philippians 3:12 f Paul says, "Not that I have already obtained it or am already perfect. . . . I do not consider that I have made it my own." This is quite the contrary of a fides apprehensiva. It is the attitude of humble uncertitude which has at all times been that of devout persons in the Church. Catholic tradition insists that an individual cannot as a rule claim certitude of salvation unless he has received a special revelation.

Luther tried to explain this passage from Philippians in accordance with his doctrine. He takes it as scriptural evidence to show "that even Christians feel the weakness of their faith and are tempted by desolation on account of their sense of sin." The "weakness of faith" consists according to him in the frequent failure of attempts at putting down remorse by exercises in certitude: "It takes tremendous effort to grasp this by faith in such a way as to be able to believe and say, 'I have sinned and yet not sinned,' so that the conscience may be defeated."[37]

But this is surely not the sense of St. Paul's text. After the words quoted he continues, "I press on to make it my own, because Christ Jesus has made me his own." This "pressing on" certainly does not consist, as Luther intimates, in exercises of asserting individual certitude or suppressing the consciousness of sin, but in the fulfilment of the apostolic task, which is the proclamation of the gospel, that is, a work.

The passage quoted above from the Scholia on Isaiah reveals the most essential difference, in fact the radical opposition, between Luther's practice of "asserting" and the thought of the New Testament. The opposition consists in the different attitude toward sin. Luther's certitude of salvation is continually threatened by the consciousness of being a sinner. An essential feature of his notion of faith is self-assertion in opposition to

98

this consciousness. He asserts, "I have sinned and yet not sinned."
This paradox is only superficially similar to paradoxical statements
of St. Paul like that of 2 Corinthians 4:8 f: "We are afflicted in every
way, but not crushed; perplexed, but not driven to despair; . . .
struck down, but not destroyed." Romans 8:31-39, quoted above,
also shows that the Church of the New Testament was aware of
being threatened by many perils. This passage enumerates forces
and threats but says of all of them that they cannot separate us
from Christ's love. One thing is not mentioned, and this is precisely what was for Luther the threatening force par excellence,
namely sin, or rather the consciousness of having sinned.

The individual in the New Testament cannot "state with certitude"
his own salvation because his final and eternal salvation is also
dependent on the good works in which he has to actualize the grace
he has received. In the case of St. Paul, the work required of him
is primarily his missionary activity, as, for example, in I Corinthians 9:16. He admonishes the Galatians not to be mistaken about
the fact that their ultimate destiny will also depend on their works.
"Works of the flesh, " which are all sorts of sin, will produce
"corruption, " but works done under the guidance of the Spirit,
which are exactly what the New Testament means by good works,
will bear as their fruit "life everlasting" (Galatians 5:18-23;
6:7-10). As the works are an abiding task, there remains an uncertainty with regard to eternal salvation. Certitude here would
amount to presumption. Luther, whose conscience was always
very sensitive, was not unaware of this spiritual fact.[38] Nevertheless, he thought that in order to secure salvation a Christian
had to assert his being in God's grace or mercy "with certitude"
and thereby to stifle stings of conscience.

According to II Peter 1:5-10 it is works by which we have "to
confirm our call and election." Luther, however, thought he could
adapt this passage to his system too. II Peter 1:9 censures sinners,
"because they have forgotten that they were cleansed from their
old sins." Luther claims that this refers to "ingratitude for the
baptism they had received" and "to their wicked unbelief."[39]
But he ignores the context, which leaves no doubt that those who
"have forgotten" their baptism are people who fail to do works
corresponding to the baptismal cleansing or grace, works deriving
from faith: self-control, patience, piety, charity. Loss of faith
is not envisaged, for in verse 1 it is presupposed that the recipients
of the letter are faithful. In other writings, Luther offers the explanation that the good works mentioned in the Epistle are a test
of (reflexive) faith. He thinks that if a man finds himself doing

good works he may take this as a token of his faith being right, since true faith must actuate a man to do good works. Thus he may once more state God's favor toward him when he observes himself doing good works.[40] The confirmation of election spoken of in the II Peter text would thus depend on a person's asserting the goodness of his works and consequently their and his being agreeable to God.[41] But it goes without saying that this anthropocentric theology misses the sense of the text on which it claims to be based. The election of the person doing good works can be confirmed only by God, who rewards merit, not by man's reflex thought.

According to the New Testament, incertitude of salvation does not arise from a man's conscience reproaching him for his sins, but from the conviction that the actions of the justified one, who has obtained the grace of being guided by the Holy Spirit, will be judged, and it is uncertain whether he will persevere until the end in faith and love actuated in good works. Therefore, incertitude is an incentive, not to be stifled by asserting one's own salvation, but to "make sure" the gift of grace by doing good works with "every effort" (II Peter 1:5) and "with fear and trembling" (Philippians 2:12). The same idea is at the bottom of all exhortations in the Epistles. Because Paul is "apprehended" by Christ, he must "press on" to reach the goal. Because it is God himself who in the Philippians "works both the will and the deed," they must "work out their salvation in fear and trembling" (Philippians 3:12 f; 2:12 f).

The relationship between the community's consciousness of salvation and the individual's zeal for self-sanctification is brought out clearly in the First Epistle of St. John (3:2 f). The community's certitude is expressed in the words, "We know that when he appears, he shall be like him." Then, the necessity for self-sanctification is emphasized, and it is significant that the text here uses the singular: "Every one who thus hopes in him purifies himself, as he is pure." So the individual's certitude is one of hope, which though is not absolute because its fulfilment depends on man's self-purification as well. It is still a confident hope because it is comprised in the absolute certitude that the community as a whole will attain the goal which in later theology is described as the beatific vision.

A special case is II Timothy 4:7 f. Here, for once, an individual speaks of his being certain of his salvation: "Henceforth there is laid up for me the crown of righteousness, which the Lord, the righteous Judge, will award me on that Day." But it has to be borne in mind that the speaker of these words has reached the

100

end of his earthly career. He is awaiting martyrdom in the near future. He cannot work any more. It is therefore an exceptional situation which here makes possible a certitude of salvation. And the ideas associated with this certitude in no way fit in with Luther's system. For the text quoted is preceded by the words, "I have fought the good fight, I have finished the race, I have kept the faith." The statements of this passage manifest the conviction that it is not faith alone which secures final consummation, which is Luther's doctrine. On the contrary, the "crown of righteousness" is laid up not only for the faith which the speaker has "kept" but also for his "good fight," that is, his work. The Apostle's assurance is thus based on the fulfilment of his task too, which, according to Luther's doctine, would be plainly condemnable. Even the idea of Christ the Judge, which Luther strove to oust from the domain of justifying faith, is included in the author's assurance, which is a firm hope of being rewarded by the Judge.

Luther, however, ventured to adapt even this text to his system. According to a sermon preached in 1532, "the crown of righteousness which the Apostle expects is not to be understood as blessedness but as the glory and honor which will be granted to the true worker and warrior according to the measure of faithfulness and his exertion in working and suffering."[42] In Luther's words, "Before Thee, I am a sinner. But because I have served the ungrateful world, He will award me the crown. This however is not salvation; but the renown, the crown, the glory, and the honor will be there."[43] But this is a wrong exegesis. "The crown of righteousness" spoken of in the text is beatitude, and the crown is expected to be awarded on the ground of faith and works.

Luther liked to allude to James 2:19, "You believe that God is one; you do well. Even the demons believe, and shudder."[44] He took this passage to be a biblical argument for his view that faith which was merely an acknowledgment of facts was insufficient. But this cannot be the sense. First, St. James does not discountenance belief in facts as Luther does, but approves of it, in accordance with other New Testament texts which describe faith as obedient acknowledgment of the facts of redemption, not as a believer's assertion of his ego's salvation. Second, the text shows that the devils are far from remaining unmoved by their belief in facts, for they shudder. The most important point is that, thirdly, the reason for the imperfection of the faith censured by St. James is not that the believer cannot assert his own salvation--no believer in the New Testament asserts his salvation in order to obtain it--but the fact that such faith is not supplemented by works. The Apostle clearly expresses this: "Do you want to be shown, you foolish fellow, that faith apart from works is barren?" (James 2:20). In this idea James fully agrees with Paul, who says that the only thing which counts is "faith working through love" (Galatians 5:6).

Evaluation of Luther's doctrine

Whenever Luther tried to demonstrate his theory of faith from Scripture he could not but twist the texts. That the doctrine of reflexivity is contrary to Scripture is shown by the strained nature of Luther's arguments in favor of the doctrine. Moreover, such a doctrine, if maintained, would eliminate an essential trait of New Testament spirituality, namely the inclusion of a Christian's consciousness of salvation in the consciousness of belonging to the sacred community of the Church. It was not Scripture that dictated the new doctrine; instead, the doctrine was used as the chief hermeneutical tool in the interpretation of Scripture.

Luther himself described his principle of interpretation in this sentence: "This much is beyond question, that all the scriptures point to Christ alone."[45] This means that his interpretation claims to be christocentric. But what does this christocentrism imply in the actual context of the Reformer's thought? As Althaus rightly observes, it implies "interpretation understood in terms of the gospel of justification by faith alone."[46] Justification "by faith alone" is received, according to Luther "in the form of faith," as Althaus pertinently comments,[47] and the essential trait of this faith is the pro me. But this is the ego's bending back on itself within the very act of faith. Consequently, the "christocentrism" of Luther's exegesis is ultimately based on the doctrine of reflexivity. Only those texts of the New Testament which can be used to stir up or strengthen this sort of faith are acknowledged as properly "gospel." The rest is interpretation of the law or exhortation meant for preparing a soul to apprehend the gospel.[48]

Although Luther's conception of faith is alien to Scripture and to all Christian spirituality and teaching before his time, it was regarded by him as the very essence of Christianity. It could not but produce far-reaching and fatal changes in the whole system of the Christian religion. It was therefore in fulfilment of the Church's sacred duty to guard the deposit of faith (See 1 Timothy 6:20) that the Council of Trent anathematized the new doctrine.

Carefully stating the erroneous doctrine in Luther's own words,
canon 14 of the Decree on Justification (January 13, 1547) declares:

> If any one says that a man is absolved from his sins and
> justified because he believes with certainty that he is
> absolved and justified; or that no one is truly justified ex-
> cept him who believes he is justified, and that absolution
> and justification are effected by this faith alone: let him be
> anathema.[49]

Results of reflexive faith in Luther's theology

The most important alteration concerned the doctrine of love.
It is inexact to describe as personalism the religion of Luther's
Protestant period, in which everything is centered around the concept of reflexive faith. An interpersonal relation involves trust
and respect for the partner. In religion, the analogous act is
adoration of the Divine Person of Christ and participation through
him in the trinitarian love which, itself a Person, is the relationship between the Father and the Son. If, however, a man makes
his partner in an interpersonal relationship the object of calcula-
tion or the instrument for obtaining or securing a profit through
the relationship of trust, then that relation is already deranged
or destroyed. This is exactly what happens in reflexive faith. In
particular, love--the most sublime of interpersonal relations--
is paralyzed. It is most impressive to observe how the idea of
love of God fades in Luther's works from about 1518 onward. The
fact, too, that Luther never developed a truly trinitarian devotion
is significant in this connection. It is true that the Reformer constantly urges love of one's neighbor. But he did not regard this
as an outcome of the primary love of God.[50] For him, brotherly
love had no meaning for eternity but was righteousness confined
to this world,[51] and a test of the success of reflexive faith--as
we saw above while considering Luther's exegesis of 2 Peter
1:5-10. Luther can say, "Love God in his creatures; he does not
want you to love him in his majesty."[52] The ego, bending back
on itself in the very act of faith, cannot start out from itself as
sound faith does. Thus there remains no scope for a love, which,
lost in the adoration of its object, God, forgets its subject. It
is noteworthy in this connection that Luther eliminated the ado-
rational hymn "Laudamus te . . ." and the eucharistic Preface
from the formulary of his "German Mass." The atrophy of
personalism and love of God is also consistent with his denial of

103 / Hacker

merit. For the idea of merit implies the freedom of God in his relation to his creature and involves personalism even more, since what is valued positively by God is only work done in love of God.

A spirituality like Luther's which has a keen awareness of the majesty of God, but then ousts love of God, quite naturally falls prey to dread and anguish. Luther clearly had a disposition for mysticism, which his early, pre-Protestant predilection for St. Bernard and Tauler significately indicates. Luther's destiny was not a mysticim of light, but one of darkness. His early works show that he was familiar with an experience of darkness in con-nection with his "theology of the cross."[53] But the doctrine of reflexive faith, ruling out love of God, has spoiled this mystical vein.[54]

Perhaps Luther had a real experience of consolation and peace only once in his life, namely in early 1518.[55] His doctrine of reflexivity then induced him to identify psychic peace with grace and to make the assertion of one's own salvation a means to recover peace and a duty. But this method was bound to fail. For the surest way to make consolation impossible is to struggle for it deliberately.[56] So Luther's later spirituality was a permanent fluctuation between the frightening experience of incertitude, which may be described as a degradation of the mysticism of darkness, and the mental struggle for certitude in which the struggle always fails but is continually resumed. This fluctuation is systematized in Luther's antithetical thinking, in which des-pair becomes a substitute for contrition as the condition for the reception of grace, and the hearer's consolation upon apprehend-ing the gospel as meant "for me" becomes identified with faith and grace.

The doctrine and spirituality of the sacraments underwent a thorough mutation. Sacraments became exercises in certitude. The remembrance of my baptism is an occasion for asserting God's favor toward me. Absolution, since 1520 no longer proper-ly counted as a sacrament, directly confers certitude, when the penitent hears and believes the words spoken to him. In the Eucharist, the main thing is hearing the words of institution. In hearing the "for you" included in them, the believer should realize that he is one of those included in the "you." The Real Presence is an excellent help to realize Christ's favor to me. The ecclesial dimension of the Eucharist, emphasized by Luther as late as 1519, dwindles away in his writings from 1520 on-wards. Since all sacraments are efficacious only through the medium of words, they can be altogether replaced by scriptural words or expositions of them that are apt to arouse reflexive faith.

The concept of the Church is of course completely altered too. The Church is reduced to an organization enabling the formation and development and maintenance of reflexive faith. In 1520, Luther taught his students, "In matters of faith, every Christian is to himself Pope and Church."[57] This shows graphically how fatal the new conception of faith was to become to the Church. For practical purposes Luther later emphasized ecclesiastical organization, but the seed once sown has continued to grow.

The ego in faith today

I would like to indicate briefly the relevance of Luther's central idea to the disputes of our own days. Reflection on one's own ego, in the conviction that it is essential for gaining one's ultimate stand in Being, after its first emergence in Luther's religious thought, was secularized in some tenets of German Idealism and Existentialism. These philosophies then jointly engendered anthropocentric trends even in Catholicism. Investigation into Luther's "ego-in-faith" inevitably affects one's estimation of those trends and vice versa. A critique of Luther's conception of faith does not, as Father Otto H. Pesch thinks,[58] imply that the mentality of a past period of history, namely the Middle Ages, is posited as absolute. On the one hand, there was reflection on one's own self even in antiquity and in the Middle Ages. On the other hand, the undeniable fact that such reflection is a distinctive feature of modern times does not legitimize the reflexive faith as an application of modern thought to Christian spirituality and theology. Catholics, after all, have been modern men too. St. Ignatius of Loyola and the French spirituality of the 17th and 18th centuries exemplify that self-reflection can even quicken and deepen genuinely Catholic thought and help men to lead a really Christian life. The destructive novelty of Luther's doctrine is not the mere fact of reflection on one's own self but the claim that a special sort of reflection, namely the individual's asserting his being in God's grace, is the justifying element in faith and thus indispensable for salvation. Thus, in Luther we see the rise of what was perhaps the first form of an anthropocentric theology.

Introduction to Harry J. McSorley, C.S.P.

Harry J. McSorley is a native of Philadelphia who entered the Paulist
congregation in 1953 after completing his undergraduate studies at Buck-
nell University. After philosophical and theological studies at St. Paul's
College in Washington, he was ordained to the priesthood in 1960 and
then began research in Protestant theology and ecumenical questions at
the Johann Adam Moehler Institute in Paderborn, Germany. In 1961 Father McSorley entered doctoral studies under Michael Schmaus in the
Munich faculty of Catholic theology, where he began intensive research
on the Reformation confrontation between Luther and Erasmus on the
freedom of the will. After work in the Protestant faculties of Heidelberg
and Tübingen, he received the doctorate, summa cum laude, in Munich
in 1966.

Since returning to the United States in 1966, Father McSorley has
taught Ecumenical Theology and Ecclesiology at St. Paul's College and
has taken part in the official Lutheran-Catholic Theological Consultation.
In the summer of 1968 he was visiting professor at Luther Theological
Seminary in St. Paul.

Father McSorley's dissertation on the Luther-Erasmus debate was
published in German in 1967 as the first volume of a new series, Beiträge
zur ökumenischen Theologie, edited by Heinrich Fries of Munich's Catholic Ecumenical Institute. This work gives us a major survey of the
doctrines of sin, grace, and freedom through Scripture, the Fathers,
and Church teaching, and then turns to a careful analysis of the background
and contents of Luther's great work, De servo arbitrio, written in response to Erasmus in 1525.

Father McSorley's work exemplifies the valuable contribution of careful
historical work to the ecumenical dialogue. The following essay shows
how he has sifted out two distinct auguments in Luther's assertion of the
bondage of the will. His significant evaluation of Luther's basic point,
the need of grace in every human action relevant to salvation, is set
against the background of the denial of this doctrine in one school of late
medieval scholasticism. McSorley delineates sharply the ambiguity of
Erasmus' position and thus by attending to the immediate context of
Luther's defense of grace he makes possible an important Catholic reassessment of Luther's role in the history of Christian thought.

Father McSorley's book appeared in English in early 1969 as a joint
publication of a Lutheran and a Catholic publishing house (Augsburg and
Newman) under the title, Luther: Right or Wrong?

Notes begin on page 199.

Erasmus versus Luther--
Compounding the Reformation Tragedy

Harry J. McSorley, C.S.P.

The Protestant Reformation included many positive aspects of
Church renewal, some of which have come to be appreciated and
assimilated by Roman Catholicism only as recently as the Second
Vatican Council. The tragic dimension of the Reformation lies in
the fact that the Reformers were unable to carry out their reformation program in union with the Roman Church but "were separated
from full communion"[1] with that Church. This was a tragic separation "for which" as Vatican II pointed out, "men of both sides
were to blame."[2]

Elsewhere[3] we have suggested that one of the blameworthy aspects in the pre-Reformation Church was the lack of vigilance
on the part of the Church's official pastors and teachers. The
neglect by popes and bishops to attend to their chief function of
feeding the flock of Christ with the word of God was one of the
major causes not only of the widespread theological unclarity
in Luther's time, but also of the emergence, in the Ockham-
Biel school of late medieval Nominalism, of a Catholicism that
was not fully Catholic.[4]

We have argued in the aforementioned work that Luther, in his central and original reformation protest, was a Catholic reformer, a defender of the traditional Catholic faith against an un-Catholic error that was widespread in the German Church of his day. A series of complicated developments involving mutual misunderstanding and often blameworthy attitudes, accusations, and conduct on both sides turned what was originally a Catholic protest into a movement that eventually led to the tragedy of the division--still not fully healed--of Western Christianity.

It would be a gross over-simplification to say that the sixteenth century separation was due solely to misunderstanding, even though, as the ecumenical theology of our time has amply demonstrated, serious misunderstandings there were. There were also real disagreements, especially after Luther's excommunication, which continue to the present day and are the object of the ongoing ecumenical-theological dialogue.

A first misunderstanding

One disagreement that convinced the Catholics that Luther was a genuine heretic and not simply a misunderstood radical was Luther's necessitarianism. In the Bull, Exsurge Domine, of June 15, 1520, Pope Leo X censured forty-one propositions taken from Luther's works as "respectively heretical, or scandalous, or false, or offensive to pious ears, or seductive of simple minds and as opposed to Catholic truth."[5]

The thirty-sixth of the censured propositions reads as follows: "Free will after sin is an empty word; and when a man does what is in him, he sins mortally."[6] This proposition is an exact rendition of a thesis that Luther drew up for the Heidelberg Disputation in 1518.[7] The language is indeed a radical departure from the ecclesial tradition, which always affirmed the existence of free will (liberum arbitrium) before and after man's fall into sin.[8] The meaning that Luther attaches to this radical-sounding thesis, however, is a genuinely traditional meaning.

In the "proof" which Luther offers for his thesis it is clear that he is not denying man's power of free choice. In complete fidelity to John 8:34 ff. and to Augustine, both of whom he cites, Luther is teaching nothing more than the biblical-Catholic tradition that man's free will, apart from grace, is unable to please God and is thus capable only of sin.[9]

The drafters of Exsurge Domine focused solely on Luther's

radical language in censuring the Heidelberg thesis. They showed
no apparent concern for its biblical-Catholic meaning. When they
censured the proposition this, in Luther's eyes, was tantamount
to a censure of Christ and of the gospel. It was for him final proof
that the Pope was the anti-Christ, evidence that the Pope would not
allow the gospel to be preached.[10]

At this point in our consideration of the genesis of the Reformation separation we see indications of tragic misunderstanding: the
papal party sees Luther as one who denied man's power of free
choice; Luther interprets Exsurge Domine as a denial of the gospel of justification by grace. Neither side did justice to the other,
neither really heard the other's concerns.

With Luther's reply to Exsurge Domine, the Reformation tragedy is compounded. The tragedy is no longer confined to misunderstanding and to lack of openness on both sides. Luther gives the
Roman Church evidence that he has really departed from the Catholic faith. And in reply to Luther, as we shall see, the foremost
thinker of the Roman Catholic Church in the first half of the sixteenth century--Erasmus of Rotterdam--gives Luther real evidence that the course of protest Luther had taken was right!

Luther's response and new argument

Luther defended the propositions censured by Exsurge Domine
in his Assertio onmium articulorum . . . per bullam Leonis
X novissimam damnatorum.[11] When he comes to defend proposition thirty-six--the one dealing with free will--Luther stresses
the primacy and centrality of this question by saying:

> In the other articles on the papacy, councils, indulgences
> and other unnecessary trumpery, the levity and foolishness
> of the Pope and his associates ought to be tolerated, but in
> this article, which is the most important of all and the
> greatest of our concerns, one must grieve and weep that
> these wretches so rave.[12]

In defending his thesis on the bondage of the will to sin, Luther
repeats the arguments from Scripture and from Augustine that he
used in the Heidelberg Disputation. But there is an important difference. He adds a new argument that comes neither from Scripture
nor Augustine--nor from anywhere in the Christian tradition. It
is the argument that the will is not free because all things happen
by absolute necessity:

> . . . it is necessary to revoke this article. For I have
> wrongly said that free will before grace exists in name
> only. I should have said frankly: "free will is a fiction,
> a name without a correspondent in reality." Because no
> one indeed has power freely to think of good or evil, but
> (as the thesis of Wiclif condemned at Constance correctly
> teaches) all things happen by absolute necessity. This
> is what the Poet meant when he said: "all things are
> determined by a fixed law." And Christ says in Matt. 10:
> "The leaf of a tree does not fall to the ground without the
> will of your Father . . ." and in Is. 41 he insults them
> when he says: "Do good or evil if you can."[13]

Such an argument gives an entirely new ring and meaning to
Luther's doctrine of servum arbitrium. First of all, if all things
happen by absolute necessity, then the assertion which Luther
makes in earlier and in later writings--that man has liberum
arbitrium "in inferioribus"--is meaningless.[14] Luther's original
understanding of servum arbitrium as man's bondage to sin now
becomes a doctrine which imposes absolute necessity and excludes
free will by the very fact that we are creatures, not because we
are sinners.[15]

Secondly, the fact that Luther cites Virgil, a fatalistic pagan
poet, to support his thesis of absolute necessity is an a priori
indication that this concept of servum arbitrium is neither strictly
biblical nor Christian. The two biblical texts Luther adds to
his citation from Virgil have no probative value for the thesis:
"all things happen by absolute necessity."

Luther, passionately convinced of the rightness of his mission
to defend the gospel of grace against the Pope and his theologians,
clearly tries to prove too much here. Searching for any argument
he can find to support the biblical-Augustinian doctrine of fallen
man's bondage to sin, he finds one that is both unnecessary and
unfortunate--two constitutive elements of all tragedy. He does
not need the necessitarian argument, for his case from Scripture
and tradition is strong enough--if only he could get a hearing! The
use of the necessitarian argument is likewise most unfortunate for
it gives the Catholics corroborating proof that he is truly a heretic,
a new representative of the old Manichaean denial of free will.

Erasmus intervenes

Luther's Assertio encountered swift opposition from Catholic apologists. We are concerned here with only one of these replies. De libero arbitrio diatribe sive collatio, written in 1524 by Erasmus of Rotterdam.[16] This was the book which directly provoked Luther's major systematic work, De servo arbitrio.

By the middle of 1522 Erasmus had made known his intention to write against Luther.[17] Whereas the attacks on the Assertio by such opponents of Luther as John Cochlaeus and Henry VIII centered mainly on the theses concerning the sacraments which were censured in Exsurge Domine, Erasmus concentrated on proposition thirty-six. In a letter to Zwingli of August 31, 1523, Erasmus listed the doctrine of servum arbitrium as one of Luther's three fundamental errors.[18]

The book which A. von Harnack has judged to be "the crown"[19] of Erasmus' works was completed on May 13, 1524. De libero arbitrio is written with such characteristic Erasmian moderation, elegance and gentleness that some have taken this as an indication of a lack of Erasmus' personal involvement in the question.[20]

Erasmus divides his book into four parts: I an introduction; II a presentation of biblical texts which speak in favor of free will; III an explanation of the texts which seem to negate free will; and IV a formulation of his own view and an evaluation of the views of others.

Three things strike us about De libero arbitrio that enable us to see more clearly how the reformation tragedy was compounded. First, Erasmus shows little appreciation of the genuine meaning of Luther's thesis of the unfree will, namely, that the will of fallen man apart from grace is totally incapable of doing anything for salvation, totally unfree to do anything that is good in God's sight. Instead of coming to grips with this biblical concept of man's slavery to sin, Erasmus concentrates his attention on the secondary, non-biblical supporting argument which Luther used in the Assertio--the argument from the absolute necessity of all events.

Repeatedly Erasmus attacks the view that all things happen "by mere necessity."[21] In the eyes of Erasmus, Luther's thesis of servum arbitrium is simply one more example of determinism or necessitarianism, to be ranked alongside the deterministic doctrine of Manichaeus and the necessitarian doctrine supposedly held by Wiclif.[22] Once again we perceive the absence of the spirit of dialogue, the failure of one to grasp the central concern of the other.[23]

Secondly, and more unfortunately, we find the leading scholar of the Roman Church doing a bad job in presenting the Church's teaching on free will. Erasmus defines free will as "the power of the human will by which man can apply himself toward or turn himself away from the things which lead to eternal salvation."[24]

This is a seriously defective definition of free will. Instead of defining free will in terms of the ability to choose between certain alternatives, Erasmus defines free will in terms of salvation--without mentioning grace![25] Erasmus gives no hint in his definition that man the sinner is enslaved to sin until he is liberated by grace. The definition is surely one of the "extraordinary blunders" which, according to P. Hughes, characterize De libero arbitrio.[26]

In his reply to Erasmus, Luther seizes upon the definition and attacks it repeatedly as Pelagian. The definition undoubtedly gave Luther a basis for such an assault. In fairness to Erasmus however, it must be noted that he speaks of the need for grace many times in his book. While Luther was right in severely criticizing Erasmus' definition, his accusation that Erasmus was a Pelagian is exaggerated and unfair.[27]

A third striking fact about De libero arbitrio is Erasmus' unawareness that the Church, centuries before, had taken an official stand against a modified version of Pelagianism that came to be known, late in the sixteenth century, as Semipelagianism. Erasmus was not alone in his unawareness of the Second Council of Orange (529 A.D.) and its confirmation by Pope Boniface II in 531. As H. Bouillard has pointed out, the decrees of Orange II were in some way lost during the middle ages and are cited by no authors from the tenth until the mid-sixteenth centuries.[28] This did not mean that the doctrine of Orange II was lost. Such biblically oriented theologians as Bernard, Anselm, Thomas Aquinas, and Gregory of Rimini, who recognized Augustine as their theological master, especially in the doctrine of grace, were all agreed that the sinner is a slave to sin unless he is liberated by the prevenient grace of Christ. Thomas, without knowing of the decrees of Orange II,[29] was even able to say that it is a "truth of faith" that the very beginning of faith is in us from God.[30]

But with theologians who are not known for their biblical exegesis such as Ockham and Biel, or for their recognition of Augustine as the "doctor gratiae," such as Erasmus,[31] one finds a departure from the Catholic tradition--biblical, Augustinian, conciliar, Thomistic and Lutheran--that the grace of God is necessary for the very first step towards justification.

Luther's original reformation protest was directed precisely against Biel and others who held that the sinner, by his own un-aided natural powers of reason and free will, could initiate--and to a certain extent merit! (de congruo)--the grace of justification.[32] As we have said earlier, following Lortz, Luther was indeed rejecting a Catholicism that was not fully Catholic.

Now, several years after his excommunication, Luther finds the leading Catholic intellectual saying that the following Neo-Semipelagian position is a tenable option: ". . . [H]aving not yet received the grace which forgives sin, man can, by his natural powers, perform works which, as they say are morally good, by which justifying grace is merited not de condigno but de congruo . . ."[33]

The teaching which--unknown to Erasmus--had been defined by the Second Synod of Orange and had been called a "truth of faith" by Aquinas is labeled by Erasmus as "probable opinion" (sententia probabilis) held by Augustine, Thomas and Bernard:

> . . . [T]hose who are farthest removed from Pelagius attribute much to grace and almost nothing to free will although they do not take it away completely. They deny that man can will good without special grace and they deny that he can begin, make progress or become perfect without the principal and perpetual aid of divine grace.[34]

Both of these opinions, says Erasmus, fit his definition of free will. He rejects neither view, but is personally inclined toward the one that attributes more to grace.[35]

Erasmus reveals his total unawareness of the Church's rejection of Semipelagianism in the Hyperaspistes, his lengthy response to Luther's reply to him in De servo arbitrio. Of the Ockham-Biel opinion, Erasmus says that as far as he knows it has not been rejected by the Church.[36] Further, developing the concept of "natural" or "common" grace that he had mentioned in De libero arbitrio,[37] Erasmus distinguishes a "human faith," which is "a type of knowledge preparatory to the light of faith," from a "faith which through grace justifies." Then he explains:

> . . . as there are degrees of justice, so there are degrees of gifts until you reach that which is merely natural. But even this is grace, since God is the author of nature. Thus Augustine is needlessly afraid of saying that the initium gratiae arises from man.[38]

Erasmus seems completely unaware that Pelagius had said exactly the same thing to Augustine: free will is a donum Dei; therefore no other donum is necessary! In this sense Pelagius could also say as Erasmus does: "We ascribe everything to God's goodness."[39]

Erasmus seems to offer as his own opinion the following:

> We assent--and that is something we can certainly do by our natural powers. I am not speaking of the assent which justifies, but of that which in some way prepares us.[40]

Compare this teaching with that of canon four of the Second Council of Orange:

> If anyone contends that, in order that we might be cleansed from sin, God awaits our will, but does not confess that even our will to be cleansed takes place through the infusion and the operation of the Holy Spirit in us, he resists the Holy Spirit himself saying through Solomon: "The will is prepared by the Lord" [Proverbs 8:35: Septuagint]. He also resists the sound preaching of the Apostle: "It is God who works in you both the willing and the accomplishing . . . " [Phil. 2:13].[41]

Compare Erasmus' view also with the later teaching of Trent that was defined in 1547:

> [The Council] declares that the beginning (exordium) of justification in adults must be taken to be the prevenient grace from God through Jesus Christ . . . so that those who are turned away from God through sins are disposed by his grace awakening and aiding them to turn to their own justification by freely assenting to and cooperating with that grace . . ."[42]

We have not compared Erasmus' opinion to the teachings of Orange II and Trent in order to indict Erasmus as a heretic. His unawareness that the Church had once taken a definitive stand in favor of the doctrine of fallen man's bondage to sin exculpates him from the charge of formal error or heresy.[43] That the decrees of the Second Council of Orange went astray and that a new form of the old Semipelagian error arose among late medieval theologians would seem to be more than anything else the result of negligence in the exercise of the Church's teaching office.

We have called attention to Erasmus' lack of sensitivity to this Neo-Semipelagianism simply to illustrate what Lortz has has called the "theological unclarity" in the Church on the eve of the Reformation and prior to the Council of Trent; further, to show how inept was the response of the Church's leading intellectual to Martin Luther's protest. We are likewise able to see how Luther would be all the more convinced of the rightness of his cause after reading Erasmus' De libero arbitrio.

Luther on the bondage of the will

Luther responded to Erasmus after more than a year's delay with what is unquestionably his foremost systematic work, De servo arbitrio.[44] Luther once again makes it clear, as he did in the Assertio, that the thesis of the bondage of the will is his central concern. He says to Erasmus at the close of the book:

> I give you hearty praise on this . . . account--that you alone, in contrast with all others, have attacked the real thing, that is, the essential issue (res ipsa; summa caussae). You have not wearied me with those extraneous issues about the papacy, purgatory, indulgences and such like--trifles, rather than issues . . . . You, and you alone, have seen the hinge on which all turns (cardo rerum), and aimed for the vital spot (iugulum).[45]

As we have already indicated, Luther pounces upon Erasmus' highly inadequate definition of free will and accuses him--quite unfairly--of being worse than the Pelagians. Luther also rightly criticizes some of Erasmus' questionable exegesis. For example, in dealing with John 15:5: "Without me you can do nothing," Erasmus says that "nothing" here can mean "that which is of little moment."[46] Luther spends several pages attacking this interpretation,[47] and in doing so, he is on the side of Thomas Aquinas[48] and the Second Council of Orange.[49]

As in the Assertio Luther here offers a two-fold defense of his thesis of the bondage of the will: by a necessitarian argument[50] and by a massive biblical argument.[51]

We find his necessitarian argument here, as before, both unnecessary and unfortunate. It proves too much in that it denies that man has free will not because he is a sinner but because he is a creature. Furthermore, it makes it quite difficult to see how we can be free in regard to lower things (in inferioribus), since these too are foreseen by God.

"It is," says Luther, "fundamentally necessary and wholesome for Christians to know that God foreknows nothing contingently, but that He foresees, purposes, and does all things according to his own immutable, eternal and infallible will. This bombshell knocks 'free-will' flat and utterly shatters it."[52]

It follows "by resistless logic," he adds, "that all we do, however it may appear to us to be done mutably and contingently, is in reality done necessarily and immutably in respect of God's will."[53] We believe that a painstaking exegesis can absolve Luther of the charge of absolute necessitarianism, determinism or fatalism.[54] Nevertheless, his theology suffered severely from the use of this argument.

By dissolving the traditional dialectic of grace and free will into a doctrine of the unfree or necessitated will, with or without grace, Luther is unable to affirm the free-decision character of faith. It is likewise very difficult to see how Luther can affirm that evil is caused by free will[55] if God's foreknowledge destroys free will.

These theological embarrassments are aptly but frighteningly illustrated by Luther's celebrated image:

> Man's will is like a beast standing before two riders.
> If God rides, it wills and goes where God wills. . . .
> If Satan rides, it wills and goes where Satan wills.
> Nor may it choose to which rider it will run, or which
> it will seek; but the riders themselves fight to decide
> who shall have and hold it.[56]

Erasmus had given Luther ample reason to believe that the Reformation was going in the right direction. Luther in turn, with his continual use of the necessitarian argument against free will, convinced the Catholics all the more that he was really a heretic.

Having traced the manner in which Luther and Erasmus compounded the Reformation tragedy, we need not end on such a dreary note. We should keep in mind two things. First, as we have pointed out, Luther's necessitarian argument against free will is not essential to his original and abiding evangelical understanding of man's bondage to sin. The argument, furthermore, was never officially embraced by the Lutheran confessional writings. Today it is almost impossible to find a Lutheran theolo-

116

gian who would defend such a concept of the bondage of the will.

As for Erasmus, it is sufficient to point out that his views on grace and free will are not normative for Roman Catholics. The Catholic commitment to the grace of God is recorded above all in Scripture and in the Councils of Orange II, Trent, Vatican I and Vatican II.[57]

Secondly, in De servo arbitrio Luther presents the most powerful biblical argument for fallen man's bondage to sin that the Church had heard since St. Augustine.[58] Such a reformation proclamation was truly needed in the first quarter of the sixteenth century. It is no exaggeration to say that until the Council of Trent reaffirmed what was taught by the Second Council of Orange, Martin Luther was one of the few theologians in Germany who unhesitatingly defended the biblical and Catholic teaching on man's bondage to sin. He proclaimed that fallen man could do nothing whatever without grace to prepare himself for salvation. This he did at a time in which many, many Catholics--including Erasmus--had either lost this truth or were uncertain about it.

Introduction to Peter Manns

Peter Manns pursued his theological studies at Bonn and Mainz after military service during the Second World War. Shortly after his ordination to the priesthood in 1951 he became a consultant in Joseph Lortz' division of the Institute for European History in Mainz. Manns' early research treated the history of medieval and early modern spirituality. In 1953 he published a survey of recent work on Fénelon, and in 1966 he edited the collection, Die Heiligen in unserer Zeit (Mainz: Matthias Grünewald).

In August 1966 Manns took part in the Third International Congress for Luther Research, where he made important critical interventions on behalf of the "historical Luther" against modernizing interpretations of an existentialist tendency. As long-time co-worker with Joseph Lortz, Manns is acutely aware of Luther's highly original style of thought. He insists on the need for constant and explicit attention to the polemical or pastoral situation out of which Luther spoke. Manns' concern for methodology led to the publication of a monograph, Lutherforschung heute--Krise und Aufbruch (Wiesbaden: Franz Steiner, 1967), in which he carries on a detailed argument with Otto H. Pesch, O.P. Manns finds Pesch's program of a systematic confrontation with Luther seriously defective, primarily because it would neglect history in order to dialogue with the Luther of modern, doctrinally oriented Luther interpretations-- which for Manns are too much the product of contemporary philosophical prepossessions. Further, Manns feels that Pesch's choice of Thomas Aquinas as the main dialogue-partner for Luther is ill-advised. Manns finds in the tradition of monastic theology--especially in Bernard of Clairvaux--Catholic thought of a style that is especially appropriate for comparison with Luther.

The following essay demonstrates the kind of historical reading of Luther which Manns sees as absolutely necessary. Luther is not a thinker whose teaching can be moulded into an orderly and intelligible unity separable from his original living context. Luther was a wholly involved theologian, and his presentation of the interrelation of faith, hope, and charity in the Galatians' Commentary was deeply marked by this involvement. Luther's deepest intention becomes utterly clear, as he rejects any salvational value in human effort independent of God's grace. But when Luther turned to explain the role of human activity under God's influence, he became unclear and his polemic inhibited development of a theology of good works, charity, and advance in righteousness, all of which he affirmed in embryonic form. Thus Peter Manns finds in a prized Reformation document a central concern that is fully Catholic and a series of undeveloped Catholic themes which a Lutheranism uninhibited by polemic could well bring to maturity.

This study appeared originally in the Festschrift for Hubert Jedin, Reformata Reformanda (Münster: Aschendorff, 1965). With permission of the author, the editor of this volume has simplified and condensed some of the original footnotes.

Notes begin on page 205.

Absolute and Incarnate Faith-- Luther on Justification in the Galatians' Commentary of 1531-1535

Peter Manns

The problem

In both content and style, Luther's passages on faith and good works are quite varied, depending on whether he is speaking as a Reformer, as a theologian and exegete, or whether, as a preacher and director of souls, he is struggling to determine the exact relations between these two realities. His Reformation witness on justification--"from faith alone and without works"-- articulates with kerygmatic clearness and forcefulness the core of a doctrine which, as the articulus stantis et cadentis ecclesiae, decides simply the truth or falsity of faith. For genuine faith waits for its salvation from God, not from man. Over against this clear witness stand those statements in which a biblical text or situation at hand makes Luther strive to give a positive explanation of the relationship between faith and good works. Despite Luther's steady concern and polemical rigor, these latter statements never attain theological clarity. As a consequence we are confronted

with the peculiar phenomenon that Luther's statements on faith
and good works draw attention both to the central witness of
the Reformation doctrine of justification and as well to its central problem.

This situation, in turn, has had a lasting effect on the course
of subsequent history. Lutheranism, and Protestant interpretations of Luther in general, have adhered to a doctrine as binding
and as ecclesially divisive, while the meaning of this doctrine
has been at the same time subjected to widely divergent and even
contradictory interpretations. The evidence for my assertion is
to be found primarily in the rich and valuable secondary literature
that has been devoted to this question beginning with K. Holl.[1]
Exceptions aside,[2] in spite of ever-repeated readiness for ecumenical dialogue, such scholars agree that a dividing line appears in the question of good works that now as then separates the
Reformation from the Catholic confession of faith. Correspondingly, the same conception is defended by many Catholic scholars.[3]
On closer examination, however, this consensus loses much of
its impact because it lacks unity in its theological foundation.
Consequently, some writers, along with J. Lortz and under his
influence, regard the fixed boundary as false and assert the
Catholicity of the fundamental Reformation concern.[4]

The present study will attempt to support and confirm the same
thesis with regard to Luther's doctrine of justification. At the
same we dedicate our study in homage to Hubert Jedin whose
studies of the Council of Trent, as well of Seripando and Con-
tarini, are of great importance in this context.[5]

The framework of an essay naturally forces me to limit my
topic. The question itself dictates that priority be given to the
analysis of Luther's text, and that a detailed treatment of secondary literature be restricted. Even without direct treatment of
their works my contribution will serve in the dialogue with such
authors as P. Althaus,[6] W. Joest,[7] and A. Peters,[8] to all of
whom the writer is deeply indebted. In accordance with a methodical desideratum of Luther scholarship, we shall limit ourselves
to Luther's major Commentary on Galatians, which in the past
has been cited frequently in connection with our theme, but which
as yet has not been given exhaustive consideration.[9]

The major Commentary on Galatians of 1535-1538, a revision
of Luther's lectures of 1531, is peculiarly adapted to the aims
of our study.[10] The mature Reformer did more here than simply
treat the doctrine of justification in a thematic fashion.[11] The
work is a massive and unmistakable affirmation that the article

on justification is central to his own deepest concern. For Luther
the doctrine of justification, not an existential theology of the Word,
served as the foundation which could not be lost without destroying
the whole of Christian doctrine[12] and the Church itself.[13] As a
consequence, the doctrine of justification contains the very condition through which separation from the Roman Church would lose
its reason and basis:

> Once this has been established, namely that God alone
> justifies us solely by His grace through Christ, we are
> willing not only to bear the pope aloft on our hands but
> also to kiss his feet.[14]

Luther's statements must moreover be understood in terms
of specific situations. At times he felt the necessity of emphasizing once again for Christians, through instruction, defense, and
polemic, the central concern of the Reformation upheaval. For
in addition to the "papists" new enemies of the Gospel had arisen
who seemed all the more dangerous to Luther because they
stemmed from his own camp. They were, on the one hand, the
Anabaptists, enthusiasts, sacramentalists, and sectarians,
and on the other hand, the Antionomians (whom the expanded
Preface in 1538 singles out explicitly[15]) and libertines. While
the former denied justification through grace and faith through
new emphasis on works and the Law, the latter compromised
the Gospel by abolishing the Law or by the foul conclusion,
"Then let us not do any works!"[16] Luther views all of his opponents simplistically as foxes, who have different heads but
whose tails are all knotted together.[17] In light of the dismal
situation in his own Church, Luther's presentation of Galatians
assumes the function of spiritual self-justification and of defense
against the temptation to think carnally and to despair over his
own work.[18]

It is no wonder, then, that Luther seeks defense for his doctrine
and consolation in this distressing situation by taking refuge in
the Epistle to which he felt himself wedded[19] and which he considered superior to the Epistle to the Romans.[20] It is also no
wonder that in no other of Luther's writings do we grasp so
clearly his need to compare and identify himself in all things
with the Apostle.[21]

Whoever is familiar with Luther's style of thought knows how
the situation of a many-sided defence or attack affected the way
he expressed his deeper theological intention. The editor of the

Weimar volumes containing these lectures spoke of a theology grown huge through conflict. [22] We may assuredly interpret this as indicating that Luther was captivated by his polemic. The result is not a darkening of his purely religious concern[23] but the introduction of an inhibition that prevented Luther from giving a clear, theological exposition of his deepest intention. On the other hand, this situation of an all-fronts defense also carries with it important advantages. Formally, there is a noticeable simplification of his theological method and manner of expression. Regarding content, there is an appreciable refinement of his whole concern through varied expressions corresponding to his constant change of fronts.

The following analysis seeks to discover, amidst changing and polemically fixed formulations, how Luther understood the relation between faith and good works in justification at the level of his basic point of departure and central concern. In line with the text he was explaining, Luther characterized justification by faith basically in terms of a defense against Jewish legalism, which he identifies with papist justification by works. In the search for positive statements on this point, we should not dwell on formulations whose basic thrust is negative. In terms of the theological and controversial tradition, Luther saw justifying faith as a part of the problem of the theological virtues, faith, hope, and charity. In consequence of this context, Luther opposed passionately the doctrine of "faith formed by charity" as the sublime camouflage for justification by works. Here the negative tendency is dominant. However Luther was also aware that St. Paul argued for an interrelation of the effects stemming from the theological virtues. Although Luther accentuates the primacy of faith almost to the point of excluding all else, he still feels obliged to determine more carefully the relation of faith to the other virtues. Our analysis will show somewhat surprisingly that he found no difficulty in determining the relations between faith and hope, and that in this context he made some significant statements on the good works and activity of Christians. Luther's exposition of the relation between faith and charity appears then as very important. In a re-interpretation typical of the Reformation, charity becomes the specific support of good works, a fact that conceals Luther's much deeper understanding of agape. We will try especially to indicate the point of departure of this latter idea and develop a reflection upon it.

124

Absolute and incarnate faith

We shall begin by ascertaining a point which will help us to
confine the field of study considerably and focus on the real
problems. The great majority of characteristic central statements in which Luther radically excludes good works from
justification are exclusively concerned with a works-righteousness in which one's own human effort to fulfill the Law denies
the total dependence of man on Christ's work of salvation and
the grace of God.[24] What primarily concerns Luther is the
elimination of a heresy that must also be sharply repudiated
from the point of view of properly understood Catholic doctrine.
The relevant passages on this point do not require further
examination within the scope of our theme. However, what we
have here ascertained is of further importance in light of the
fact that Luther's fundamental position also influences his attempt to portray the role of good works under grace for justification. Luther's endeavor to defend the role of grace in justification
against the incursion of good works is totally justified if we consider the over-emphasis on works in late scholasticism and in
ecclesiastical practice. He sees with utter clarity the danger
of mixing justification by faith and justification by works,[25] or
Gospel and Law,[26] and denies the possibility of a middle-way
between them. On the other hand, there is no denying that this
sollicitude brings with it a negative tendency and almost a complex against good works that seriously hinders Luther in his attempts to portray positively the role of human activity under the
influence of grace. The Commentary we are studying documents
impressively Luther's nervousness and peculiar uncertainty. He
goes so far as to make preparation for a defeat at the hands of
the proponents of the righteousness of works. If their exegesis
prevails, he plans to snatch victory by having recourse to Christ
the Lord of Scripture in opposition to the biblical witness to
good works.[27]

Accordingly, in Luther's positive assessment of the role of
good works under grace in justification there is not the theological clarity that characterizes his denial of works-righteousness.
Instead, the relevant statements developing our theme are ambigu-
ous, contradictory, in need of clarification, and therefore misleading.[28] In interpreting this phenomenon it seems to us decisive
that one can give a straightforward explanation in terms of Luther's
hermeneutic situation. We touch on the tragedy of the Reformation
when we realize that Luther's lack of clarity stems from the lack of

clarity on the part of this theological opponents, and when we grasp that it was the necessity of defending grace that encumbered his theological treatment of good works under grace. At the same time, we must not lose sight of the immense difficulties entailed in a positive presentation of the problematic of justification. No Catholic system has been successful in dealing with the mystery of the free action of man under grace with final clarity. From this vantage point we understand the basic paradoxical tension of Luther's starting point. The new way that Luther tried to follow does not a priori lead to an un-Catholic conclusion. Consequently, we propose to pose the question in a manner keeping close to reality and avoiding the pitfalls of subsequent systematization.[29]

Undoubtedly Luther's most interesting and most promising attempt to relate faith and good works was his application to this problem of the analogy with the hypostatic union of divine and human natures in Christ. No other than the great ecumenicist, Père Yves Congar, believes he finds here documentation for his thesis that the inadequacies of Luther's doctrine of justification are connected with deeper defects in his Christology.[30] In distinction from O. Modalsli, who devoted a special chapter to this "incarnate faith,"[31] Congar deserves credit for having sketched out the problem at hand with total clarity.

Luther begins his attempted explanation in his exegesis of the difficult passage from Galatians 3:10. Luther draws attention to the fact that Scripture speaks of "faith" in entirely diverse ways: sometimes "outside of good works," in the sense of "fides abstracta vel absoluta"; and at other times "along with good works," in the sense of "fides concreta, composita seu incarnata." This diversity is analogous with Scripture's statements about Christ.[32] According to Luther, this analogy leads to the following set of correspondences.

"Fides absoluta," i.e., the faith that is the exclusive cause of justification without works,[33] corresponds to the divinity of Christ which alone makes our Lord Creator, King, and Savior.[34] "Fides incarnata," on the other hand, i.e., the faith that works through "faithful doing" in the works of faith[35] has its Christological counterpart in the divinity conjoined with the humanity,[36] that is, with the composite and incarnate Christ.[37] This association leads Luther to speak of justifying faith according to the analogous Christological notion of the communication of idioms. Just as the creation of everything can most truly[38] be ascribed to the infant in the manger[39] or the liberation of Israel from the hands of the Egyptians to Jesus as man,[40] even though he effected them only

through his divinity, "so justification is attributed to incarnate faith
or to faithful doing."[41] The parallelism is complete. To Jesus
as man and to incarnate faith one can ascribe, simply but truly,
what is actually effected only through the divinity of Christ and
absolute faith. Luther's Christological axiom, "Everything is
. . . attributed to the man on account of the divinity,"[42] has as
its soteriological counterpart the statement, "Everything that
is attributed to works belongs to faith."[43]

Consequently, as these remarks show, the humanity of Christ
and the works of the believer have no independent function with
regard to redemption and justification, respectively. They are
simply modes of transparency for what in fact is alone effective
--the divinity and bare faith: "Therefore in theology let faith always be the divinity of works, diffused throughout works in the
same way that the divinity is throughout the humanity of Christ."[44]
In a passage which P. Congar makes the basis for his case,
Luther synthesizes his thought in seemingly complete, scholastic
concentration:

> Thus a theological man is a man of faith. In like manner,
> a right reason and a good will are a reason and will in
> faith. Thus faith is universally the divinity in the work,
> the person, and the members of the body, as the one and
> only cause of justification; afterwards this is attributed
> to the matter on account of the form, to the work on ac-
> count of the faith. The kingly authority of the divinity is
> given to Christ the man, not because of His humanity but
> because of His divinity. For the divinity alone created
> all things, without the cooperation of the humanity. Nor did
> the humanity conquer sin and death; but the hook that was
> concealed under the worm, at which the devil struck, con-
> quered and devoured the devil, who was attempting to
> devour the worm.[45]

Passages of this sort might discourage us from posing Luther
against Luther in order to work out an intricate interpretation of
the deeper intention hidden beneath this apparently clear theological
formulation. Nonetheless we believe we must disagree with the
conclusions arrived at by P. Congar.

If we understand this passage in its context, two points can be
proven. First, the lack of clarity in Luther's Christology is not
the cause of the lack of clarity in his doctrine of justification.
Rather, it is the polemical captivation with the assertion of justi-

fication by faith alone that moves Luther to propose a Christological justification of this doctrine. This ad hoc Christological construction is obviously forced and too strongly contradicts Luther's other Christological statements to qualify as a valid theological expression of his thought. Second, this also holds analogously for the intended statement of the relation between faith and works, which is Luther's main purpose here. This first observation poses no problems. However, the second point will require a further elaboration.

The fundamental defect in Luther's construction of a Christological comparative scheme lies in the fact that it almost exclusively discusses divine acts (creation of the world, the miraculous deliverance of the Israelites, etc.) in terms of the communication of idioms. Christ's theandric act of redemption is mentioned only peripherally in the mythological allegory of the fish-hook and the bait. The aim of this one-sided approach is obviously the exaltation of "fides absoluta" by comparison with the corresponding divinity of Christ. Where this context of defence of "bare faith" is not present, Luther's commentary focuses his Christological statements most often on the theandric acts of Christ's passion, death, and resurrection. This is true of the many passages in which the suffering and death of Christ lead Luther to refer to Him as our "Mediator," "High Priest," and "Priest,"[46] or those which speak of the fulfillment of the Law through Christ.[47] Consequently, the neutralization of Christ's human cooperation in the comparison with faith and good works cannot be taken as typical of Luther's Christology.

Even P. Congar has found too narrow E. Vogelsang's assertion that Luther rarely refers to Christ as Mediator.[48] But Congar feels that in a modified form it is correct, namely, insofar as Luther links the notion of Christ as Mediator with the notion of the "compassionate Savior" (in contrast with Christ as Judge), and above all because he thinks that Luther's writings subsequent to 1517-1520 seldom mentioned Christ as "mediator of our merits."[49] But just such formulations show up in different passages of the Commentary on Galatians,[50] a fact we see as supporting our thesis of Luther's richer Christology. Luther stresses total dependence on the saving work of Christ to the exclusion of mere human merits.[51]

These passages show that Luther does not hold fast to the Christological position he developed in seeking to systematize the relation of faith and works. Thus it seems to us wrong to draw wide-ranging consequences from statements like "Here all is attributed to Jesus the man on account of the divinity." It goes without question that Luther is concerned to adhere to the position of Chalcedon in his Christology. This alone, of course, does not eliminate the lack of clarity that P. Congar has criticized. The inaccurate formulations can be explained by Luther's lack of interest in a Christology as such. Beyond this, one can speak of Luther being inhibited from giving an exact theological account of how the theandric acts of Christ entail a true and actual co-operation of the humanity in salvation. There can be no doubt that this inhibition with regard to Christology is grounded in the difficulty Luther found with regard to human cooperation in the area of justification. Still, it is typical of Luther's deep-lying inhibition in this matter that he does not let himself fall into a formally heretical formulation. Luther neutralizes and diminishes the human element in the divine-human activity without contesting the reality and necessity of the Incarnation. The forced conclusion in Luther's attempt to interpret the redemption in the image of the "fish-hook" and "bait" displays all too clearly the unresolved tension between the two concerns, the affirmation of "God alone" in justification and of "God incarnate" in soteriology. As well, we see the impossibility of a theological resolution: "Therefore the humanity would not have to accomplish anything by itself; but the divinity, joined with the humanity, did it alone."[52]

Luther does not here set "divinity by itself" unambiguously over against "the humanity by itself," but speaks in a peculiar fashion of "the divinity, joined with the humanity." Thus only the exclusion of the wholly independent activity of Christ's human nature is theologically clear here. The extent of the independent activity of the divinity and of grace, implicit in the context, remains unclear because at the same time Luther holds fast to the incarnate conjunction of divinity and humanity, of faith and works. Luther's position appears to be contradictory because by defending the total dependence of salvation and justification on grace he seems to exclude precisely what, at other times, he wishes to include with grace.

Thus the great opportunity is lost for developing the seminal idea of "fides incarnata" by interpreting faith's passage into works (Werk-Werdung) according to the analogy of God's becoming man (Mensch-Werdung). On the other hand, there can be no doubt that it was Luther's intention to solve the problem of justification from the doctrine of the Incarnation. Our conclusion that the theological formulation is not adequate to this basic idea should not lead us to conclude that we must challenge, or even deny, the intention itself. A detailed analysis shows quite clearly that it is the polemically encumbered question of cooperation that causes Luther's peculiar fluctuations and inclination toward one-sidedness. Whenever Luther confronts the problem of justification as a case of applied Christology as he did here, he is apprehensive of endangering both the divinity and grace with a "monophysitical" or "monistic" attempt at a solution.[53]

There are, of course, other statements contrary to these that attempt to determine the effective nature of faith completely in terms of the Incarnation:

> Therefore faith always justifies and makes alive; and yet it does not remain alone, that is, idle. Not that it does not remain alone on its own level and in its own function, for it always justifies alone. But it is incarnate and becomes man; that is, it neither is nor remains idle or without love.[54]

Luther's attempts to determine the relation between faith and good works in terms of the parable of the tree and its fruits also fit into this connection:

> First there must be a tree, then the fruit. For apples do not make a tree, but a tree makes apples. So faith first makes the person, who afterwards performs works.[55]

Here Luther emphasizes the primacy and priority of grace without denying the necessity of works. But once again Luther's inhibition is noticeable. It is significant that Luther avoids the verse that closes the parable in Matthew: "Every tree that does not bear good fruit is cut down and thrown into the fire" (Matthew 7:19). Luther is reluctant to define good works as a condition or a co-cause of salvation. Nevertheless the positive inclusion of good works in the life of faith is dominant in these passages, to the extent that they are viewed as a necessary fruit and result.[56] Luther goes even further in this direction when he makes the authenticity of justifying faith dependent on such effectiveness:

> He who wants to be a true Christian or to belong to the kingdom of Christ must be truly a believer. But he does not truly believe if works of love do not follow his faith.[57]

However Luther did not succeed in specifying good works in the sense of free cooperation in such a way that, without denying or limiting grace, they might be seen to have true causality and necessity for salvation. But it does not follow from this, as P. Congar indicated,[58] that he denies all cooperation, or so radically asserts God's operation that all other activity is excluded.

Therefore Luther's emphasis on <u>fides</u> <u>absoluta</u> attains only a negative theological clarity in the denial of any form of justification by works. In spite of the conflict of intentions we pointed out, Luther's positive portrayal remains open to realizing the intention of <u>fides</u> <u>incarnata.</u>

"Faith is nothing without hope"

If the openness of "faith alone" to good works, as we have examined it so far, resembles a damaged rampart, we find an entirely different situation when we come to consider the relation of faith to hope. To continue the imagery, we might say that Luther opens all the gates when hope seeks entrance into the fortress of faith. This extraordinary openness has according to Luther's texts several bases. Luther regards hope as the theological sister-virtue to faith, so strongly related to it that in very fact the two of them can hardly be distinguished.[59] In addition, hope lacks a direct connection with works and cooperation, so that Luther's easily triggered defense mechanism does not spring to action. Finally, the question does not bring him into close contact with the scholastics. For them he has but one cutting remark: "The sophists have really sweat over this issue."[60] This state of affairs is all the more interesting since it can only be explained as an unintentional misunderstanding or neglect of the scholastic positions. It can be said with certainty that Luther's treatment of hope would have turned out differently had he taken it up in terms of the scholastic idea of "hope formed by charity" or in terms of a secret identification of hope and the love of concupiscence. This situation explains a general characteristic of Luther's statements about hope. In the absence of polemical contact with his opponents, the slumbering scholastic in Luther stirs! Among the handwritten notes that contain Luther's lecture preparations, we find a scholion of the mature Reformer that could not be more scholastic in style.[61] In a fashion quite foreign to biblical expression, Luther distinguishes the relations of hope to faith by bringing them under the following points of view: "1. <u>Subiecto</u>; 2. <u>Officio</u>; 3. <u>Objecto</u>; 4. <u>Ordine</u>; 5. <u>A Contrariis</u>."[62] The scholion concludes with the surprisingly straightforward statement:

> Just as prudence is vain without fortitude
> so faith is nothing without hope. . . . Just

as fortitude without prudence is temerity,
so hope without faith is presumption of the spirit.[63]

Thus the much abused scholastic mode of thought comes to a thoroughly positive issue by clarifying the presentation of a point of view that, despite its strange clothing, is fully Protestant.

This emphasis leads first of all to a determination of the idea of faith which, in the delineation from hope, displays traits that are nearly suppressed in other contexts where Luther's fiducial faith is predominant. The intellect, instruction, and knowledge, as well as the truth and its defense against error and heresy, form the characteristics of faith in complete alignment with tradition. Here, hope is connected with the will, with admonition, encouragement, and perseverance, and has goodness as its object. Its work is the overcoming of temptation.[64] As this classification shows, faith here is thoroughly in need of supplementation through hope and does not assume, as so often, the rank of a Protestant universal virtue.[65] These passages are even more important for our theme in light of the fact that in them Luther concedes decisive functions to hope with regard to righteousness and justification.

Faith grasps righteousness only in a limited manner, and needs development in two respects. First, righteousness looks toward being revealed since throughout this life it is concealed in coexistence (simul) with ever-present sin. Second, righteousness requires real development since faith merely conveys the first fruits of the Spirit and the beginnings of the death of the flesh, such that now we are "not yet wholly righteous." According to Luther the proper object of hope is our endurance until the full development of the righteousness received only limitedly in faith.[66]

Luther makes use of a typical distinction to characterize this two-sided need of development: "Thus our righteousness does not yet exist in fact (in re), but it still exists in hope (in spe)."[67] This distinction, which Luther used frequently in his early writings, is a favorite of the existentialist Luther interpreters, since the opposition between res and spes seems to call into doubt the reality of righteousness as given here and now.[68] It is extremely important to note that the application of this pair of ideas, when seen in this context and the wider one of Luther's whole thought, completely excludes the existentialist reduction of reality and so the distinction provides us important hermeneutic assistance.

As we hinted above, faith-righteousness, according to Luther, is limited insofar as it coexists with the ever-presence of sin for the duration of this life. This means that righteousness is hidden from human awareness beneath the opposing experience of struggle in a conscience dominated by the sense of sin.[69] In this situation, hope functions to give a "most important and most pleasant comfort."[70] What Luther means by "comfort" becomes clear from the admonition whereby we are to comfort our troubled brethren:

> Brother, you want to have a conscious righteousness; that is, you want to be conscious of righteousness in the same way you are conscious of sin. This will not happen. But your righteousness must transcend your consciousness of sin and you must hope that you are righteous in the sight of God. That is, your righteousness is not visible and it is not conscious; but it is hoped for as something to be revealed in due time. Therefore, you must not judge on the basis of your consciousness of sin, which terrifies and troubles you, but on the basis of the promise and teaching of faith, by which Christ is promised to you as your perfect and eternal righteousness.[71]

If we omit for now the question of the nature of ever-present sin,[72] we can see that Luther clearly ascribes reality to faith-righteousness, and that hope does not await righteousness, but its disclosure. Thus Luther can say, ". . . we wait by hope for that righteousness which we already possess by faith."[73] If my own self-awareness forces me toward the conclusion that I am besieged and overwhelmed by sin, faith asserts that this conclusion is in fact not true. The believer, therefore, has to follow the Word of God, not his own self-awareness.[74]

Consequently, when Luther contrasts the distinction between "not yet in fact (in re), but still in hope (in spe)" he is not speaking of the reality and existence of righteousness but of the mode of its givenness, which in turn determines the way in which it is experienced. In re, that is, directly and really, we do not experience righteousness, but rather the sin which conceals righteousness. Only faith believes in righteousness as already given, through confidence in Christ and the Word of God--a righteousness that not only is not perceptible, but which goes directly against our real experience of sin. In this situation it is hope that promises a troubled faith, at least in spe, what it lacks in re, namely, the disclosure at the end of time of the righteousness that up to now lies hidden.[75]

According to Luther, then, faith and hope are related to righteousness in different ways. Faith has to do with a righteousness which is neither visible nor perceptible, while hope refers to the righteousness to be revealed. Thus Luther can distinguish between the two virtues in scholastic style according to their objects, wherein the concept res again plays an important role. In his preparatory note, for instance, his third distinction is:

> Thirdly, faith and hope differ with regard to object. Faith has as object the word about the reality (verbum rei) and the promise of realities, that is, of the truth. Hope's object is the reality of the word (rem verbi) or the reality promised, for it looks to goodness.[76]

Again the use of the concept res is at first confusing. If we understand the distinction to mean that faith has no more than "the word about the reality and the promise of realities" as its object, while hope has "the reality of the word or the reality promised" then, contrary to the interpretation given above, we would conclude that only the hope that grasps toward the Eschaton lays hold of real righteousness while faith must be satisfied with the mere word and the mere promise. Taken in context, however, the strictly futuristic interpretation is untenable. For "the word about the reality and the promise of realities" is the object of faith insofar as it is known as "truth."[77] If this does not rule out faith as merely believing something true and the knowledge of purely future promises, still the truth of faith, as Luther understands it, does not have as its content purely eschatological salvation. As we have already seen, "the truth," particularly as it is understood by Luther, coincides more with righteousness which we "already possess" in faith,[78] and which gives us the right to regard the dominance of sin, that as a fact (re ipsa) fills our experience, as untrue.[79] The purely future interpretation is even more contrary to Luther's firm conviction that faith in God's word grasps Christ, and makes us share in His righteousness,[80] whereby union with Christ is secured as a real communion of life as against all forms of spiritualistic reduction.[81] Therefore when Luther associates "the word about reality" and not "the reality of the word" with faith, he is not denying the reality of what is grasped in faith. Luther simply means that in this life we possess the res of righteousness only through faith in the Word, and that it is not yet experienceable as res. This experience is something we can only await in hope and thus can only anticipate.

134

If the reality of the righteousness of faith is thereby guaranteed against dangerous misconceptions, we must nevertheless
be aware of the fact that Luther sets hope in a uniquely realistic
relationship to res. Hope is oriented directly to "the reality of
the word or the reality promised" as it is to be given to us completely at the end of time through revelation.[82] Nevertheless,
we would not grasp Luther's thought properly if hope were taken
to be a purely eschatological expectation. Analogous to the veritas
of faith, hope has bonitas as its object. What Luther means by
these original formulations is clear if we replace the abstract
"reality of the word" with the concrete "righteousness" and equate
it with bonitas. Hope, then, has to do with the good, in which righteousness is visible to the extent that it moves out of concealment.
Thus, according to Luther, hope does not await the revelation of
righteousness simply as an event at the end of time. Rather it is
actively involved, here and now, in the process of revelation.
Consequently, "expectation" is not for Luther the primary, nor
the proper, concern of hope.

More typical activities of hope include exhortation, encouragement, daring, endurance, and struggling. Thereby it enters into
the process and advances it. Thus Luther can say that in the battle between faith and the devil, hope takes up the concerns of faith
and leads to victory:

> Then my battling hope grasps what faith has commanded;
> it becomes vigorous and conquers the devil, who attacks
> faith. When he has been conquered, there follow peace
> and joy in the Holy Spirit.[83]

The real relation of hope to righteousness becomes still more
significant if we consider that Luther assigns to it as object not
only "righteousness to be revealed" but also "righteousness to be
advanced." There is such a tight connection between the revelation
and advance of righteousness that basically they have to do with
two aspects of the same development. For righteousness is "revealed" to the degree that it grows toward its perfection. With
regard to the participation of hope in the vital process of increasing
realization of the embryonic righteousness that is given us, Luther
says:

> We have indeed begun to be justified by faith, by which we
> have also received the first fruits of the Spirit; and the
> mortification of our flesh has begun. But we are not yet

perfectly righteous. Perfect justification remains to be done, and this is what we hope for.[84]

The consummated righteousness of heaven can first of all be "expected" by hope only as an eschatological gift.[85] On the other hand, this expectation has immediate significance in the struggle for perfection. Therefore it is anything but a passive waiting. It instills the forbearance whereby we endure the conflict of the continuing battle[86] and it confers upon our struggle the necessary perseverance: "Thus we began by faith, we persevere by hope, and we shall have everything by revelation."[87] Still the activity of hope does not exhaust itself in anticipation, endurance, and perseverance. Luther concedes yet more active functions to it when he allows it to intervene directly as the "leader in war"[88] and as "theological fortitude"[89] in the struggle for the real perfection of faith-righteousness.

Thus we see most clearly not only the distinction between the two virtues, but the true dependence of faith on hope for supplementation. For although faith precedes all else as the beginning of life, insofar as it apprehends Christ in knowledge and as theological prudence, it nonetheless requires hope, directly and unconditionally, wherever communion with Christ introduces the believer into the crosses and battles of a life conformed to Christ.[90] Regarding hope's share in this life, Luther does not hesitate to ascribe to it the "victory" in the battle.[91]

Therefore it remains true that Luther does not maintain the exclusiveness of sola fide with regard to hope. His startling assertion--"faith without hope is nothing"[92]--cannot be dismissed as an over-subtle formulation. It must be taken as a serious theological statement.[93] It is highly significant that within the scope of our problematic Luther conceives the function of hope as true and real efficacy, that is, as a work that must be carried out for our salvation. Hope masters the deadly crisis in which our faith in hidden righteousness would otherwise succumb to the contradiction posed by the overpowering experience of sin. As we have seen, hope is not restricted merely to making the tension tolerable by assuring us, to a degree corresponding to the level of temptation, that we can expect righteousness at the end of time.[94] Rather, it enters directly into the battle against sin and the devil, and thus struggles actively for the revelation and perfection of the righteousness given now only in a hidden and seminal fashion. As "the leader in battle" hope is in control of the situation and comes to the aid of faith through the real experience of the victorious

136

power of resistance.[95] Here the overpowering exclusiveness of
the awareness of sin is not only mitigated, but fundamentally
neutralized.[96] What makes such a positive assessment of hope
possible for Luther is ultimately the conviction that "battling
hope" is grounded totally in Christ and totally in the mystery of
a life conformed to Christ. When it permeates and activates
the whole man, it is not the case that our achievement and power
need be introduced or contributed by us independently of Christ.
Therefore, hope's activity in no way endangers the truth of faith
that our righteousness is through Christ alone--a point Luther
did not neglect to mention in this context.[97] However, since the
full gratuity of justification is guaranteed, Luther does not hesitate to specify faith, hope, and love itself as functionally interrelated powers of the new life.[98] Thus our idea of hope receives
a final confirmation in light of the fact that Luther says of the
man struggling for perfection:

> Thus a man is whole and perfect in this life, both inwardly
> and outwardly, until the revelation of the righteousness for
> which he looks, which will be consummated and eternal.[99]

"In the place of charity, we place faith"

We are now brought to our third topic, the relation between
faith and charity. It is of particular importance for our theme
because the discussion of good works in the scholastic tradition
had its theological locus precisely in this context. It suffices
simply to recall the scholastic doctrine of "faith formed by
charity," which was often documented by Scripture passages such
as Galatians 5:6: "fides quae per charitatem operatur." This points
immediately to the polemical tension[100] that determined Luther's
hermeneutical situation, making it very difficult, if not impossible,
to give clear expression to his own deeper intention while rejecting
opposing positions. Although Luther is ordinarily aware of the
distinction between theological interpretations of dogma and the
binding doctrine of faith, in this case the doctrine of the scholastics[101] becomes the very essence of what is Catholic and papist.
This he opposes defiantly with his evangelical witness without
regard for his own more nuanced theology of agape. The Catholic
emphasis on charity leads him to dethrone it and replace it with
faith alone. "Such are the dreams of the scholastics. But where
they speak of love, we speak of faith."[102]

In light of our problematic, we must beware of taking at face value this truly revolutionary alteration of a consecrated ranking. Rather, we must investigate what exactly Luther rejects with the scholastic idea of charity and what he puts in its place in the name of faith.

With regard to Luther's rejection of charity, it seems best to omit a detailed methodical examination of the scholastic doctrine in question.[103] The problems that would face us could not be handled with the necessary thoroughness within the scope of this article. In addition, such a restriction seems justified by reason of the data in Luther. The Reformer does make occasional distinctions between his scholastic opponents and their respective schools of thought,[104] but he otherwise omits a detailed confrontation with individual thinkers. His procedure is summary in form and is limited to the rejection of a doctrine indicated by a brief formula which, despite the subtler differences, he takes as typical of scholasticism as such. Consequently we shall focus our attention on the content of Luther's objections insofar as they bring to light his deeper intention. Still this necessary precaution, however, does not prevent us from charging late scholasticism with a dangerous lack of theological clarity at least with regard to the points discussed here. The Ockhamist assertion of a love of God "by one's own natural powers"[105] is all we need to know to make Luther's position, as well as his excitement, quite understandable.

Luther's statements against scholasticism are primarily of a defensive nature. He defends the central position of faith in the work of salvation and resists the superiority of the charity that would be the "form" of faith, making faith nothing but the "pura materia charitatis."[106] From this viewpoint Luther can so speak of the scholastic doctrine:

> According to this malignant figment of the sophists, faith, that miserable virtue, would be a sort of unformed chaos, without any work, efficacy, or life, a purely passive material.[107]

Luther, however, cannot simply rest the matter here. Because of his understanding of faith, his defense necessarily goes over to the offensive. For whoever makes faith into a miserable, needy virtue and then points to charity, in the sense of moral activity, as the way to salvation blasphemes against God and separates us "from Christ the mediator and from the faith that grasps Christ."[108] The double thrust against <u>charitas</u> is obvious here. First, Luther attacks it insofar as it suppresses the faith that brings righteousness by grasping Christ. Second, he attacks it because it replaces the grace coming from the mediation of Christ in favor of moral effort. Since we will deal further with the first aspect, we shall first confine ourselves to the second. It may come as a surprise, but it is a fact that Luther rejects charity because he believes he has discovered in it a subtle cover for works-righteousness. He not only directs this point against Scotus and Ockham, but against high scholasticism as well. Luther knows they connected love with justifying grace, but he treats this grace as "a work and gift required by the Law," so that ultimately only the good works count with reference to eternal life as due them.[109] In this polemical perspective, charity slips wholly over to the side of the Law and works, according to Luther, and thus stands in sharp contrast to faith and grace. For instance in his exegesis of Galatians 3:12, Luther argues that the Law and charity are identical, because the former commands nothing else but charity. If according to Paul, however, the Law commanding charity conflicts with faith, then it follows that "therefore charity too is not from faith."[110] According to Luther, Paul clearly decides in favor of justification "from faith alone," which he distinguishes sharply from the Law and love.[111] But the "false and godless gloss of the sophists," that is, the doctrine of "faith formed by charity," mixes faith and the Law: "Hence the gloss of the sophists, which joins the Law to faith, is false and wicked; in fact, it extinguishes faith and puts the Law in place of faith."[112] In the same vein, Luther says that the papists pervert the Gospel when they, in the name of love, once again set up the Law and require works: "Therefore they make of the Gospel a 'law of charity.'"[113] By doing this they reject Christ, the proper "object of the Gospel," who is neither Law nor good work.[114] For of Christ, who proclaims the Gospel as "a divine work granted to me out of pure grace,"[115] Luther asserts:

> Christ is not the Law; He is not my work or that of the Law; He is not my love or that of the Law; He is not my chastity, obedience, or poverty. But He is the Lord of life and death, the Mediator and Savior of sinners, the Redeemer of those who are under the Law.[116]

When the Gospel, at the core of its message, proclaims Christ as Mediator, Savior, and Redeemer, then it is proclaiming deliverance and justification through a faith that grasps this Christ:

> The true Gospel, however, is this: Works or love are not
> the ornament or perfection of faith; but faith itself is a
> gift of God, a work of God in our hearts, which justifies
> us because it takes hold of Christ as the Savior.[117]

Here, as in our first consideration of <u>fides</u> <u>incarnata,</u> it is
extremely important to note what exactly is meant theologically
by Luther's rejection of "charity informing faith." For here
also, taken strictly, Luther is rejecting nothing other than a
doctrine that, under false reference to the theological virtue of
charity, once again establishes the Law and requires works for
justification and salvation making the mediation of Christ, his
blood and his wounds, superfluous. Whenever Luther rejects
good works in the context of the doctrine of justification, the issue
is not simply good works and charity, but laws and all works of
the Law.[118] We see that this negative determination does not
answer our question even though it is an important element of the
answer we are seeking.

We must recognize also that Luther does not make it easy for
us to specify the content and significance of the works of love
which he himself withdraws from his condemnation. Moreover,
precisely at this point his thought appears to be particularly
fixed through polemics, since he always views charity in light
of the doctrine of "faith formed by charity" and thus in com-
petition with faith.

As a consequence of his struggle against the work-oriented and
legalistic charity he sees in scholasticism, Luther insists first
that true love can only result from union with Christ--from faith
and grace.[119] This initial determination coincides with the parable
of the tree. Just as the tree comes before the fruit, so grace and
faith come before love--or, true love and its works can only be
conceived as the fruits of faith.[120] Insofar as Luther means the
total dependence of charity on grace, this position does not present
the slightest difficulty, since he is here emphasizing a basic Catholic truth. The problem begins when he seems to formulate so
exclusively the "consecutive" relation of love and its works to
grace and faith that any "final" reference of charity to salvation
by reason of grace becomes impossible.[121] In the case of love,
Luther seems to go even further. There are a number of quite
important statements in which love is clearly not viewed as the
necessary fruit of faith, but as an independent and optional addition.

For instance, when Galatians 5:14 praises the command to love one's neighbor as the fulfillment of the whole law, Luther holds that this makes no demand of the Christian. What is required, rather, is only faith in Christ, in whom we are perfected and have all things. Love, on the other hand, appears in this context as something added on which frees the Christian from the Law but is left to his own discretion:

> Now if to faith, the worship that is most pleasing to God, you want to add laws, then you should know that in this very brief commandment, "You shall love your neighbor as yourself," all laws are included.[122]

Along this line of determination, Luther characterizes faith as intolerance and inflexibility, and love as tolerance and maximum flexibility.

> Love "bears all things, believes all things, hopes all things, endures all things"; therefore it yields. But not faith; it will not stand for anything. . . . So far as his faith is concerned, therefore, a Christian is as proud and firm as he can be (superbissimus et pertinacissimus).[123]

As in the case of fides incarnata Luther makes use of a comparison that turns out unhappily from the viewpoint of Christology:

> At this point faith makes man God (II Peter 1:4). But God does not stand for anything or yield to anyone, for He is unchanging. Thus faith is unchanging. . . . But so far as love is concerned, a Christian should yield and stand for everything; for here he is only a human being.[124]

All of these statements ultimately climax in an idea of Luther's which A. Nygren has presented in his highly reputed study[125] as the genuine Reformation understanding of agape--which is thought to entail the fundamental overthrow of the Catholic synthesis centered on charity. The agape spoken of here is God's love for us which gives and pours itself out into the lowliness of humanity, but without empowering the Christian to begin a response to God in an ascending love.[126]

The starting point for this position can be easily found in our last quotation from Luther. In faith, man orients himself upward toward God and toward his own divinization. But in love one descends as a mere human to pour oneself out in the realm of change and need. Luther expresses the same thoughts in his commentary on Galatians 5:6, where his text spoke of "fides per charitatem efficax."

> Paul is describing the whole of the Christian life in this passage: inwardly it is faith toward God, and outwardly it is love or works toward one's neighbor. Thus a man is a Christian in a total sense: inwardly through faith in the sight of God, who does not need our works; outwardly in the sight of men, who do not derive any benefit from faith but do derive benefit from works or from our love. [127]

Analogously, in the exegesis of Galatians 5:13, Luther interprets the commandment to love our neighbor as defending the freedom given us in faith:

> Therefore, the apostle imposes an obligation on Christians through this law about mutual love in order to keep them from abusing their freedom. Therefore the godly should remember that for the sake of Christ they are free in their conscience before God from the curse of the Law, from sin, and from death, but that according to the body they are bound; here each must serve the other through love, in accordance with this commandment of Paul. [128]

If we gather Luther's statements together in a kind of synopsis, then the Reformation understanding of charity takes on the following form. Charity does not have to do with God, with existence coram Deo, with our divinization, nor with the intus of interiority, but rather with man, with existence coram hominibus, with our humanization, and with the foris of external works. Charity does not liberate us in conscience from the curse of the Law, from sin, and from death, but rather it merely protects the freedom we gained in faith through service according to love. Finally, charity does not belong to the unchanging and eternal domain of God, of the Spirit, and of truth, but rather is restricted to the fleeting, changing domain of the flesh where the requirement arises of service to the neighbor both in tolerance and according to the Law and its provisional works. Above all else, charity is no longer an independent virtue that has a constitutive significance as a power (a virtus) with respect to salvation. At best, charity is a proper answer that follows faith "as a kind of gratitude." [129]

142

Strictly speaking, charity is nothing but the external function of faith itself.[130]

Luther, therefore, gave his opponents their full due on the field of battle. He returned attack with attack, and, unfortunately, one-sidedness with one-sidedness. He unmasked the papist charity as works-righteousness, secured the claims of justifying faith, and--sad to say--his victory is clearly at the expense of the charity that he did not at any price want to renounce. Amidst the shadows of polemics, charity is imperceptibly forced to the place where his scholastic opponents had ostensibly situated faith. Stripped of its old predicates and functions, it is now the pura materia and misera virtus[131] that henceforth must serve as a "maidservant" to humanity. Charity's bridal role has been lost to faith.

It is not so much the expulsion of charity by faith from its rela- tion to salvation, however, that is so questionable in this Reforma- tion re-interpretation of love. We shall, in fact, attempt to show that this exclusiveness of faith presupposes a positive relation to charity which, although Luther was incapable of formulating it, nonetheless is part of his deeper intention. Much more problemati- cal is the unbiblical and violent denial of a love for God that reaches God precisely in the neighbor much more than through the neighbor or immediately. Luther distorts the incarnate unity of the command to love--a unity which is maintained in the much-abused scholastic doctrine in the remarkable thesis that love of neighbor, as a theo- logical virtue, has God as its formal object. Admittedly, this doctrine is seldom thought through to the end. From Luther's point of view, however, it should be noted that perhaps love preserves for itself a direct relation to the beloved Lord, precisely in its kenosis of the transition from the divine bride to the serving maid.

A final problematical--and surprising--point is the peculiar dis- placement of love, as understood in the Reformation, into the area of works, Law, and precepts. Does love, according to Luther, really exhaust itself in works that God does not need, but which have significance only for our neighbor? Can one really defend Luther's expulsion of love into the area of the second table of the Law? Our questions point to the polemical fixations of the Re- formation notion of agape which should caution us against simply accepting Luther's re-interpretation with all seriousness. His statements are neither as certain or precise as they pretend to be. Luther's uncertainty and inhibitions are more noticeable than usual when his opponents hide themselves behind First Corinthians 13, as if behind their wall of bronze. His categorical judgment-- "But they are men without understanding . . . they cannot grasp or see anything in Paul"--is an inadequate response to the problems that this chapter posed for him throughout his life. Luther's obstinate "sola fide, non fide charitate formata . . ."[132] is a confessional decision, not a theological solution. Therefore we have good reason to examine even the programmatic statements of the Reformer in terms of Luther himself. He even appears to demand such a critical examination in connection with his important commentary on Galatians 5:6, in which no less a problem than that of the "whole Christian life"[133] is handled with determination typical of the Reformer. In this exposition Luther finally admits that his view of the "form of Christian life" deals only with the factual interaction between the two virtues. An examination of the nature of faith and charity still remained: "One has not yet said what faith is and what love is; for this is another matter for discussion."[134] In the same passage, Luther refers to his statements concerning the internal nature, power, and use of faith. An equally complete treatment of charity, of course, would be sought for in vain in the Commentary on Galatians, although remarks such as those related to Galatians 5:14 seem to presuppose one.[135] Consequently, our interpretation must work through the many isolated statements, and should neither shrink away nor lose heart from apparent (or glaring) contradictions.

It would be an easy thing to show that the fixations we found above in the Reformation understanding of love stand in contradiction to, or at least in distinction from, other statements. There are numerous examples in which charity is not conceived as a facultative addition but as a necessary fruit of faith.[136] No less numerous are examples that upset the fixation on interhuman charity and emphasize the biblical unity of love of God and love of neighbor.[137] Other passages give importance to the attitude and affection of charity in opposition to works.[138] Others give charity its place in the Gospel instead of under the Law.[139] But it seems best to forego a complicated examination of individual examples in order to pursue Luther's fundamental conception. As we have pointed out several times before, this is concealed behind his polemics, but it is in no sense negated or abandoned.

A casual or systematically oriented reading of the Commentary on Galatians could be misled by the notion that with reference to justification and salvation Luther grants constitutive meaning only to faith and not to love. Over against this incisive and, in fact, revolutionary alteration of the traditional ordering of the virtues and fundamental powers of the new life, we must take careful account of the fact that Luther consistently identifies full righteousness and holiness with love, not with faith:

> If we were pure of all sin, and if we burned with a perfect love toward God and our neighbor, then we would certainly be righteous and holy through love, and there would be nothing more that God could require of us. That does not happen in this present life but must be postponed until the life to come.[140]

Consequently, the primacy of faith is only provisional and temporary, lasting as long as the perfect and eternal righteousness of love is held back. Moreover, the true goal of faith is consummation in love. Only love remains, while <u>fides</u> and <u>spes</u> come to an end with the completion of love.[141] And if the perfect love of the future life is held back, it in no way follows that love does not now determine our lives. Before pursuing this line of thought, let us seek a deeper understanding of the passage just quoted. It is supported by Luther's theology of the Law, especially as it was worked out in his early writings. According to it, the Law not only requires works, but requires them in the sense of a willingness to obey that expresses one's loving surrender of will and heart. This required surrender in love does not exhaust itself in the intentional simplicity of a love purified of every element of self-relatedness, but rather demands the full liberty, spontaneity, and enthusiasm of heartfelt surrender. The self-seeking of the old man must change into the "<u>concupiscentia charitatis</u>."[142] Thus the Law becomes a fundamental but saving demand placed on man which he cannot fulfill. It brings man to realize his inability of fulfilling the Law through his own power. It exposes the ever-presence of sin in all of its ramifications and thus drives a man into the arms of Christ where, through grace, the process of fulfilling the Law and the new life begin.

Precisely this notion can be found in many passages of the Commentary on Galatians, where it is presupposed as a basic conviction. Luther's position is that the Law requires the adoration of God in fear, love, and faith. But men offend against this law insofar as they deny love to God through works-righteousness and hence love only themselves.[143] Wherever the Law exposes sin and increases it with its requirement of love, the accusing and condemning function of Law climaxes in man's experience "that he not only does not love but hates and blasphemes God, the supremely good, with his most holy Law."[144] The relation of man to the Law, therefore, resembles that of the Jewish people to Moses, or that of the student to his teacher. They fulfill the requirements (which should be fulfilled willingly and joyfully) only out of fear of punishment and under the constant threats of the law-giver and the master of the rod.[145] Thus Luther says of the Law:

> If it justified, certainly men would love it, delight in it, and embrace it with a will that would be inclined toward it, not away from it. But where is that will? . . . Therefore their fleeing shows the infinite hatred of the human heart against the Law.[146]

It follows that it is not so much crass sins such as murder, adultery, and theft, that make fulfillment of the Law impossible, but much more the inner sins of which human reason is utterly ignorant, such as reluctance and rebellion against God.[147] They add up to the odium cordis with which human self-love responds to the requirement of unselfish love of God. Therefore if we only "listen" a little to Luther's texts, we discover there the central agape, or eros, motif.[148]

But what is the significance of this future love for our present life, which, according to Luther, shares in righteousness only through faith?[149] We hinted already that love, as the goal of the life-process governed by faith and hope, cannot be without meaning for this life. Luther, however, obviously goes further by regarding love (which in its complete form is reserved for heaven) as already the formative power of the new life. For as "fruit" of the Spirit,[150] of grace, and of faith, love is free from the blasphemous claim and impossible duty of gaining, or of having to gain, righteousness through works. Thus nothing else stands in the way of its inclusion. This unique relation between charity and good works is all the more noteworthy since Luther denies this doing to faith: "Faith does not perform works; it believes in Christ the Justifier. And so a man does not live because of his doing, he lives because of his believing. Yet a believer does keep the Law."[151] The division of functions is clear. Faith justifies; the justified man, however, follows the Law, or at least begins its fulfillment. It is evident that the fides incarnata, or faith become flesh and man, leads to love, or is even identical with it.[152] In reference to hope, Luther expresses the same functional connection in the following manner: "Thus we must always trust and

and hope, and we must always take hold of Christ as the Head and Source of our righteousness. . . . we should take pains to be righteous outwardly as well . . ."[153] External righteousness, therefore, is ascribed to charity, as well as to effectiveness in works, while faith remains restricted to what is internal. If we compare this position with the passage cited above,[154] we notice a significant change in meaning. Here the concern is no longer with the negatively-tinged externality of the body-flesh as opposed to the interiority of the spirit, but rather with the manifestation and actualization of the reality that is given only internally in faith. Luther defends himself here against the scholastic idea of charity, which, with its empty well-wishing and as a mere inhering quality, shows itself to be a caricature, "a completely bare, meager, and mathematical love, which does not become incarnate . . . and does not go to work."[155]

If, along with Luther, we view love in this perspective, then the constricted ideas we criticized above may be understood as polemical attitudes that fundamentally go against his deeper intention. For if faith takes on flesh in love in order to live out the gift of righteousness in increasing fulfillment of the Law, then the good work directed to mankind and manifesting itself externally is nothing but the expression of the final and inner surrender of love that God requires of us under the Law--a love in which God Himself is the object.[156] Much to our surprise, then, charity, which is assumed to be degraded in the Reformation outlook, turns out after all to have a central role to play. Luther not only conceives of charity as the goal of the life beginning with faith in Christ, but also as the power that actively and operatively leads us toward this goal.

However, we should not lose sight of the fact that this charity striving for perfection does not yet entirely fulfill the Law, and that the Christian must for the remainder of this life have faith so as to retain righteousness and salvation. In order not to misunderstand this practical primacy of faith, it is of extreme importance to determine exactly love's need for supplementation. In his commentary to Galatians 5:17 ("Caro enim concupiscit adversus Spiritum"), Luther deals with our question rather thoroughly. Following the Scriptural text, Luther takes the opposition between flesh and spirit to be a battle that all the saints (and consequently we also) experience[157] and that we all have to endure for our salvation. According to Luther, it is the opposition of the flesh which prevents us from fulfilling the Law: "The flesh prevents us from keeping the commandments of God, from loving our

neighbors as ourselves, and especially from loving God with all
our heart."[158] The non-fulfillment of the Law is not from the
evil of our works, but rather from the attitude (not the surrender
in charity) out of which the works proceed. It is important to note
that Luther in no way completely denied this attitude to the Christian. In an important way love is already the master of the heart,
namely in the operative readiness of the will for surrender in
love. What is lacking now is spontaneity and enthusiasm:

> The good will is present, as it should be--it is, of course,
> the Spirit Himself resisting the flesh--and it would rather
> do good, fulfill the Law, love God and the neighbor.[159]

Indeed, this good will is not able entirely to break the opposition
of the flesh and thus it does not attain the desired willingness,
but at the same time it is not an empty and ineffective velleity.
As an operative will of love, rather, it already determines the
situation that through its intervention undergoes a definite transformation. For the Spirit makes the opposition against the flesh
fruitful and puts the will in the position to deny the concupiscent
flesh its victory.[160] Luther expresses this transformation of the
situation even more distinctly when he says of the Spirit operative
in the will of Love: "The Spirit rules and the flesh is subordinate
. . . righteousness is supreme and sin is a servant."[161] In a
thoroughly logical manner, Luther also modifies his statement
of the simul iustus et peccator, replacing the total double qualification with two partial qualifications:[162] "They know that they
have partly flesh and partly Spirit."[163]

This makes it unmistakably clear wherein love requires supplementation through faith. If, with Luther, the lack of fulfillment of the Law is viewed in light of James 2:10,[164] then, of
course, the real need for supplementation is extended to total
dependency. Whoever does not attain the spontaneity of surrender in love trespasses against the whole Law and is thus
wholly dependent on faith to gain righteousness.[165] From this
vantage point, the kerygmatic pathos of the demand for "faith
alone," as well as the theological tendency (polemically sharpened)
toward a complete suppression of love through faith, takes on new
meaning. On the other hand, a context has been established that
makes this phenomenon of suppression intelligible and removes
its one-sided sharpness. Luther's aggressive words "in the place
of charity . . . we place faith"[166] are relentless only when set off
against only a charity masking justification by works.[167] But with

148

regard to love properly understood, there is a change of relationship so that love assists and gives the needed supplementation.
Faith assists charity by grasping Christ and his righteousness
so that the pervading sin of imperfectly fulfilling the Law is not
imputed against us.[168] Faith also supplements love to the extent
that it becomes operative out of its communion with Christ. Thus
faith fills out in steady growth, by becoming flesh in charity,
the given milieu of righteousness. It is characteristic of this
synthesis of mutual complementation that Luther does not hesitate
to ascribe even now to the faith that takes hold of Christ what will
constitute the perfection of love in the future, that is, the spontaneous and joyful surrender of the heart:

> Coming at a predetermined time, He truly abolished the
> entire Law. But now that the Law has been abolished, we
> are no longer held in custody under its tyranny; but we
> live securely and happily with Christ, who now reigns sweetly
> in us by His Spirit.[169]

This highest attribution does not belong to justifying faith in
itself, but only to faith that ends the struggle victoriously in conjunction with hope and charity. Thus Luther speaks of "the weakness of faith in the pious," a faith that still lacks joyful certainty
and purity of heart.[170] With regard to an operative faith, however, we can attribute to it what can be said of love alone only
with considerable restrictions: "When Christ has been grasped
by faith . . . then I do good works, love God, give thanks, and
practice love toward my neighbor."[171] From this point of view,
the dethroning of love through faith, as discussed earlier, becomes practically unobjectionable. For here Luther's theology
presupposes a functional context that makes possible a trans-
ference of the predicates in line with the communication of idioms.
What in the full sense belongs only to the charity of the future
life is ascribed to faith now in view of Christ and the perfection
in love that he will bring about. For the duration of the present
intermediate life, in which full victory still lies ahead, despite the
fundamental overcoming of the flesh, the surrender of faith sub-
stitutes for the surrender in love. Faith serves both to shelter
and to promote charity, a situation corresponding to the present
hiddenness (Luther's absconditas) of our salvation. In this interpretation, the sola fide formula loses all of its aggressive pointed-
ness. Here again we are face to face with the tragedy of the polemical captivation that prevented Luther from fully formulating

and developing the beginnings (that are clearly there) of a valid determination of the relationship between faith and charity.[172]

If this approach makes clear the significance of faith for love, the converse question--what is the significance of charity for justifying faith?--is still left open. It is in accord with Luther that we pose this question because, as we saw above, he describes the function and operation of the love already given in a thoroughly realistic manner. Charity, while referred to faith for supplementation, is nonetheless at work positively insofar as it adheres to the Law with a good will and strives for the perfect willingness of total surrender.[173] Charity works negatively insofar as it hinders the powerful evil self-love[174] from bringing concupiscence to its perfection.[175] Luther, therefore, is entirely correct in characterizing the present, interim state with the quantitative partim-partim denomination, whereby the visibly real, partial actualization of the Law is ascribed to love.

This conclusion leads to some important questions for further research, which cannot be avoided in our problematic, but which also cannot be dealt with exhaustively. On the question of the reality of the righteousness developed in connection with charity, we refer back to our discussion of the "righteousness to be revealed and advanced" in our section on hope. The problem of whether the incipient and imperfect charity is already real love (although a love in need of development) must, as we see it, be solved in an analogous sense. The clearly documented idea of genuine development, which by its nature can only occur during our present life,[176] excludes the notion of the dialectical and absolute new start of a constantly repeated semper incipiendum.[177] Luther's realistic statements about incipient love and fulfillment of the Law[178] can be explained only in terms of the embryonic first fruits of the Spirit[179] that grow toward the true and perfect charity of heaven in a real, though hidden, process. With regard to the substitutionary function of faith, we must refer to all the statements that ascribe a real and transforming effectiveness to faith and to Christ present in faith.[180]

Finally, in our perspective the sin remaining after justification loses much of its shocking offensiveness. As our analysis has shown, it coincides concretely with the ultimate inability of love to attain spontaneous and joyful surrender.[181] As a consequence, Luther himself speaks of "the remains of sin"[182] that are an utterly serious matter for the believer in the sensitivity of his love and in light of the divine demand.[183] The remnants are in truth overcome as sin so that henceforth they must serve life.[184]

Although all of the related problems are not hereby solved,[185] the remaining sin does not offer a serious argument against the reality of love and righteousness. In functional conjunction with the powers of the new life, with Christ and with the Holy Spirit, this "sin" experiences a change in meaning, making it necessary to distinguish it strictly from sin as such. Luther justly affirms the prevalence of righteousness and life over sin when he says in one of his <u>partim formulae</u> (with reference to the flesh and the Spirit in man):

> We are partly sinners and partly righteous. Yet our righteousness of Christ . . . vastly surpasses the sin of the entire world.[186]

The role of charity in the formation and preservation of the "righteousness to be revealed and advanced" is considerable, so considerable in fact that the question concerning the relevance of charity to salvation is inescapable from the texts. Therefore, let us pose the question directly: Would it be contrary to Luther's deeper intention to attach to the contribution of charity, as he himself describes this, the predicate "necessary for salvation"? We are well aware of the problematic and the implications involved in such a thesis. At issue is an answer that can be verified and in fact shown to be necessary by arguments from fundamental positions. It is not however an answer that can be found explicitly in Luther because, against the background of the polemical situation, he was incapable of posing the corresponding question.[187] Admittedly, throughout studies of Luther we find it constantly asserted that the Reformer denied charity any constitutive significance in the question of justification and so was opposed to charity being seen as necessary for salvation.[188] It is then affirmed that he admitted or demanded charity as the fruit and consequence of a righteousness already given and present. In the course of this study, we have raised as an objection against this argumentation that Luther's statements should not be over-interpreted. Theologically, the only conclusion that follows unambiguously from them is the radical exclusion from justification and righteousness of a charity which as a masked works-righteousness expels Christ and grace from their salvific function. The specification of charity as the fruit of faith, however, only signifies that even the effectiveness of charity must be derived entirely from grace and that it must not deny the gratuity of salvation.[189] Both demands, the negative as well as the positive, are in accord with the Catholic understanding of what is necessary for salvation and thus do not imply a contradiction to our thesis.

Luther's preference for the abridged parable of the tree, where he did not cite Matthew 7:19 ("Every tree that does not bear good fruit is cut down and thrown into the fire."), indicates all too clearly the inhibition that troubled him. W. Joest tried to show in his very perceptive analysis that Luther excluded from the realm of grace the final, or purposeful, reference of good works to salvation as well as the corresponding imperative of the Law. Here Luther substituted a view of good works as consequences flowing naturally from righteousness and the corresponding indicative of the Gospel.[190] However, has Luther thereby also denied the new and different imperative--the nova lex of the Gospel?[191] W. Joest is well aware of this problem and wrestles with it, finally proposing, not the Calvinistic third use of the law, but a "practical use of the Gospel."[192] Thus, the Gospel does not say, "You must do this in order to gain that . . ." but speaks parenetically, "You may do this, because that is given you . . ." Ultimately, though, this idea does not go beyond affirming the dialectical opposition of Law and Gospel.[193] As a systematic theologian, Joest succumbs to the temptation to fit Luther's ideas into a system that, so far as its complexity goes, is ultimately easier to demonstrate from Scripture than from the Reformer himself.[194]

With full respect for Luther's theological genius, we prefer an interpretation that makes allowances for his hermeneutical situation and is open for the possibility of a theological failure where this better explains the phenomena. It seems to be incontestable that Luther finds himself in an inescapable circle with regard to the problem to be solved. He does not get beyond the negative limits of his deeper intention because he does not dare attempt the development of the positive principle that is justly required. Luther's inhibition stems from his deep insight into the Pauline theology of law and grace, as well as from his defensive fear of works of the law. At times, for instance in reference to Romans 11:6, he views as insoluble the problem of safeguarding the gratuity of the justification merited by Christ and bestowed in faith, if righteousness ultimately depends on the works of a love that must merit salvation through the perfect fulfillment of the Law. Luther's inhibition is characteristically noticeable when, without a touch of polemic, he says of the perfect fulfillment of the Law through love in the hereafter: "Then we would certainly be righteous and holy through love, and there would be nothing more that God could require of us."[195] Implicitly, then, Luther is trapped by the paralyzing notion that complete fulfillment the law in perfect charity could make grace superfluous! Instead of making it clear that, of course, the most perfect effectiveness of love depends no less on grace than the total surrender of faith, Luther shifts the apparently insoluble problem from this life to the hereafter: "That does not happen in this present life but must be postponed until the life to come."[196] It is only the dismal portrayal of man's incapability of achieving such a love and the emphasis on his captivity in sin[197] that bring saving grace once again into view.

Did Luther actually defend the notion that righteousness, holiness, and love cease to be effects of grace in the eschatological consummation? Did he really think that the total surrender in love is restricted by the requirements of the Law? If we wish to avoid attributing such absurdities to the Reformer, there remains only the simple explanation that he was unable to pose the question about a cooperation necessary for salvation but possible only through grace, because of the pressures under which he did his thinking. This solution is not a psychological one that takes us away from the objective problem, for Luther's thought is directed toward defense against and attack upon an opposing heretical thesis. Against this he asserts the principle of grace, which he thought had been denied. Whenever he seeks a positive assessment of charity, he runs up against a concealed, fixed conception according to which love, in terms of the doctrine of faith formed by charity, belongs on the side of Law, works, and merit. In an analogous connection sin, faith, and grace are also opposed to these. Luther does not intend these fixations and connections theologically, and much less does he demonstrate them. On the contrary, they go against his own intention and conceal the most basic principles of his religious and theological conception. As our analysis has shown, sin and love, for Luther, are utterly inseparable. We experience the true nature of sin, and our enslavement to it, only because of the command of love. Only by suffering because of sin and enduring the fate destined for it does love, in conformity with Christ, mature into perfect charity. Therefore, by the logic of his own principles Luther should have applied the paradox of sin and grace, as found in Scripture, to charity. His polemical stance against the scholastic idea of charity, however, forced him to do this only under the negative aspect, while the positive aspect (which is there in germ) is concealed and distorted in Luther's own thought by the polemic.

This situation has to be kept in mind if we are to understand Luther's sola gratia correctly, e.g., as it is repeatedly presented with growing intensity in his image of the tree and its fruit. That the tree produces the fruit and not the fruit the tree has, for Luther, primarily only this meaning: the works of love proceed as the fruits from grace, faith, and justification, not the other way around. Images aside, good works are the effects and the results of the righteousness received in faith by grace, and are not its cause. The aim of the polemical thrust in Luther's imagery is clearly that justification is the pure gift of grace. True, justification is necessarily operative bearing fruit in good works, but the works may never be associated with the command or the claim of having first to merit or want the justification that is given. The obvious misunderstanding is clarified immediately if we realize that Luther is not here opposing human cooperation as such, but rather the works of the law understood as bringing righteousness (the opinio iustitiae[198]), and the scholastic doctrine of charity which Luther has stamped as works-righteousness.[199]

This imagery contains another typical Reformation nuance if, along with Luther, we see symbolized in the tree the person of the Christian as the doer of good works.[200] In this interpretation, Luther's speaks against an externalized, reified, and mechanical understanding of justification which, by accentuating works, habits, and qualities, forgets that the person, the heart, the intention must take on life from and before God before this life can take form in works. Man becomes a person before God through faith in Christ.[201] This fact points to the mystery of the faith that takes hold of Christ,[202] from which, as we indicated above, faith develops even now the active and inner surrender of spontaneous action that as such belongs to charity.

If we put together both interpretations of the parable of the tree, then according to Luther the following requirement emerges: The Christian, blessed through the grace of God with the righteousness of Christ, is free from the Law and its command that we merit salvation under our own power through good works. With the support of the Lord, he has his hands free to fill out the space of life granted him with freely done good works through the power of the Spirit and following the movement of his heart.[203] What Luther means, in line with his defensive position, is totally clear, namely, what is to be rejected is the inner bondage of the "iustitiarius" who seeks to merit beatitude, not spontaneously, enthusiastically and joyfully, but through forced good works under threat of punishment and promise of reward.

Thus, because of his polemics, Luther's statements appear to entail a fundamental rejection of the necessity of human cooperation in salvation, as is consistently affirmed by Protestant and Catholic scholars. But when these statements are subjected to critical examination and are understood in terms of Luther's basic conception, we arrive at a different conclusion. All they unequivocally require is that the activity leading to salvation be seen as totally dependent on grace as its cause and that personal and free surrender be recognized as the form of a life in grace. Luther, as a matter of fact, does not direct himself to our question about the necessity of good works, but he does emphasize the necessary connection between faith and good works. It is a point in favor of our thesis that, in his interpretation of the parable of the tree, he restricts his emphasis to the efficient causality of grace.[204]

Whenever his words are directed precisely to a negative point, however, they are then directed only against works-righteousness.[205] In line with the inner logic of his principles, though, Luther can conceive and express a much closer relationship between faith and good works and almost utter what we have been looking for. This occurs in the few, but very important, statements in which he makes the authenticity and justifying power of faith dependent, not simply on good works, but on the transformation of faith into good works through love.[206] An exaggerated fear of works-righteousness and a legitimate concern for the grace of justification prevented Luther from taking the last intellectual step toward openly expressing in paradoxical unity both the necessity for salvation and the total gratuity of charity, as entailed in his principles. For what inhibits him in the question of the necessity of charity for salvation seems to be already overcome in his understanding of charity. If the law can be fulfilled only in the total and spontaneous surrender of love, then the Law is not only excluded as a way of salvation because it asks too much of man, to say nothing of the perverse course of legalism, but it becomes also clear that the Law's demands aim ultimately at the transcendence of the Law as Lex and its inner transformation (not its substitution or alteration) in the Gospel.

We should not, therefore, as do the Protestant scholars, become entangled in the confining alternative of lex implenda or lex impleta,[207] but must think Luther's principles through to the end as part of the adventure of faith. What is intended is the paradoxical fact that the claims of the Gospel are total but that the content of these claims overcomes once and for all the Law and legalism. For if God wants our love as a condition for salva-

tion then he is thereby indicating to us a way of salvation that
can be followed only in communion of life and destiny with
Christ and only through grace. Such a course still remains
pure grace when we have fulfilled the law of charity through
the power of the new life. As a consequence, we do not succumb
to the faulty argumentation Luther ascribed to the sophists, who
saw the passage from precepts to eternal life as simply a matter of external performance.[208] We also avoid the dialectical
circle that does not go beyond the perpetual opposition of "you
must" and "you may." Along with Luther, we understand the
mystery of love through grace in terms of the mystery of righteousness to be advanced and revealed, whereby through faith
we now possess love--the perfection of which we struggle for
in hope against ever-present sin. The specific originality of
Luther's doctrine of justification is not thereby violated. We
do go beyond Luther--however, following his basic principles
--by simply expanding the simul of "sin and righteousness"
by means of this other simul: our effort as necessary for salvation and pure grace, servitude and freedom, purposeful striving
and spontaneity. Thus we come to a doctrine of justifiction in
which absolute faith truly becomes incarnate faith through active
charity. This doctrine remains in its substance true to the Reformation, even as we seek to give theological expression to
Luther's deeper Catholic intention.

Introduction to Warren A. Quanbeck

Warren A. Quanbeck has taught theology at Luther Theological Seminary in St. Paul, Minnesota, since completing his doctoral studies at
Princeton in 1948. In 1957 he contributed a seventy-page study of
Luther's early exegetical principles to the volume Luther Today. On
the Commission on Theology of the Lutheran World Federation, he was
active in the discussions on the doctrine of justification prior to the
1963 World Assembly of the Federation in Helsinki. He is now Vice-
Chairman of that Commission.

Professor Quanbeck attended the Second Vatican Council as an official observer and contributed to both of the dialogue volumes on the
Council produced under Lutheran auspices. In Dialogue on the Way
(1965) he collaborated with George Lindbeck in narrating the course of
Lumen Gentium through the Council discussions and voting. In Challenge
and Response (1966) Professor Quanbeck analyzed in detail the Decree
on the Pastoral Duties of Bishops. He is currently a member of the official Lutheran-Catholic Theological Consultation in the United States.

Afterword

Warren A. Quanbeck

For most Protestants Roman Catholic studies of Martin Luther call up images of popular pamphleteering in which Luther is portrayed as a degenerate monk who, to satisfy his carnal appetites, was willing to defy his superiors, utter heresies and blasphemies, destroy the unity of christendom and plunge Europe into the horrors of the wars of religion. To those better informed the Catholic contribution means Heinrich Denifle and Hartmann Grisar, scholars who brought massive theological learning to the study of Luther and his writings, but who emerged with a portrait not greatly different from that of the pamphlets. Luther was for them still the fallen monk, who distorted the doctrine of the church to find an easy peace with God. Grisar differed from Denifle in the sublety of his portrait, seeing Luther as a man of great gifts but the victim of self-deception rather than the deliberate liar, the man of gross appetites and foul mouth.

Specialists in the study of Luther were aware of a new and different approach to the Reformer among Roman Catholics in the

more irenic approach of men like Karl Adam but especially in
the work of Joseph Lortz and in the circle of scholars influenced
by him. In these men an attempt is made to appraise Luther as an
important event in the history of the church, seeking to get behind his polemics to discern his religious and theological concerns and to estimate his importance not only for his own time,
but for the present, not only for the tradition of the churches of
the Reformation, but for world Christianity.

When the third Luther Congress convened at Järvenpää, Finland, in August 1966 one of the main lecturers was Professor
Erwin Iserloh who delivered the paper contained in this volume.
His selection as lecturer can be taken as an indication that Luther
scholarship has attained a kind of maturity, moving away from
the defensiveness of Protestant and the polemics of Roman Catholic approaches. Professor Iserloh's lecture was well received,
not just as a curiosity (imagine a Roman Catholic lecturing on
Luther at a Congress of Luther specialists!) but as a competent,
thorough, and solidly grounded work. In the discussions at the
Congress Professor Iserloh and other Roman Catholics participated
freely and constructively, showing wide acquaintance with Luther's
writings and the immense literature in the field of Luther studies.
They showed that there are at least certain aspects of Luther's
work which are more accessible or at least more readily perceived by scholars in the Roman Catholic tradition than by many
Protestants. The discussions left the impression that a new and
fruitful stage has been reached in Luther studies through the
fraternal discussion among specialists from different confessional and cultural backgrounds, through which may emerge a richer
and deeper understanding of the total Luther, the man, the believer, the theologian, the churchman.

The essays in the present volume go far to give substance to
these impressions. There is solid learning, a detailed knowledge
of the immense literary output of Luther himself, and broad acquaintance with the voluminous material in monographs. Roman
Catholic Luther scholarship is quite clearly no longer a branch
of theological polemics, but is historically informed, theologically sensitive, and possesses a genuine interest in the message of
the Reformer.

These essays manifest also an appreciation of the man Martin
Luther in his diverse aspects: the blunt and earthly German
peasant, the tormented monk who seeks peace with God through
intense and anguished struggles, the churchman with an impas-
sioned love for the gospel and the scriptures, the poet of great

verbal dexterity and power, the theologian of penetrating insight and unusual gifts for simple and clear exposition, the preacher whose power and eloquence emerge even from the printed page, the rugged controversialist, the gentle pastor.

The fairness of these contributions is also notable. None of the authors fells compelled to withhold critical judgments, but they attempt, and with considerable success, to give objective presentations of Luther's position in the setting of his time. A truly dialogical approach has been achieved in most of them, listening with patience to what Luther has to say, probing to make sure that they have grasped what point he is trying to make, estimating the influence of the controversial situation upon his choice of language and method, and seeking to give a fair appraisal of his significance for the present theological situation. It is to be hoped that Protestant Luther scholarship will in decades to come be correspondingly less defensive of the Reformer's reputation and permit him to be seen, not as a plaster saint, newly whitewashed for public exhibition, but as he is, "warts and all." One suspects that the Luther who emerges from the new dialogical approach will be a more impressive historical figure than either tradition has been able to perceive to date.

As intimated above, the specifically Roman Catholic background and training of these authors seems to contribute some special insight to the study of Luther. A number of such aspects may be mentioned.

1 The fact that scholastic theology is still to some extent a living world of thought in the Roman Catholic Church enables Catholic scholars to get at some things in Luther more easily than Protestants can. Luther's background in late medieval Catholic theology and piety is accessible to Protestants only through a laboriously achieved act of historical imagination. Catholics who live in a world still continuous in many respects with that of Luther seem to have a feeling for that world and a kind of natural sense for the relationships of the various pieces of cultural furniture. Catholics too can blunder in reading nominalistic scholasticism as though it were identical with derivative thomistic thought, but the historically informed among them apparently have sensitive ears to the overtones and nuances that some moderns have difficulty with.

2 The churchly Luther emerges from the Catholic portrait with a new vividness, so that Protestants can acknowledge with feelings of recognition the appropriateness and truth of the portrait. The polemics of the past four centuries have deterred most Protestants

from dwelling on resemblances between the reformer and his contemporaries. Unfortunate tensions between institutional churches and between the churches and the university theological faculties have also contributed to the obscuring of this aspect, for university professors, however fair minded and objective, have not been anxious to do their opponents' homework. Luther and his theology have taken on a predominantly academic appearance as a result of the highly academic character of much research. The contributions of Lortz, Iserloh, Manns and Pesch help recover neglected dimensions of Luther the pastor, the spiritual adviser, the biblical expositor, the preacher.

3 Luther's concern for religious experience also emerges in fuller detail in these essays. The use of Luther scholarship as a part of the armory of theological controversy in modern Protestantism has occasionally stressed overmuch Luther's rejection of the enthusiasts, Anabaptists and other aspects of the left wing of the reformation. The bias against mysticism both in Ritschlianism and Barthian theology has also shown up in the colors chosen for Luther's portrait. But Luther was concerned for personal appropriation, for effective congregations, for faith working in love, and this comes out clearly in these essays. Even where the exposition by Protestants has been ample and clear, the Catholic contribution adds color and depth to the picture. Lennart Pinomaa, for example, has effectively shown the existential, rather than scholastic character of Luther's theology. The comparison in depth with Thomas in the work of Pesch adds not only additional illustrative material but enriches our grasp of Luther's methodology.

4 These attempts to make sense of Luther within the world of contemporary Catholicism also offer useful suggestions for methodology. The examination of language, style, method and exegetical technique in the work of Lortz, Manns, Hacker and Pesch follow the lines of modern linguistic analysis and literary criticism, and suggest that much work of this kind will appear in the next few years. The development of Luther research seems to require more detailed studies in Luther's theological vocabulary, his categories of thought and theological method, in order to come to grips with questions now on the horizon, the meaning of faith, the problems of ethics, the law, the church and eschatology.

Joseph Lortz deserves special gratitude as the pioneer of modern Catholic research in Luther. The combination of insight and courage which is needed to break with accepted patterns of interpretation, especially in a situation where passions run high, is sufficiently rare to be worth mention. All students of Luther are indebted to him for the impulse which he has given to a new situation in scholarship.

Lortz' essay in this volume gives a richly suggestive sketch of Luther as man and theologian. The appreciation of the Catholic richness of his thought, the fullness of his activity as believer, prophet and battler, the prominence of volitional and emotional elements in his personality, his pastoral concern for the relationships of men with God--all of these elements help the novice to sense something of Luther's greateness and importance. Even the experienced Luther scholar will be helped by them to see Luther in clearer focus. The discussion of Luther's theological style is of especial interest today in view of the concern for problems of hermeneutics and theological method. Little of this material is really new, and yet its presentation in a compact and clear statement gives a telling portrait of Luther.

Iserloh's essay was especially well received at the Luther Congress in Finland in 1966. The author's mastery of Luther's thought was apparent both in the essay and the discussion which followed. Inasmuch as both traditional Lutheran confessionalism and much of modern Luther research have tended to minimize the importance of mystical elements in the mature Luther, Iserloh's stress on their continued importance in Luther's growth and thought are stimulating and suggestive. The one-sided and abstract imputation theology of much of Lutheran scholasticism had already been called into question by the earliest elements of the Luther revival as in Theodosius Harnack. The delineation of the enduring patristic and especially Augustinian elements in Luther is however a valuable aid to keeping the questions in focus. Iserloh is perhaps most helpful in indicating the inner connections of Luther's mysticism, his theology of the Cross, and his use of the Augustinian motif of sacramentum and exemplum. His insistence that Luther did not divorce scientific theology from a concern for spirituality is also a useful corrective to some overly academic treatments of the reformer.

Hacker focuses on a question which has been at the center of the stage since Bizer's germinal book Fides ex Auditu appeared. He demonstrates that all the evidence has not yet been gathered, and that we do not yet comprehend all the movements in Luther's early development. His method is also suggestive, for a detailed examination of Luther's theological vocabulary in its context seems necessary for the development of our understanding. He shows what most students of Luther were already, at least

in a vague way, aware of, that the reformer is not as precise in
his theological terminology as modern conventions of writing require.
The contemporary analyst of Luther's language is indeed frequently frustrated and annoyed by his habit of shifting the content or
emphasis in traditional terms without notice. But while Hacker has
made a significant contribution to the discussion of Luther's inner
development, his work is flawed in two ways. He is not sufficiently patient to wait to find out what Luther is saying, but bears in
upon him like a prosecuting attorney who is already convinced of
the guilt of the culprit in the witness chair. Adequate interpretation
begins with faithful listening and a serious attempt at appreciation;
but this has no part in Hacker's method. A second weakness of his
work is his failure to observe that Luther's usage and his own frequently diverge and that he reads his own meaning into Luther's
vocabulary. Remission of sins for example is for Hacker apparently a narrow and precise term, somewhat similar to what it became
in some later Lutheran scholastic theologians. For Luther remission of sins is a capacious summary term, standing for the sum
total of what God offers us in Christ.

McSorley's handling of the problems of De Servo Arbitrio is a
good example of dialogical theology. The exposition of the historical background of the diatribe enables him to see how both sides
in the discussion furnished fuel for their opponents, and to recognize that Luther was unfairly condemned while at the same time
his language gave his opponents a handle against him. Luther was
right in rejecting an uncatholic Catholicism and yet his argumentation was unfortunate. McSorley rightly calls attention to the inconsistency of the necessaritarian argument, which still strikes
readers of the book as a defense of determinism. Like the contributions of Manns and Pesch this essay helps to clear away misunderstandings of terms and intentions which have unfortunately
persisted through four centuries of polemics. That each side
comes to understand the other in terms of its best representatives,
and that they understand the real thrust of the others' argument
and its religious and spiritual concerns is a fruitful possibility
in the present, as it has not been for centuries.

Manns also performs this useful ecumenical task of eliminating
misunderstanding and clarifying the concerns of the participants
as well as the issues in the discussion. His handling of the problem
of faith and good works makes clear that Luther was concerned to
eliminate the heresy of denying man's total dependence upon the
grace of God in Christ, but that the controversial setting prevented him from formulating an adequate statement of the place

164

of good works in the Christian life. Instead, however, of using this as an occasion for partisan rejoicing, he points out that no Catholic system has succeeded in dealing with clarity with the mystery of man's free action under the grace of God. He then uses the analysis of Luther's handling of the faith-works, faith-hope, and faith-charity complexes as opportunities to show his purpose, the complexity of his terminology, and the multiplicity of the devices he uses to express the various aspects of faith. The essay becomes not only an effective exposition of a problem in the theology of Luther, but an indication of the persistent difficulties which confront us in our search for solutions today. His emphasis upon the dangers of abstracting Luther from his historical context for systematic confrontation with contemporary theologies is a useful warning, for especially in the case of Luther, the historical context is necessary for adequate understanding.

Manns' insistence that not Thomas but Bernard is the appropriate theologian for confrontation for Luther carries the same historian's warning to systematicians, and rouses our interest in having some one undertake the task. But whatever historical difficulties beset his path, Pesch performs a striking feat in showing common or complementary theological thrusts operating through quite different theological methods. We are embarrassed to discover how vain and fruitless many exercises of traditional Kontrovers- theologie have been in comparing incomparables, in assuming identity of meaning because the same words are used, or in missing common concerns beneath divergent terminology. It is one of the great theological assets of our time that historical- critical method has equipped us with means to realize the variety of theologies with which the New Testament expounds the mystery of God's activity in Christ, the number of different theological methods used through the centuries of the church's existence to communicate this message to the world, and the variety of vocabularies and images which are available to articulate theologies in our time. We are given a new theological situation. We are not imprisoned forever in the fruitless repetition of old quarrels, but by use of new methods accessible to us can find areas of agreement where formerly discord reigned, and move on to the discussion of the questions which are genuinely significant. When we are realistically modest about our theological achievements, we recognize that the problems are not solved, but still waiting for solutions which may emerge from constructive dialogue.

WA   D. Martin Luthers Werke, Kritische Gesamtausgabe (The Weimar Edition: Hermann Bohlaus Nachfolger, 1883--). References give volume, page, and line number.

WABr   The Weimar Edition, Briefwechsel (1930--). References give volume, page, and line number, followed by the number of the letter referred to.

WATr   The Weimar Edition, Tischreden (1912--). References give volume and page number, followed by the number of the recorded table remark.

LW   Luther's Works--The American Edition, published in fifty-five volumes by Concordia Publishing House of St. Louis and Fortress Press of Philadelphia, 1955--. References give volume and page number, with the name of the translator of cited passages following in parentheses.

Bondage   Martin Luther on the Bondage of the Will, a translation of Luther's De Servo Arbitrio of 1525 by J. I. Packer and O. R. Johnston (London: James Clarke, 1957). Citations used with permission.

Pauck   Luther: Lectures on Romans (The Library of Christian Classics, Volume XV), translated and edited by Wilhelm Pauck (Philadelphia: The Westminster Press. © 1961, W. L. Jenkins). Citations used with permission.

ET   English translation.

ST   St. Thomas Aquinas, Summa Theologiae.

NOTES TO JOSEPH LORTZ
The Basic Elements of Luther's Intellectual Style

1 H. Boehmer, Luther in Light of Recent Research, trans.
 Carl F. Huth (New York: The Christian Herald, 1916), p. 7.
2 W. Link, Das Ringen Luthers um die Freiheit der Theologie
 von der Philosophie (Munich: Kaiser, ²1955), pp. 22-66.
3 A. Brandenburg, "Um die Deutung der Theologie Luthers,"
 Theologische Revue 60 (1964), p. 82.
4 What we refer to is not precisely the same as the kaleido-
 scope of interpretations of Luther which Gerhard Ebeling
describes and even justifies. See Ebeling's Luther-Einführung in
sein Denken (Tubingen: Mohr, 1964), p. 12. We do not find fault
with the differing images of Luther that successive generations
draw out of the vast fullness of the Reformer. The true problem
arises from the contradictory interpretations, and this especially
in the more recent studies, which have paid such close attention
to Luther's intellectual makeup. This leads us to ask about the
unity or disunity of Luther himself--a question about which we
must come to a commonly accepted opinion, if men are to avoid
despairing of the worth of scientific historical theology in Luther's
case.
5 R. Hermann, Luthers These: Gerecht und Sünder zugleich
 (Gütersloh: Mohn, 1960), p. 1f. See R. Kösters' series of
articles on Hermann's interpretation of Luther, Catholica 18
(1964), 48-77 and 193-217; 19 (1965), 138-162 and 171-185.
6 P. Althaus, Die Theologie Martin Luthers (Gütersloh: Mohn,
 1962), p. 8. ET: The Theology of Martin Luther, trans.
Robert C. Schultz (Philadelphia: Fortress, 1966), p. vi, where
"Ozean" is palely translated as "a way of thinking."
7 See W. von Loewenich, Luther als Ausleger der Synoptiker
 (Munich: Kaiser, 1954), p. 10.
8 The Reformation in Germany (New York: Herder and Herder,
 1968), Vol. I, pp. 207 f.
9 I do not mean this in the sense of K. A. Meissinger's first
 volume, Der katholische Luther (Munich: Leo Lehnen, 1952),
where he defended the Catholic orthodoxy of the young, pre-Reformation Luther. Rather, I would want to show the presence of
lifelong Catholic elements in Luther, against the position of the
Protestant scholar, W. von Loewenich, in "Der katholische
Luther," in Dank an Paul Althaus, ed. W. Künneth and W. Joest
(Gütersloh: Bertelsmann, 1948), pp. 141-150.

10 Editor's Note: Since the writing of this article, Professor
   Lortz has developed this topic in two Festschrift articles:
"Zum Kirchendenken des jungen Luther, " in Wahrheit und Verkündigung (Schmaus Festschrift. Paderborn: Schöningh, 1967), pp. 947-
986; and "Reformatorisch und Katholisch beim jungen Luther (1518-
1519), in Humanitas-Christianitas (von Loewenich Festschrift.
Witten: Luther Verlag, 1968), pp. 47-62. His latest publication,
"Sakramentales Denken beim jungen Luther, " appeared in the 1969
Luther-Jahrbuch.
   11 The Reformation in Germany, Vol. I, pp. 434-436.
   12 R. Hermann, "Das Verhältnis von Rechtfertigung und Gebet, "
      in Gesmamelte Studien zur Theologie Luthers und der Re-
formation (Göttingen: Vandenhoeck und Ruprecht, 1960), p. 12.
   13 From Luther's marginal notes to Tauler (ca. 1516) WA 9,
      98, 21.
   14 WATr 4, 577 f., no. 4915. LW 54, 370.
   15 WATr 3, 411 f., no. 3558. Cf. also WATr 1, 146, no. 352.
      LW 54, 50 f.
   16 W. von Loewenich, Luthers Theologia crucis (Munich:
      Kaiser, 41954), p. 183.
   17 H. Grisar, Martin Luther - His Life and Work, trans. F.
      J. Eble (Westminster: Newman, 1950). Paul J. Reiter,
Martin Luthers Umwelt Charackter und Psychose (Copenhagen:
Levin and Munksgaard, 1937-1941). Erik H. Erikson, Young Man
Luther (New York: Norton, 1958). See also E. Grossmann, Beiträge
zur psychologischen Analyse der Reformatoren Luther und Calvin
(Basel: S. Karger, 1958).
   18 We can omit a detailed presentation of this difficult material.
      The neat distinction between experienced sin and non-expe-
rienced justification is far from doing justice to the totality of
Luther's statements on this point.
   19 Note Luther's frequent praise of the "verbum audible, " or
      of the "vocale verbum" in WATr 1, 26, no. 76; and 2, 299,
no. 2031.
   20 WATr 5, 204, no. 5511. See also WATr 3, 210, no. 3173a:
      "I can't combine brevity and perspicacity the way Philip
[Melanchthon] and Amsdorf can."
   21 See Luther's large commentary on Galatians, LW 26-27.
   22 The Reformation in Germany, Vol. I, p. 172. Cf. H. Grisar,
      Luther, trans. E. M. Lamond, Vol. IV (St. Louis: B.
Herder, 1917), p. 344.
   23 See Luther's severe rejection of Agricola for hypocrisy and
      decimating all moral order and discipline. WA 50, 465.

24 Ibid.

25 WA 6, 528,24 and 529,11. LW 36, 60 f.

26 WA 7, 219,17.

27 "Paulus und das Luthersche simul iustus et peccator,"
Kerygma und Dogma 1 (1955), p. 312 f.

28 L. Ihmels, Die christliche Wahrheitsgewissheit (Leipzig:
A. Deichert, 1902), p. 19. E. Bizer, Fides ex auditu
(Neukirchen: Erziehungsverein, [2]1961), p. 129.

29 WA 1, 353,11. LW 31, 39. Earlier he named theses he
was sending or having sent to Johann Lang "paradoxa"
three times, and once with forceful irony "kakadoxa." WABr 1,
103,7 ff., no. 45 (letter of Sept. 4, 1517); and 1, 121,4 (letter
of Nov. 11, 1517 with which Luther sent the 95 theses to Lang,
which he also expressly judged to be "orthodoxa").

30 See especially the rich exposition of Romans 4:7 from
1515-1516, WA 56, 269,25 ff. (Pauck, 124 ff.). Also, in
the large commentary on Galatians, WA 40II, 23 f. (LW 27, 20 f.).

31 WA 39I, 563,13 and 564,4.

32 See the remarks on this point by Gerhard Ebeling in his
Luther-Einführung in sein Denken. "The central problem
we face in Luther's thought is how to unify these two apparently
contradictory viewpoints." (p. 160) "The issue precisely is to
grasp the internal connections between Luther's apparently contradictory series of statements." (p. 161) "What is most notable
in [Luther's] thought is how the basic antithetical structure has
both contradictory and non-contradictory elements." (p. 163)
"Temporally, things are sharply distinguished, and nonetheless
they are tightly interrelated, that is, sin, grace, law, gospel."
(p. 165) However one may evaluate these ingenious distinctions,
I do not find them in the gospels, and not even in a fully assimilated
St. Paul. What we have in Luther is a forced development working
on from the idea of kenosis. Also, there is an attempt to construct
a partial unity out of statements that are brought together in affirming and denying the same thing.

33 This position is based on a vast number of texts in which
Luther employs a paradoxical structure. Luther spoke
explicitly of his position in Thesis 21 of the Disputation on the
Incarnation in 1539: "[Christian truth] is indeed not against the
truth of dialectics, but is outside, inside, above, below, before,
and beyond such truth." WA 39II, 4,34.

34 Lectures on Romans, WA 56, 341,30 (Pauck, 203). See
also my exposition of these lectures in the Trierer Theologische Zeitschrift 71 (1962), 129-153 and 216-247. But the older

Luther, especially, knew a pleasure in obeying the law: "Thus
Christ's office is as well to restore the human race in this life
to its lost innocence and to a pleasurable obedience to the law.
. . . Thereby, he becomes a law for us, and obedience becomes
in some way pleasurable." WA 39I, 375, 4.

35 W. von Loewenich, Luthers Theologia crucis, p. 111.
36 "The one faith is the same as the other . . . since they
    both cling to the offspring of Abraham, that is to Christ,
one before, the other after his coming." WA 10I/2, 5, 19 ff.
37 Vraie et fausse Reform (Paris: du Cerf, 1950), p. 448,
    where Congar cites G. Faure.
38 Congar, ibid., p. 447 f.
39 E. Wolf, in Evangelische Selbstprüfung (Stuttgart: Kohl-
    hammer, 1947), p. 150 on Luther, and p. 143 on Calvin.
Also F. M. Braun, Neues Licht auf die Kirche (Einsiedeln and
Cologne: Benzinger, 1947).
40 WA 39I, 104, 11 ff. LW 34, 173 f. Luther formulated even
    more radical paradoxes in his exposition of Ps 117. WA 31,
249, 21 ff. (LW 14, 31): "God's faithfulness and truth always must
first become a great lie before it becomes truth. . . . In short,
God cannot become God unless he first becomes a devil. We cannot go to heaven unless we first go to hell. We cannot become
God's children until we first become children of the devil. . . .
The godless do not go to hell without first having gone to heaven.
They do not become the devil's children until they have first
been the children of God." And 250, 24 f. (LW 14, 32): "To sum-
marize, the devil does not become and is not a devil without first
having been God." (Trans. Edward Sittler) -- Surely, it is not
out of place to express a modest doubt about the propriety of this
verbositas. We add an example from Luther's Lectures on
Genesis: "Therefore we should know that God hides Himself under
the form of the devil." WA 44, 429, 24. LW 7, 175 (P. D. Pahl).
41 WA 18, 310, 16. LW 46, 29 (Charles M. Jacobs). See the
    similar statements, such as WA 11, 252, 2 (LW 45, 91 f.)
and WA 51, 270, 15 ff. (LW 12, 150 f.).
42 See Albrecht Peters, Glaube und Werk (Berlin and Hamburg:
    Lutherisches Verlagshaus, 1962), and Ole Modalsli, Das
Gericht nach den Werken (Göttingen: Vandenhoeck und Ruprecht,
1963). Also W. von Loewenich, Luther als Ausleger der Synoptiker
(Munich: Kaiser, 1954).
43 As with Bernard, what is decisive for Luther is the never
    ceasing striving for what is better.
44 See above, p. 15.

45 WA 40I, 141,16f. LW 26, 72 (J. Pelikan).

46 WA 31II, 249,10 (from the 1529 lectures on Isaiah).

47 WA 29, 556,17. This experience has more general validity: "Let him who will start attempt this. He will see and experience how exquisitely difficult it is for a man who has devoted his life to holiness by works to rise out of this and bring himself with wholehearted faith to the one and only mediator." WA 36, 372,25f.

48 WATr 5, 210, no. 5518. LW 54, 442f.

49 WATr 3, 678f., no. 3874. LW 54, 287.

50 WA 32, 123,18.

51 WA 44, 767,18f. LW 8, 256 (P. D. Pahl).

52 WA 44, 806,12. LW 8, 308 (P. D. Pahl). Also 807,9f. LW 8, 309.

53 W. von Loewenich, Modern Catholicism, transl. R. H. Fuller (London: Macmillan, 1959), p. 102.

54 WA 34II, 148,10f.

55 WABr 1, 391,97ff.; no. 174.

56 WA 10II, 107,9.

57 WATr 5, 168,35, no. 5468. See LW 54, 476.

58 H. Bornkamm, "Luther als Schriftsteller," in Formenwandel --Festschrift für Paul Böckmann (Hamburg: Hoffmann und Campe, 1964), p. 104.

59 WA 40I, 458,13-38. LW 26, 294f. (J. Pelikan). Immediately following, Luther added, "Neither the devil nor any self-righteous person can rob you of this answer or refute it. You are safe in the sight of God; for your heart is fixed on the object of faith, who is called Christ." 459,19ff. LW 26, 295f. (J. Pelikan).

60 WA 40I, 266,15ff. LW 26, 155 (J. Pelikan). Later: "He does not truly believe if works of love do not follow his faith." WA 40II, 37,16f. LW 27, 30 (J. Pelikan).

61 WA 40I, 21,33. See P. Manns' treatment of this passage, pp. 131-137, in this volume.

62 WA 40II, 38,9.

63 WAT r 2, 244, no. 1877. LW 54, 165.

64 WA 33, 167,17f. LW 23, 109.

65 "I say what I feel. I miss more than one thing in this book, and it makes me consider it to be neither apostolic nor prophetic. . . . Finally, let everyone think of it as his own spirit leads him. My spirit cannot accommodate itself to this book." WADB 7, 404,4ff.25f. LW 35, 398f. (Trans. C. M. Jacobs, revised by E. T. Bachmann).

66 WA 17II, 137,4ff.

67 Bernard: "Thus the Apostle judged that a man is justified

gratis through faith." Sermon on the Annunciation I, 3 (Patrologia Latina, Vol. 183, Col. 384A). Thomas: "Therefore there is no hope of justification in these (in the law), but in faith alone." Lectures on St. Paul's Epistles, on 1 Tim, 1. III, 21 (on 1 Tim 1, 8).

    68 WA 40I, 181,11. LW 26,99 (J. Pelikan).

    69 WA 12, 189,23 f. LW 40,34.

    70 J. C. Hampe, Ende der Gegenreformation? (Stuttgart: Kreuz Verlag, 1964), p. 378.

Luther's Christ-Mysticism

1 History of Dogma, trans. N. Buchanan (New York: Russell & Russell, 1958), Vol. 6, p. 97.
2 Ibid., p. 98.
3 Ibid., p. 99.
4 Described, but not defended by Bengt Hägglund, "Luther und die Mystik," in The Church, Mysticism, Sanctification and the Natural in Luther's Thought (Philadelphia: Fortress Press, 1967), p. 86.
5 WA 1, 557,25-32. LW 31, 129 (C. W. Folkemer).
6 WA 1, 378,21 ff. LW 31, 75 (H. J. Grimm).
7 "Luther und der deutsche Geist," in Luthers geistige Welt (Gütersloh: G. Mohn, [4]1960), p. 292.
8 Der Weg zur Reformation (Munich: Kaiser, 1965), p. 87. See also p. 106.
9 See, for instance, the large commentary on Galatians of 1531, WA 40I, 520,2; and a sermon of March 1, 1534, WA 37, 314,15, which was printed in 1544 (WA 52, 179,22).
10 See, for instance, B. Moeller, "Tauler und Luther," in La Mystique rhénane (Paris: Presses Universitaires, 1963), pp. 157-168; K. Grunewald, Studien zu Johannis Taulers Frömmigkeit (Diss. Leipzig, 1930), esp. pp. 50 ff.; and F. W. Wentzlaff-Eggebert, "Studien zur Lebenslehre Taulers," in Abhandlungen der Preussischen Akademie der Wissenschaft (1940), p. 50.
11 See A. Wikenhauser, Pauline Mysticism (New York: Herder and Herder, 1960).
12 "Hence the speculation of the sectarians is vain when they imagine that Christ is present in us 'spiritually,' that is, speculatively, but is really in heaven. Christ and faith must be completely joined. We must simply take our place in heaven; and Christ must be, live, and work in us. But he lives and works in us, not speculatively but really, with presence and power (vivit autem et operatur in nobis non speculative, sed realiter, praesentissime et efficacissime)." WA 40I, 546,6.23 ff. LW 26, 357 (J. Pelikan).
13 "Simul gemitus et raptus: Luther und die Mystik," in The Church, Mysticism, Sanctification and the Natural in Luther's Thought, ed. Ivar Asheim (Philadelphia: Fortress, 1967), 20-59.
14 Like Tauler, Luther uses the term "Lesemeister" to indicate a master of theory, as against the preferable "Lebemeister,"

a guide for life. WA 6, 291,30.

15 We do not have the space to present the many-sided influence
of Augustine on Luther through the piety and theology of the
Augustianian order, through Johann Staupitz, and through Luther's
wide reading (at least from 1509 onward) of Augustine's works. I
have treated some of this material in "Luthers Stellung in der theol-
ogischen Tradition, " in Wandlungen des Lutherbildes, ed. Karl
Forster (Würzburg: Echter Verlag, 1966), 13-47.

16 "True theology is practical, and its foundation is Christ,
whose death is appropriated to us through faith. However,
today all those who do not agree with us and do not share our
teaching make theology speculative because they cannot free themselves from the notion that those who do good [will be rewarded].
This is not what is written, but rather, 'whoso feareth the Lord,
it shall go well with him at the last' [Ecclus. 1,13]. Accordingly,
speculative theology belongs to the devil in hell. So Zwingli specu-
lated . . ." WATr 1, 72, no. 153. LW 54, 22 (T. G. Tappert).

17 "Züge spätmittelalterlicher Frömmigkeit in Luthers Theologie, " in Zeitschrift für Theologie und Kirche 62 (1965),
381-402, esp. p. 395. On the piety of the devotio moderna, see
my essay, "Die Kirchenfrömmigkeit in der 'Imitatio Christi, '"
in Sentire Ecclesiam, ed J. Daniélou and H. Vorgrimler (Freiburg: Herder, 1961), 251-267, esp. p. 257 ff.

18 WA 3, 124,33 ff.

19 This negative theology is one "qua Deus inexpressibiliter
et prae stupore et admiratione maiestatis eius silentio
laudatur, ita ut iam non solum verbum minus, sed et omnem
cogitatum inferiorem esse laude eius sentiat." WA 3, 372,13 ff.
For Luther this negative theology contrasts with the disputatious
theologians he knows, but such theology is not valued: "non
coronat ullum ulla universitas, nisi solus Spiritus Sanctus."
372,25.

20 WA 3, 124,33 ff.

21 WA 56, 298,25 ff. Pauck, 154.

22 WA 56, 299,27 ff. Pauck, 155 f.

23 So M. Elze, "Züge spätmittelalterlicher Frömmigkeit, " p.
399.

24 Sermon on the Song of Songs, 3,2; 41,2; 62,7.

25 The Mind's Road to God, ch. 4.

26 WA 9, 98,14-27. The note ends with these words: "Theologia
autem propria de spirituali nativiate verbi incarnati habet
unum necessarium et optimam partem. Haec non sollicita est et
turbatur erga plurima et contra peccata crescit et pugnat ad virtutem

sollicita, ubi illa victrix vitiorum triumphat." lines 23-27.

27 Luther could have learned this idea of Dionysius from Gerson's De Theologia Mystica. See Gerson, Oeuvres complètes, ed. P. Glorieux, Vol. III (Tournai: Desclée, 1962), p. 252 f.

28 WA 57III, 197,19 f. See also Luther's use of this division in his scholion on Hebrews 5:12, WA 57 III, 179,5-15.

29 WA 9, 98,33 f. Also 100,28 f.

30 On Ps 5, 12, in his exposition of 1519-1521, Luther warned against mere study of what Dionysius wrote on mystical theology: "Vivendo, immo moriendo et damnando fit theologus, non intelligendo, legendo aut speculando." WA 5, 163,28 f. In a table remark in 1533 Luther included St. Bonaventure among the worthless speculative theologians: WATr 1, 302, no. 644 (LW 54, 112). In the First Disputation against the Antinomians (1537), Luther spoke of the spiritual harm he had himself suffered by seeking the direct union with God described by Dionysius. WA 39I, 389,18 ff.

31 WA 9, 103,41.

32 "For our righteousness looks down from heaven and descends to us. But those godless men have presumed to ascend into heaven by means of their righteousness and from there to bring the truth which has arisen among us from the earth." WA 2, 493, 12 ff. LW 27, 225 (R. Jungkuntz). See also WA 4, 647,19 ff.; 6, 562,8 ff.; 39I, 389,10 ff.

33 WA 16, 144,3 ff. (Sermon on Exodus [1524]); WA 9, 406,17-23 (Sermon on Genesis [1519-1521]); WA 43, 72,9--73,13 (Lecture on Genesis [1535 ff.]; LW 3, 275 f.).

34 "Züge spätmittelalterlicher Frömmigkeit," p. 392 f.

35 WA 57 III, 114,17 ff.

36 WA 56, 392,28--393,3 (emphasis added by Luther). Pauck, 264.

37 WA 56, 446,31 ff. Pauck, 327.

38 WA 56, 447,3 ff. Pauck, 327.

39 WA 40I, 229,15 ff. LW 26, 129 f. (J. Pelikan).

40 "Dionysius, who wrote about 'negative theology' and 'affirmative theology,' deserves to be ridiculed. . . . But if we wish to give a true definition of 'negative theology,' we should say that it is the holy cross and the afflictions in which we do not, it is true, discern God, but in which those signs are present of which I have already spoken." WA 40 III, 543,8 ff. LW 13, 110 f. (P. M. Bretscher).

41 WA 43, 202,16 ff. LW 4, 93.

42 WA 5, 204,25 ff.

43 WA 19, 223,15 f.

44 Ibid., 229,31.

45 WA 56, 368,27 ff. Pauck, 233.

46 WA 56, 250,8 f. Pauck, 103. Also ibid., 392,32 and 446, 32 (Pauck, 264 and 327).

47 WA 5, 165,21 ff.

48 WA 57III, 129,21 ff.

49 WA 4, 265,30.

50 WA 57III, 144,10 ff.

51 Ibid., 185,2 ff.

52 Ibid., 153,9 f.

53 WA 2, 504,6 ff. Also 535,24: "Credere enim in Christum est eum induere, unum cum eo fieri." LW 27, 241 and 289. Further: WA 4, 408,22 ff.

54 WA 1, 28,40.

55 WA 40I, 285,5. LW 26, 168. Even W. von Loewenich speaks of a Christ-mysticism in connection with Luther's idea of faith, and of Luther's use of images drawn from St. Paul and from mysticism to describe the Christian's union with Christ. Luthers Theologia crucis (Munich: Kaiser, [1]1929), p. 135 f. Whereas the first edition of this book affirmed an absolute opposition between Luther's theology of the cross and medieval German mysticism, the fourth edition of 1954 modified this position to a large extent (p. 246 f.).

56 WA 2, 146,14 f.

57 WA 57III, 178,10 ff. and WA 8, 111,33 ff.: ". . . in illum nos rapi de diem magis voluit, non in acceptis consistere, sed in Christum plane transformari." LW 32, 235.

58 WA 8, 112,5 f.

59 "Et haec est ars christianorum, a meo peccato transilire ad Christi iustitiam." WATr 2, 468,20, no. 2457a.

60 "And this is the reason why our theology is certain: it snatches us away from ourselves and places us outside ourselves, so that we do not depend on our own strength, con- science, experience, person or works but depend on that which is outside ourselves, that is, on the promise and truth of God, which cannot deceive." WA 40I, 589,25 ff. LW 26, 387 (J. Pelikan).

61 WA 40II, 527,9 f.

62 "This attachment to Him causes me to be liberated from the terror of the Law and from sin, pulled out of my own skin, and transferred into Christ and his kingdom." WA 40I, 284,16 ff. LW 26, 167 (J. Pelikan). In his lecture on the same

verse (Galatians 2:20), Luther told how Paul seeks "to drive us
to Christ and tear us away from works." Ibid., 1. 9. Luther then
speaks of our union with Christ as a "conglutinatio." Ibid., lines
6.24; 285,25. LW 26, 167 and 168.

63 WA 36, 285,1.

64 WA 57III, 224,13 ff.

65 Over against the scholastic idea of grace as a quality hidden
    in the heart, "we teach and believe differently about grace,
namely, that grace is the continuous and perpetual operation or
action through which we are grasped and moved by the Spirit of
God so that we do not disbelieve His promises and that we think
and do whatever is favorable and pleasing to God. The Spirit is
something living, not dead. Just as life is never idle, . . . so the
Holy Spirit is never idle in the pious, but is always doing something
that pertains to the Kingdom of God." WA 40II, 422,28 ff. LW 12,
377 f. (J. Pelikan).

66 From Luther's lecture on Gal 3,28 in 1531. WA 40I, 546,
    3 ff. See above, p. 173, n. 12, for the printed version of this
passage.

67 An example of this would be Rudolph Hermann's comment
    on the passage in Luther's response to Latomus we cited
above, p. 176, n. 57. Hermann will not see the "in Christum
plane transformari" as a fulfillment of God's graciousness to us
in faith. He sees it as questionable that a transformation into
Christ is God's will for us. Luthers These "Gerecht und Sünder
zugleich" (Gütersloh: Mohn, ²1960), p. 280.

68 WA 40III, 738,5-17. See also 739,13 ff. At WA 40 I, 241,
    13 ff. Luther argued from the intimacy of the marital em-
brace that justification is a union of Christ with faith alone, with
works banished from this private chamber. LW 26, 137 f.

69 WA 40I, 589,25 ff., cited above, p. 176, n. 60.

70 WA 40II, 422,3 ff. On this "experience of faith," see von
    Loewenich, Luthers Theologia crucis, 4th ed., pp. 118-
121.

71 "In form this crying and sighing is that amid your trial you
    do not call God a tyrant, and angry judge, or a tormentor,
but a Father--even though the sighing may be so faint that it can
hardly be felt. By contrast the other crying is very great and is
felt very strongly, when in genuine terror of conscience we call
God wicked, cruel, an angry tyrant, and a judge." WA 40I, 591,
31 ff. LW 26, 389 (J. Pelikan). At 40III, 542,9 f. Luther spoke of
the unutterable sighs which reach to God, about which we cannot
give an account but which can only be sensed and experienced.

See LW 13, 110 f.

72 In this section I am greatly indebted to the unpublished
    study of T. Beer, "Die Grundzüge der Theologie Luthers
im Lichte des katholischen Glaubens." Still, I do not agree with
Beer's conclusions. See also W. Maurer, Von der Freiheit eines
Christenmenschen (Göttingen: Vandenhoeck und Ruprecht, 1949),
pp. 55-77; F. W. Kantzenbach, "Christusgemeinschaft und
Rechfertigung," in Luther 35 (1964), 34-45; and E. Vogelsang,
"Die unio mystica bei Luther," in Archiv für Reformationsge-
schichte 35 (1938), 63-80.

73 WA 7, 25,26--26,12. Translation by B. L. Woolf, in
    Reformation Writings of Martin Luther (London: Lutter-
worth, 1952), p. 363 f.

74 WA 56, 343,19 ff. Pauck, 204 f.

75 Ibid., 267,5 ff. Pauck, 121.

76 WA 2, 145-152. LW 31, 297-304.

77 We touched briefly on the bridal relation of the soul to
    Christ in the section on faith, above. It is more immediate-
ly connected with the theme of the "happy exchange," but we cannot study it in detail. It has been investigated in Luther's works
up to 1521 by F. T. Ruhland, in "Luther und die Brautmystik"
(Dissertation, Giessen Univ., 1938).

78 WA 2, 147,26 ff. LW 31, 300 (L. J. Satre).

79 WA 40I, 285,24 ff. LW 26, 168 (J. Pelikan).

80 Ibid., 443,23 ff. LW 26, 284 (J. Pelikan).

81 "Si ipse est reus omnium peccatorum quae fecimus, ergo
    absoluti nos non per nos sed illium." Ibid., 438,8 f. LW
26, 280. Also: 448,28 ff. (LW 26, 288).

82 Ibid., 442,10 f. See LW 26, 283 f.

83 Ibid., 443,31 ff. LW 26, 284 (J. Pelikan).

84 Ibid., 284,22 ff. LW 26, 167 (J. Pelikan).

85 "A theological work is a work done in faith; thus a theol-
    ogical man is a man of faith. In like manner, a right reason
and a good will are a reason and will in faith. Thus faith is universally the divinity in the work, the person, and the members of
the body, as the one and only cause of justification; afterwards
this is attributed to the matter on account of the form, to the work
on account of the faith. The kingly authority of the divinity is given
to Christ the man, not because of His humanity but because of His
divinity. For the divinity alone created all things, without the cooperation of the humanity. Nor did the humanity conquer sin and
death; but the hook that was concealed under the worm, at which
the devil struck, conquered and devoured the devil, who was at-

tempting to devour the worm. Therefore the humanity would not have accomplished anything by itself; but the divinity, joined with the humanity, did it alone, and the humanity did it on account of the divinity. So here faith alone justifies and does everything; nevertheless, it is attributed to works on account of faith." Ibid., 417,25 ff. LW 26, 266 f. (J. Pelikan).

86 Luther's concern became clear at WA 40I, 240,21 f.: "Non quod opera aut charitatem reiiciamus, ut adversarii nos accusant, sed ex statu caussae nolumus divelli." LW 26, 137.

87 Y. Congar developed this point more fully in "Considerations and Reflections on the Christology of Luther," in Dialogue between Christians, trans. P. Loretz (Westminster: Newman Press, 1966), pp. 372-406. Peter Manns' important study of Luther's Galatians Commentary (see below) has worked out this point in greater detail.

88 This section is a condensation of my contribution to the Festschrift for Hubert Jedin, "Sacramentum et exemplum. Ein augustinisches Thema lutherischer Theologie," Reformata Reformanda, eds. E. Iserloh and K. Repgen (Münster: Aschendorff, 1965), Vol. I, 247-264.

89 Patrologia Latina, Vol. 42, Col. 889 f. ET by W. J. Oates in Basic Writings of St. Augustine (New York: Random House, 1948), Vol. II, p. 733 f. See also ibid., Col. 891 (Basic Writings, Vol. II, p. 734).

90 WA 9, 18,19 ff. This passage has been treated by A. Hamel in Der junge Luther und Augustin, Vol. 1 (Gütersloh: Bertelsmann, 1934), p. 23; and by W. Jetter in Die Taufe beim jungen Luther (Tübingen: Mohr, 1954), pp. 136-159. O. Ritschl saw in this passage a clear statement of Luther's "theology of the cross" as early as 1509. Dogmengeschichte des Protestantismus, Vol. II/I (Leipzig: Hinrichs, 1912), p. 43.

91 WA 9, 18,29 f.

92 E. Bizer, "Die Entdeckung des Sakraments durch Luther," in Evangelische Theologie 17 (1957), p. 66.

93 WA 9, 18,29.

94 "Die Entdeckung des Sakraments," p. 66 and p. 68.

95 W. Jetter saw how Luther was returning to the more ancient tradition as found in Augustine. Die Taufe beim jungen Luther, p. 139, n. 1. Jetter's conclusion, though, that Luther is playing down a present efficacy of the Passion through the sacraments is drawn neither from Luther nor from Augustine but from the apriori of a modern "theology of the word."

96 WA 4, 243,7-24.

97 Ibid., 1. 14. See also 172,27: "In abstracto loquitur, quia nos sumus eius concretum."

98 WA 4, 173,23. See also 242,6-10.

99 WA 3, 392,35--393,5.

100 Ibid., 418,19ff.

101 WA 56, 58,19. Pauck, 184, n. 17. See also the marginal gloss on Rom 6,10: 59,15ff. (Pauck, ibid.).

102 "Resurrectio et vita Christ est non tantum sacramentum, sed et causa, i.e., efficax sacramentum nostrae spiritualis resurrectionis et vitae, quia facit resurgere et vivere credentes in eam." WA 56, 51,20ff.

103 Ibid., 296,17-22. Pauck, 152.

104 Ibid., 321,23ff. Pauck, 178f. Here Luther refers to Augustine's De Trinitate passage on sacrament and example. Luther speaks further of Baptism and dying with Christ at 324,15-23 (Pauck, 181); 57,17f.; 58,4; 327,20 (Pauck, 186); 64,21. On the forgiveness of sins in Baptism, see 70,25 and 349,24 (Pauck, 211).

105 WA 57III, 222,25.30.

106 Ibid., 114,7ff.

107 "Significat et est sacramentum imitandi Christum." Ibid., 222,25.

108 Ibid., 223,1ff.

109 Ibid., 224,13f.

110 I developed this at length in my study, Gnade und Eucharistie in der philosophischen Theologie des Wilhelm von Ockham (Wiesbaden: F. Steiner, 1956), pp. 27-43.

111 WA 1, 309,18ff. W. Jetter saw in this passage against Eck the first instance in which Luther put sacramentum ahead of exemplum. Die Taufe beim jungen Luther, p. 149. This is simply not true, since from the very beginning Luther argued that the example follows the sacrament both materially and temporally. Early in the Lectures on Hebrews he emphasized strongly that they are in error who begin with the example and not with the sacrament. WA 57III, 114,17.

112 WA 2, 501,34ff. LW 27, 238 (R. Jungkuntz).

113 Ibid., 518,16. LW 27, 263 (R. Jungkuntz).

114 WA 9, 440,2ff.

115 Ibid., 11,6-19.

116 So W. Jetter, Die Taufe beim jungen Luther, p. 156.

117 For example, WA 56, 296,20ff. ("Resurrectio eius non tantum est sacramentum iustitiae nostrae, sed etiam ef-ficit eam in nobis."), cited from Pauck, p. 152, on p. 54f., above.

See also 51,20f., cited on p. 180, n. 102, above.

118 WA 10I/1, 11,1-18 and 12,12--13,2. See also Luther's sermon on December 11, 1524 (WA 15, 778,2-8).

119 WA 39I, 356,35f.

120 Ibid., 462,14ff.

121 WA 40I, 280,25ff. LW 26, 165 (J. Pelikan). See also 543, 34f. and 540,17ff. (LW 26, 355 and 352f.).

122 The opening passage of Luther's Lectures on Romans brings this out well: WA 56, 158,10-14 (Pauck, 4). See also WA 39I, 109,1ff.: "Extra nos esse est ex nostris viribus non esse. Est quidem iustitia possessio nostra, quia nobis donata est ex misericordia, tamen est aliena a nobis, quia non meruimus eam." See LW 34, 178. Heiko Oberman urged that while justice is for Luther our possessio, it does not become our proprietas. Oberman sees here a distinction of two technical terms from juridical parlance. "Simul gemitus et raptus," p. 54. This question needs further study, before we can be sure that Luther knew this distinction and that it is of help for our understanding of his conception of justification. I, for one, remain doubtful on this point.

123 Luther's sermon is at WA 4, 645-650. Tauler's can be found in Die Predigten Taulers, ed. F. Vetter (Berlin: Weidmann, 1910), pp. 201-207.

NOTES TO OTTO H. PESCH, O.P.
Existential and Sapiential Theology--
The Theological Confrontation between Luther and Thomas Aquinas

1 One can consult these more recent investigations of Luther's
   relationship to late medieval theology: B. Hägglund, Theologie
und Philosophie bei Luther und in der occamistischen Tradition
(Lund, Gleerup, 1955), and "Voraussetzungen der Rechtfertigungslehre Luthers in der spätmittelalterlichen Theologie, " in Lutherische Rundschau 11 (1961), 28-55; L. Grane, Contra Gabrielem
(Copenhagen: Gyldendal, 1962); R. Schwarz, Fides, spes und
caritas beim jungen Luther (Berlin: DeGruyter, 1962). Hägglund's
1961 article and Grane's book give helpful surveys of past research
on this question. Among the older works in this area these should
be mentioned: P. Vignaux, Luther--Commentateur des Sentences
(Paris: J. Vrin, 1935), and "Sur Luther et Ockham, " Franzis-
kanische Studien 32 (1950), 21-30; W. Link, Luthers Ringen um
die Freiheit der Theologie von der Philosophie (Munich: Kaiser,
[1]1940 and [2]1955), especially pp. 270-315; and K. A. Meissinger,
Der katholische Luther (Munich: Leo Lehnen, 1952), pp. 104-112.
The theological tradition of Nominalism, out of which Luther arose,
has been the topic of recent detailed studies: E. Iserloh, Gnade
und Eucharistie in der philosophischen Theologie des Wilhelm von
Ockham (Wiesbaden: F. Steiner, 1956); W. Dettloff, Die Lehre
der acceptatio divina bei Johannes Duns Scotus (Werl: Dietrich-
Colde, 1954); and Die Entwicklung der Akzeptations- und Verdienst-
lehre von Duns Scotus bis Luther (Münster: Aschendorff, 1963);
and H. A. Oberman, The Harvest of Medieval Theology (Cambridge,
Mass.: Harvard University Press, 1963). The discussion of late
scholasticism has been marked by sharp divergences among the
scholars (e.g., Iserloh, Dettloff, Grane, and Oberman) both regarding interpretation and evaluation of the theology itself, and
regarding its significance in the development of Luther's Reformation position. In this discussion we would agree with L.
Grane, who has proceeded along lines indicated by Paul Vignaux to
arrive at a sensitive and just evaluation of Biel's work and to prove
that at least on the question of justification Ockhamism, including
its theory of the acceptatio divina, exercised no creative influence
at all on Luther's theological development. See Contra Gabrielem,
pp. 377-388. Hägglund had already pointed in this direction in his
1961 article, pp. 51-55, and Schwarz has also said this in his
Fides, spes und caritas, pp. 1 and 14. Luther's theological
beginnings appear to be connected more with an Augustinian re-

action against the via moderna than with Ockhamism itself. Meissinger had spoken in this way in his Der katholische Luther, pp. 106-129, and Grane affirmed this--although with a different value judgment on this Augustinianism--in Contra Gabrielem, pp. 370-375 and 387 f. B. Lohse has confirmed this point recently in his article, "Die Bedeutung Augustins für den jungen Luther," Kerygma und Dogma 11 (1965), 116-135, as has E. Iserloh in his no less impressive contribution to the Jedin Festschrift, "Sacramentum et exemplum--Ein augustinisches Thema lutherischer Theologie," Reformata Reformanda, Vol. I (Munster: Aschendorff, 1965), pp. 247-264. It is still disputed whether this Augustinianism of the young Luther is already a Reformation position, i.e., whether it goes beyond the bounds within which one could attack the via moderna and still remain within the Church. This question takes us into the perennial argument about Luther's "tower experience." I have surveyed the recent discussion on this in "Zur Frage nach Luthers reformatorischer Wende," Catholica 20 (1966), 216-243 and 264-280.

2 See Meissinger, Der katholische Luther, p. 109, and Link, Luthers Ringen, pp. 191 f. The polemical attacks of the older Luther against Thomas should not mislead one into believing that he had read Thomas intensively. First, Luther had little time in his later period for careful scientific investigations. Secondly, the points Luther attacks (e.g., fides caritate formata, opus operatum, the doctrine of the obex hindering fruitful reception of a sacrament, the vis spiritualis of the sacraments, etc.) are theses of a popularized Thomism. The way Luther attacks them betrays his lack of familiarity with both the historical and systematic dimensions of these questions.

3 The recent work of Gerhard Hennig, Cajetan und Luther (Stuttgart: Calwer, 1966), has contested both our denial of a historical encounter between Luther and Thomas as well as the justification of a systematic confrontation of the two theologians. Hennig contends that Cardinal Cajetan mirrored the theology of St. Thomas and therefore made possible an actual encounter of Luther and Thomism in the Reformation era. Since Luther did meet Cajetan, Hennig would reject Joseph Lortz' contention that Luther's Reformation breakthrough rests on a lamentable mistake about what was fully Catholic, i.e., the theology of St. Thomas and the spirituality of the Roman missal. Through Cajetan, Luther learned, understood, and sharply rejected the theology of St. Thomas. On the other side, Cajetan perceived so clearly the significance of Luther's position that for the last fifteen years of

his life he did little else but continue the discussion begun in
Augsburg in 1518. Thus, according to Hennig, we need only re-
view Cajetan's critical judgments on Luther to learn what one of
the greatest Thomists saw as the challenge and as the innovation
of the Reformation. See Hennig, p. 10f. One cannot contest the
fact that Luther did meet in Cajetan a representative of Thomist
theology. But Hennig's conclusions from this fact regarding the
relation of Luther and St. Thomas are questionable. We cannot
go into a detailed study of Hennig's interpretation of Cajetan, but
we must point to two very fundamental exaggerations that flaw his
methodology. First, he admits that Luther's knowledge of Cajetan's
thinking stems exclusively from the oral statements of the Cardinal
during the hearing in Augsburg. Luther did not even have an opportunity to read the quaestiones Cajetan had drafted in preparation
for the meeting (Hennig, p. 47). We know of no further occasion
on which Luther read any of Cajetan's writings. Now, one must
ask whether an oral argument about fine points of theology is sufficient for one to really learn a comprehensive theological system
such as Thomism? Could one in this manner truly understand the
explicit and hidden motifs and orientations of a system, and then
adequately evaluate it? This is patently impossible. Second, Hennig
is simplistic in his substantial identification of Thomism and the
theology of St. Thomas. He relies on Cajetan's great reputation
in the sixteenth century as a Thomist. However, Cajetan's authenticity can only be established by a minute historical investigation. Although there is as yet no comprehensive study of this, one does not
gain the impression that Hennig is familiar with the specific conclusions already reached by research. We have indicated the main
works in our article, "Thomismus," in the Lexikon für Theologie
und Kirche, 2nd ed., Vol. 10, Col. 166f. We can note two points
against Hennig: 1) The papalist ecclesiology of Cajetan (Hennig, p.
13 and passim) is not to be simply identified with the thought of St.
Thomas. Of course, one can easily find a few texts in Thomas that
agree with Cajetan, but the context of the whole makes it clear
that in comparison with the ecclesiology of the sixteenth century
and of the present St. Thomas' view is quite critical of the Church.
See the presentation of Thomas' view of the Church by M. Seckler,
Das Heil in der Geschichte (Munich: Kösel, 1964), pp. 217-260,
where the recent literature has been surveyed. It is no accident
that Catholics like A. Dempf have accused Thomas of defending a
spiritualistic ecclesiology. 2) In criticizing the work of S. Pfürtner,
Luther and Thomas on Salvation, Hennig refers extensively to the
role of "cooperation" in the Thomistic doctrine of grace (pp. 168-

171). Although Hennig notes that Pfürtner's interpretation differs
sharply from that of Cajetan, he never goes into the question
whether "cooperation" is such an obvious part of the Thomist
teaching on grace. Both in general and regarding "merit" in particular, one can show that "cooperationism" is not a mark of Thomas'
thought on grace. I have taken this up in my major study, Theologie
der Rechtfertigung bei Martin Luther and Thomas von Aquin (Mainz:
Matthias Grünewald, 1967), pp. 659-670, 679-686, 748-758, 771-
784, and 840-880, and in a shorter study in the recent Schmaus-
Festschrift, "Die Lehre vom 'Verdienst' als Problem für die
Theologie und Verkündigung, " in Wahrheit und Verkündigung
(Paderborn: Schöningh, 1967), pp. 1865-1907, esp. 1882-1890.

    4 Via Caritatis--Theologie des Gesetzes bei Thomas von Aquin
(Göttingen: Vandenhoeck und Ruprecht, 1965), pp. 11-14.

    5 Ibid., p. 11.

    6 Other examples that can be named are Thomas Bonhoeffer
(Die Gotteslehre des Thomas von Aquin als Sprachproblem
[Tübingen: Mohr, 1961], pp. 1-3) and H. Vorster (Das Freiheits-
verständnis bei Thomas von Aquin und Martin Luther [Göttingen:
Vandenhoeck und Ruprecht, 1965], pp. 11-20). The increasing
number of Lutheran studies of Thomas (see note 10, below) show
that the matter itself is well understood, even where the purpose
has not been so expressly formulated.

    7 One example of this would be the annotations given by H.
Bornkamm to the text of the Augsburg Confession and Melanchthon's Apologia in the Latin-German edition of the Lutheran Confessional documents.

    8 Via Caritatis, p. 14.

    9 Ibid., p. 13.

    10 The most important works of Protestant scholars are these:
H. Lyttkens, The Analogy between God and the World (Uppsala:
Almquist & Wiksells, 1952), and "Die Bedeutung der Gottesprädi-
kate bei Thomas von Aquin, " in Neue Zeitschrift für systematische
Theologie 6 (1964), 274-289); P. E. Persson, Sacra Doctrina (Lund:
Gleerup, 1957), and "Le plan de la Somme et le rapport Ratio-
Revelatio, " in Revue philosophique de Louvain 56 (1958), 545-572:
M. A. Schmidt, art. "Thomas von Aquin, " in Evangelisches Kirchen-
lexikon, Vol. 3, Coll. 1429-1435; W. Pannenberg, art. "Thomas
von Aquino, " in Religion in Geschichte und Gegenwart, 3rd ed.,
Vol. VI, Coll. 856-863; G. Ebeling, "The Hermeneutical Locus
of the Doctrine of God in Peter Lombard und Thomas Aquinas, "
in Journal for Theology and the Church, Vol. III (1967), pp. 70-111,
and "Existence between God and God, " in Journal for Theology and

the Church, V (1968), pp. 128-154. Also, the works of Ulrich Kühn
and Hans Vorster, mentioned above. Some important Catholic
contributions would be the following: G. Söhngen, Gesetz und
Evangelium (Frieburg-Munich: K. Albert, 1957), and an article
with the same title in Catholica 14 (1960), pp. 81-105; S. Pfürtner,
Luther and Thomas on Salvation (New York: Sheed and Ward,
1965); R. Gerest, "Du serf-arbitre à la liberté du chrétien," in
Lumière et Vie 12 (1963), No. 61, pp. 75-120; H. Fries, "Die
Grundanliegen der Theologie Luthers in der Sicht der katholischen Theologie der Gegenwart," in Wandlungen des Lutherbildes
(Würzburg: Echter Verlag, 1966), 157-191. I myself have published the following articles: "Ein katholisches Anliegen an evangelische Darstellungen der Theologie Luthers," Catholica 16
(1962), 69-77; "Freiheitsbegriff und Freiheitslehre bei Thomas
von Aquin und Luther," Catholica 17 (1963), 197-244; "Thomas
von Aquin im Lichte evangelischer Fragen," Catholica 20 (1966),
54-78; and "Der hermeneutische Ort der Theologie bei Thomas
von Aquin und Martin Luther," Tübingen theologische Quartal-
schrift 146 (1966), 159-212. I have treated the theology of justification in a comprehensive manner in my comparative study,
Theologie der Rechtfertigung bei Martin Luther und Thomas von
Aquin (Mainz: Matthias Grünewald, 1967).

11 The investigations of U. Kühn and H. Vorster deserve a
brief introduction. Kühn begins with a critical survey of
the developing theological image of Thomas Aquinas in the past
fifty years, stressing here the gradual shift in research from
philosophical to theological questions. He will himself fill a lacuna
in the research with his study of the theology of law in Thomas.
He follows his topic through the Thomistic corpus from the Commentary on the Sentences, through the Contra Gentiles and the
shorter works, to the mature position of the Summa Theologiae.
Kühn's resulting thesis is that the old law makes sin known and
by demanding too much ensnares the person who attempts to obey
it without grace ever deeper in sin and eventual death. Man can
live according to the divine law only if this law has been interiorized as the new law of grace, which is granted by way of faith in
Christ the mediator and which then inspires one to spontaneous
fulfillment of God's will. For Thomas the old law is never a way
to self-justification, but because of its weakness leading to death
it is an indicator pointing to Christ. In spite of the continuity
between old and new, it is ultimately no more than a negative indicator. The new law of the Gospel, because it is the interiorized
grace of the Holy Spirit, has ceased to be "law" in the pointed

186

Lutheran sense of the word. In the case of Thomas, the traditional controversy between Catholics and Lutherans over "nomism" is pointless. In his final chapter Kühn confirms his thesis by taking up some detailed questions and goes on to defend Thomas' preliminary metaphysical interpretation of law in a way that will shock some Lutheran readers. Accordingly, Thomas does not work from an offensive legalistic philosophy, but from an understanding of existence under God's will which should not be foreign to Lutheran thought.

H. Vorster has seen that the common treatment of Thomas' idea of freedom as primarily a philosophical problem is too narrow. Therefore, he begins his study with an exposition of Thomas' doctrine of God. This leads him to break resolutely with the ordinary Protestant interpretation of Thomas' idea of freedom as a kind of synergism. Instead of being the classic opponent of Luther, Thomas agrees with him in excluding a human freedom over against God. God's determining influence is always prior, and thus it is not correct to speak of a decision on man's part over against God's providence, predestination and grace. Everything and everyone, including sin, is under God's universal influence. In this connection Vorster stresses the Augustinian elements in Thomas' work, and rightly sees no cause for excusing the pessimistic tones in Thomas' description of the powers of fallen man (ST I-II, 109, 2). Human freedom exists only as the infallibly certain (ST I-II, 112, 3) agreement with God's action. It is the resonance and answer to God's working, more a spontaneity and voluntariness than liberty in the strict sense. Thomas, however, does not bring this out in his terminology, as Luther does, since he continues to speak of freedom, although he uses the concept in a manner that omits decisive elements from its denotation. -- We have studied these works critically in our 1966 Catholica article, "Thomas von Aquin im Lichte evangelischer Fragen." On Vorster's study of freedom, see especially the extensive chapter on St. Thomas in Harry Mc-Sorley's work, Luther: Right or Wrong? (Augsburg Publishing House and Newman Press, 1969), pp. 138-182.

12 This has been developed in the following works: W. Joest, Gesetz und Freiheit (Göttingen: Vandenhoeck und Ruprecht, 31961), p. 201, note 56; G. Ebeling, "Die Anfänge von Luthers Hermeneutik," in Zeitschrift für Theologie und Kirche 48 (1951), pp. 189-197, and Luther--Einführung in sein Denken (Tübingen: Mohr, 1964), pp. 92-94; L. Grane, Contra Gabrielem, pp. 371f. and 374f.; and L. Haikola, Studien zu Luther und zum Luthertum (Uppsala-Wiesbaden: Lundequistska bokhandeln, 1958), pp. 7-55 and 69-103.

13 We borrow this idea of the Erkenntniswille from J. Auer,
    Die menschliche Willensfreiheit im Lehrsystem des Thomas
von Aquin und des Johannes Duns Scotus (Munich: Hueber, 1938),
pp. 23 ff. and 302.

14 The most important study is that of D. Löfgren, Die Theol-
    ogie der Schöpfung bei Luther (Göttingen: Vandenhoeck und
Ruprecht, 1960). Paul Althaus brought out the importance of the
doctrine of creation in many different books and articles.

15 WA 40II, 328,7. LW 12, 311 (J. Pelikan). For an interpre-
    tation of this text from 1532, see G. Ebeling's contribution
to the Rückert-Festschrift, "Cognitio Dei et hominis," in Geist
und Geschichte der Reformation (Berlin: DeGruyter, 1966), pp.
306-322. Luther's concentration on the question of salvation has
nothing to do with an anthropocentric and subjectivist narrowness
that is often attributed to him. His approach is merely one that
takes seriously the fact that all our understanding of God continually begins in encounter with God's own salvific action upon
us. Today, it is commonly stressed in the Catholic Church that
all theology must be "anthropocentric" in this sense. Such a view
of theology is even being discussed in recent work on Thomas
Aquinas. See, for instance, J. B. Metz, Christliche Anthropozen-
trik--Über die Denkform des Thomas von Aquin (Munich: Kösel,
1962). U. Kühn has also brought this out, Via Caritatis, pp. 124-
128 and 225-252.

16 ST I, 1, 2c and 3, ad 2. ET: Thomas Gilby, O.P., Black-
    friars edition of the Summa, Vol. 1 (New York: McGraw-
Hill, and London: Eyre & Spottiswoodie, 1964), pp. 11 and 15. I
have interpreted these texts in my 1963 Catholica article, pp.
240 f., and in Theologie der Rechtfertigung, pp. 921-935.

17 We recall how Luther contrasts philosophy/theology, letter/
    spirit, law/gospel, person/work, faith/works, freedom/
bondage, hidden God/revealed God, and so on. A characteristic
contrary example in Thomas would be ST I-II, 1-5, where the
argument starts from man's longing for happiness and procedes
step by step to prove that God alone can be the ultimate end of
man.

18 I have treated these points extensively in Theologie der
    Rechtfertigung, pp. 262 ff., 368 ff., 748 ff., and 866 ff.
See also my 1963 Catholica article on freedom, pp. 241 ff.

19 ST I-II, 112, 5. Denzinger-Schönmetzter, Enchiridion
    Symbolorum, Nn. 1533 f., 1540 f., and 1563-1566.

20 S. Pfürtner has brought this out in his book, Luther and
    Thomas on Salvation. The criticism of Pfürtner by G.

Hennig (Luther und Cajetan, pp. 168-171) is not to the point, since
Hennig falsely presupposes that St. Thomas held the "cooperationism" attributed to Cajetan. Nor do we find convincing the more
recent criticism of Pfürtner by Peter Manns in his Lutherforschung
heute (Wiesbaden: F. Steiner, 1967), p. 12, note 40. It is incontestable that Thomas uses the idea of amor concupiscentiae in his
explanation of hope, but Manns has not evaluated this fact correctly. Thomas' use of this idea can only be understood adequately
and evaluated rightly in the total context of his doctrine of the three
theological virtues. See our Theologie der Rechtfertigung, pp.
750-757, where we have also expressed our own reservations
against Pfürtner.

    21 At this point, we note that we cannot agree with the pointed
        criticism of Luther by Paul Hacker in his Das Ich im Glauben
bei Martin Luther. Hacker's objections against Luther's statuere
salutem meam are only tenable when one is thinking in terms of
theoretical certitude and of ascertaining something objectively.
But Luther's "certainty of salvation" is nothing more than the
movement of faith given by God's grace. We have reviewed Hacker's
book in Theologische Revue 64 (1968), pp. 51-56.

    22 We have already mentioned the important studies of U. Kühn,
        H. Vorster, and H. McSorley. Also: Martin Seils, Der
Gedanke vom Zusammenwirken Gottes und des Menschen in Luthers
Theologie (Gütersloh: Gerd Mohn, 1962).

    23 See the texts cited on p. 79f.

    24 See I. Backes, Die Christologie des hl. Thomas (Paderborn:
        Schöningh, 1931); T. Tschipke, Die Menschheit Christi als
Heilsorgan der Gottheit (Freiburg: Herder, 1940); and H. M.
Diepen, La Théologie de l'Immanuel (Brouges: Desclée, 1960).

    25 We have treated this more extensively in Theologie der
        Rechtfertigung, pp. 570 ff.

    26 See, for instance, WA 4, 609, 12 ff.; 1, 24, 9; 10I/1, 209, 9,
        356, 9; 10I/2, 84, 25, 297, 5; 10III, 154, 18; 21, 435, 10; 33,
154, 4 ff., 156, 6. Luther's famous statement in a letter to his
friend G. Spalatin in 1519, "Whoever wants to think or speculate
rightly about God must look before all else at the humanity of
Christ," (WABr 1, 329, 50; no. 145) has an exact parallel in Thomas
Aquinas: "If we wish to enter the holy place of glory we must enter
through the flesh of Christ, which was the curtain of divinity."
(Commentary of Hebrews 10, 20; lect. 2, no. 502). See also ST
III, 14, 1 ad 4.

    27 A characteristic text is this one from Luther's sermon on
        Exodus 12 in 1525: "The sophists have depicted how he is

both God and man, counted his bones and arms, and marvelously
mixed his two natures together. This is nothing but a sophistical
understanding of the Lord Christ. Christ is not named as such
because he has two natures. And what do I care about this? But
he bears this glorious and consoling name because of the office
and work he took upon himself. This gives him his name as Christ.
He is by nature both God and man, which is something pertaining
to himself alone. But the source of blessing and consolation is the
fact that he poured out his love to become my savior and redeemer.
What pertains to me is his office of saving his people from their
sins." WA 16, 217, 10.

28 See, for instance, WA 4, 648, 1; 2, 140, 37; 10I/2, 277, 29;
10III, 154, 18, 155, 1; 17II, 244, 27; 20, 228, 25, 229, 28; 21,
467, 12; 30I, 192, 5 (Book of Concord, Ed. T. Tappert [Philadelphia:
Fortress, 1959], p. 419); 32, 328, 31; 45, 589, 29.

29 This is brought out characteristically in Luther's Small
Catechism in the well known answer to the question about
the second article of the Creed (on redemption): "I believe that
Jesus Christ, true God, begotten of the Father from all eternity,
and also true man, born of the virgin Mary, is my Lord," Book
of Concord, p. 345.

30 See, on this, W. von Loewenich, Luther als Ausleger der
Synoptiker (Munich: Kaiser, 1954), pp. 132 ff., and E.
Wolf, Perigrinatio (Munich: Kaiser, 1962), pp. 69 ff.

31 WA 56, 272, 17. Pauck, 127.

32 WA 2, 496, 39. LW 27, 230.

33 WA 40II, 352, 8.

34 WA 39I, 492, 19.

35 WA 39I, 563, 13.

36 WA 56, 513, 17. Pauck, 402.

37 ST I-II, 113, 7; also, the even more pointed treatment in
De Veritate, 28, 9 and 28, 2 ad 10.

38 Above all other studies, R. Kösters, "Luthers These
'Gerecht und Sünder zugleich' zu dem gleichnamigen Buch
von Rudolf Hermann," in Catholica 18 (1964), 48-77, 193-217; 19
(1965), 138-162, 171-185. This series, and Kösters' 1965 Innsbruck
dissertation on the same subject, have gone over the Catholic literature on the subject. Peter Manns' contribution to this volume has
also taken up this point. The differences which will appear between
our treatment and that of Manns stem from the fact that Luther's
simul is just one aspect of a larger problem, admittedly that aspect where the problem of agreement with Catholic and Thomist
thought is most difficult. Along with Luther's simul iustus et pec-

cator, there is also a partim iustus, partim peccator in which
Luther indicates the aspect of the just man's ever imperfect growth
in new, ontological (not just imputed) righteousness. Here the moment of the simul is not stressed. We agree with the material
Manns has collected, but have reservations about his reduction of
the simul to this partial aspect. This is especially clear on p. 147f.,
below. One has the whole of Luther only by joining the two aspects,
and then adding the third variation, peccator in re, iustus in spe.

39 Luther works with these distinctions in WA 8, 96,17, 107,
     13-36; and 1, 86, 39.

40 See, for example, ST I-II, 71, 1-6; 74, 1-10; 110, 1-4;
     113, 1-8.

41 Penance is essentially complementary to charity (ST I-II,
     113, 5, especially ad 1) and lasts through one's whole life-
time (III, 84, 8c). We have dealt with this Thomistic point of departure for a simul in our book on justification.

42 ST I-II, 113, 1c and even earlier in De Veritate 28, 5 and
     28, 1 ad 12.

43 This is especially noticeable in his Lectures on Romans:
     WA 56, 348,24 (Pauck, 210). See also 275,9 (Pauck, 129).

44 It is impossible to handle the problem of concupiscence in
     Catholic theology in general and in Thomas in particular
in a few sentences. Here we can only refer to the following important works: K. Rahner, "The Theological Concept of Concupis-
centia," in Theological Investigations, Vol. 1 (Baltimore: Helicon,
1961), pp. 347-382; B. Stoeckle, Die Lehre von der erbsündlichen
Konkupiszenz in ihrer Bedeutung für das christliche Leibethos
(Ettal: Buch-Kunstverlag, 1954); S. Pfürtner, Triebleben und
sittliche Vollendung nach Thomas von Aquin (Freiburg, Switzerland: Universitätsverlag, 1958); J. B. Metz, art. "Begierde," in
Lexikon für Theologie und Kirche 2nd ed., Vol. II, Coll. 108-112,
and Christliche Anthropocentrik, p. 21, 86f., 93f.; B. Stoeckle,
"Erbsündige Begierlichkeit," in Münchener Theologische Zeitschrift
14 (1963), 225-241; R. Kösters, "Luthers These," Catholica 19
(1965), 147-160; Z. Alszeghy, "Il peccato originale nelle professione
di fede lutherane," Gregorianum 47 (1966), 86-100. We have studied
the pertinent texts of St. Thomas and compared them with Luther
in Theologie der Rechtfertigung, pp. 495ff. and 526-537.

45 Luther's position is also not strengthened by Romans 7, ac-
     cording to modern exegesis. See Paul Althaus' treatment of
this in Paulus und Luther über den Menschen (Gütersloh: Gerd Mohn,
[1]1938, [4]1963). The most recent report on the controversy on this
point, along with a new approach to a solution, is found in A. Peters,

Glaube und *Werk* (Berlin-Hamburg: Lutherisches Verlagshaus, 1962), especially pp. 166-181.

46 This has been pointed out in recent Catholic works, most pointedly in K. Rahner's *Happiness* through *Prayer* (Westminster: Newman, 1958), pp. 83-97, but also in "Questions of Controversial Theology of Justification," in *Theological* *Investigations*, Vol. IV, p. 208 f., esp. note 12; H. Küng, *Justification* (New York: Nelson, 1964), pp. 236-248; G. Söhngen, "Gesetz und Evangelium," *Catholica* 14 (1960), pp. 101-103; and R. Grosche, *Pilgernde* *Kirche* (Freiburg: Herder, 1938), especially pp. 153 ff.

47 See, for instance, W. Link, *Das* *Ringen* *Luthers* um die *Freiheit* *der* *Theologie* von *der* *Philosophie*, pp. 77 f.; and R. Kösters, "Luthers These," in *Catholica* 18 (1964), pp. 55-59. R. Hermann wrote his classic article on this point in 1925, "Das Verhältnis von Rechtfertigung und Gebet," now in *Gesammelte* *Studien* zur *Theologie* *Luthers* und der *Reformation* (Göttingen: Vandenhoeck und Ruprecht, 1960), pp. 11-43.

48 See, for example, Peters, *Glaube* und *Werk*, pp. 10 f., who bases his criticism on Link, or G. Ebeling, *Luther*, p. 268.

49 See ST I, 1, 6.

50 One should look at the following texts and compare them: ST III, 24, 3-4; I, 19, 9; 43, 2 ad 3; and III, 1, 3 ad 3.

51 We have done this in *Theologie* der *Rechtfertigung*, pp. 735 ff.

52 Karl Rahner seems to have been the first one to point this out. See *Theological* *Investigations*, Vol. IV, pp. 201-205.

53 It has often been observed that in Luther there is strangely little on love of God as the fundamental movement of the Christian life. Two excellent studies have recently presented Luther's very complex explanation of this question: on the early *Lectures* on *Romans*, J. Lortz, "Luthers Römerbriefvorlesung--Grundanliegen," *Trierer* *Theologische* *Zeitschrift* 71 (1962), 129-153 and 216-247, especially 238-247; and on the Major Commentary on Galatians, Peter Manns, "Absolute and Incarnate Faith," below in this volume, pp. 121-165.

54 See the most recent presentation by Max Seckler, *Das* *Heil* in *der* *Geschichte*, pp. 33-47. Also our article, "Um den Plan der Summa Theologiae," *Münchner* *Theologische* *Zeitschrift* 16 (1965), 128-137.

55 See, for instance, ST I-II, 109, 3c.

56 ST II-II, 23, 1; 25, 5c; 24, 2c.

57 Peter Manns has brought this argument before the public in the small book, directed principally against the present

writer, Lutherforschung heute-Krise und Aufbruch (Wiesbaden: F. Steiner, 1967).

58 The clearest sign that Scotistic personalism is still sapiential theology is perhaps the use of the theory of divine
acceptation as the basic explanatory principle regarding the relations between God and man.

59 See note 15, above.

60 WA 8, 79,21. LW 32, 190 (George Lindbeck).

61 WA 18, 644, 5. Bondage, 114.

62 WATr 3, 147,10; no. 3028.

63 WATr 4, 290,2; no. 4388.

64 In the area of justification, I have striven for completeness
   in my book, Theologie der Rechtfertigung.

65 See ibid., pp. 935 ff., for more on this point.

66 Via Caritatis, pp. 263-272, especially p. 270 f.

67 R. Guindon, Béatitude et Théologie morale chez S. Thomas
   d'Aquin (Ottawa: Editions de la Université, 1956), pp. 304-
308; M. D. Chenu, Thomas von Aquin (rowohlts monograph, n.
45), pp. 47-71; E. Gilson, The Christian Philosophy of St. Thomas
Aquinas (New York: Random House, 1956), pp. 375 ff.; and, in
dependence on these and other writers, U. Kühn, Via Caritatis,
pp. 29 f., 224, and 252.

1 The Book of Concord--The Symbols of the Evangelical
   Lutheran Church, trans. F. Bente and W. H. T. Dau (St.
Louis: Concordia, 1957), p. 160 f.

2 Inde fit, ut nullus consequatur gratiam, quia absolvitur aut
   baptizatur aut communicatur aut inungitur, sed quia credit
sic absolvendo, baptizando, communicando, inungendo se conse-
qui gratiam." WA 57III, 169, 23 ff.

3 For example, in 1535: "Fides arripit meritum Christi et
   statuit nos per Christi mortem liberatos esse." WA 42, 48,
17 f. The American Edition softens Luther's verbs to "faith ac-
quires Christ's merit and knows that through Christ's death we
have been set free." LW 1, 64 (G. V. Schick).

4 For example, WA 7, 215, 1-4, where Luther disparages a
   faith that merely believes facts to be true by putting it on a
level with believing what is said about enemies (the Turks), about
the devil, or about hell.

5 For example, WA 2, 458, 24: "Haec fides te iustificat." LW
   27, 172. Similarly, in theses 24-25 of the 1535 Disputation
on Faith and the Law. WA 39I, 46, 7 ff. LW 34, 111.

6 WA 39I, 45, 21. LW 34, 110 (Thesis 12).

7 The phrase "certo statuere" is frequent in Luther's 1531-
   1535 lectures on Galatians.

8 "Fides autem esse nullo modo potest, nisi vivax quaedam
   et indubitata opinio, qua homo certus est, super omnem
certitudinem sese placere Deo, se habere propitium et ignoscentem Deum in omnibus, quae fecerit aut gesserit: propitium
in bonis, ignoscentem in malis." WA 5, 395, 12. Other relevant
passages are WA 6, 206, 9-24 (LW 44, 25 f.); 18, 769, 4-23
(Bondage, 291 f.); and 40I, 576, 26-33 (LW 26, 378).

9 As in the passage cited in the previous footnote.

10 See, for instance, WA 1, 176, and 182 (from 1519), where
   Luther identifies peace and relief, the psychic appendage
of certitude, with forgiveness of sin.

11 In his Treatise on Good Works, WA 6, 215-216 (LW 44,
   37-39).

12 For instance, at WA 31II, 434, 34. See also WA 25, 330, 38
   to 332, 14.

13 WA 40I, 578-579. LW 26, 379-380.

14 A remarkable example is found in St. Ambrose's Treatise
   on the Gospel of St. Luke, Book II, Ch. 41 (PL 15, 1649).

15 A fine example is Luther's sermon of November 24, 1532.
WA 36, 358-360.

16 "Hanc enim novam et erroneam doctrinam putari voluit."
WA 2, 7,37. LW 31, 261. "Hanc theologiam novam videri
putant et erroneam." Ibid., 13,10. LW 31, 270.

17 Luther described what Cajetan found amiss in his idea of
faith thus: "Obiectio altera est, quod . . . dixi, neminem
iustificari posse nisi per fidem, sic scilicet, ut necesse sit, eum
certa fide credere sese iustificari et nullo modo dubitare, quod
gratiam consequatur." WA 2, 13,6-8. LW 31, 270.

18 WA 2, 13,12--16,3. LW 31, 270-274.

19 Ibid., 13,29. LW 31, 271.

20 Ibid., 13,23 f. LW 31, 271 (H. J. Grimm).

21 Ibid., 13,33 f. LW 31, 271 (H. J. Grimm).

22 Ibid., 14,16. LW 31, 272.

23 Ibid., 15,2. LW 31, 273.

24 "[Fides] quae ad effectum aliquem praesentem pertineat."
Ibid. Or it is "[fides] ad praesentem effectum destinata."
Ibid., 15,23. LW 31, 273 f. ("faith directed to the accomplishment
of an immediate end").

25 Ibid., 14,5. LW 31, 271.

26 Especially noteworthy in this connection are the expressions "superba fiducia" (WA 6, 520,4 [innocuously translated at LW 36, 46 as "firm confidence"]) and "sancta superbia"
(WA 40I, 372,21 [LW 26, 235]). Furthermore Luther can say,
"Darauf soll der Mensch frei trotzen und sich des vermessen,
dass alle Dinge Christi ohne seine Werke sein seien, aus lauter
Gnade." In English: "A man should with unrestrained defiance
and audacity insist that all things of Christ are his without his
doing works, but from pure grace." WA 10III, 350,31 f. The close
association of the terms Trotz (defiance, obstancy) and Trost
(consolation) occurring innumerable times in Luther's German
writings is also characteristic of his conception of faith. It is
defiance or obstancy that is supposed to bring about consolation.

27 For instance, he said in a sermon on Janury 1, 1517,
"Doctrina fidei hoc docet, quod homo iugiter debet intus
gemere pro gratia." WA 1, 118,37. Compare this with the texts
given above, p. 194, note 8.

28 WA 40II, 6,20 ff. LW 27, 6 (J. Pelikan).

29 The Nature of Faith, trans. R. G. Smith (London: Collins,
1961), p. 177. The anthropocentrism which was pre-formed
in Luther's doctrine of "seizing" salvation by "stating" it, is occasionally radicalized in modern existentialist Lutheranism in

statements that border on atheism. Ebeling can say that the meaning of the word "God" is the fundamental situation of man, that is,
a word-situation. Gott und Wort (Tübingen: Mohr, 1966), p. 54.
In fact, if the doctrine of reflexivity is carried to its ultimate consequences, it appears that a faith professing "God is" becomes
superfluous. In a footnote to the passage just quoted, Ebeling says
that in terms of modern logic the word "God" might be called not
an "autosematicon" but a "synsematicon." Even justification can
now be explained without at all using the word "God." See also
Ebeling's Luther-Einführung in sein Denken (Tübingen: Mohr,
1964), p. 185.

30 From Cajetan's letter of October 25, 1518, to Prince
Frederick the Wise, given in WABr 1, 234,47 f., no. 110: ". . .
de fide sacramentorum implet papyrum locis sacrae scripturae
omnino impertinentibus et perperam intellectis."

31 WA 6, 528,34 (LW 36, 60); 8, 594,6 (LW 44, 278).

32 WA 40I, 299,29. LW 26, 179 (J. Pelikan).

33 See Heinrich Schlier, Der Brief an die Galater (Meyer Kom-
    mentar; Göttingen: Vandenhoeck & Ruprecht, ²1962), p. 96 f.,
note 4, and p. 103, note 1.

34 See, for example, WA 40II, 42,10 ff. (LW 27, 34).

35 Sponsa Verbi (Einsiedeln: Johannes Verlag, 1961), pp.
    174 ff. See also the paperback excerpt, Wer ist die Kirche?
(Freiburg: Herder, 1965), pp. 31 ff.

36 WA 40I, 82-94. LW 26, 32-39. See also WA 2, 457-459
    (LW 27, 171-174).

37 Scholia on Isaiah, WA 25, 330,38 f. See also WA 31II,
    434,6 ff.

38 See, for instance, WA 40I, 578,22 (LW 26, 379). Although
    the notes taken by G. Rörer at Luther's lecture (line 2 ff.),
do not express exactly the same idea as the printed commentary,
we may be sure that the printed version faithfully renders Luther's
thought. Luther expressly sanctioned the edition by writing the
preface, "Sentio meas cogitationes esse." WA 40I, 33,4. LW 26,
x. At any rate, the large Commentary on Galatians is throughout
an authentic document of primitive Lutheranism.

39 WA 6, 529,32 ff. LW 36, 61 (T. W. Steinhäuser).

40 P. Althaus, The Theology of Martin Luther, trans. Robert
    C. Schultz (Philadelphia: Fortress Press, 1966), p. 449.

41 See, for instance, WA 6, 206,9 f.14 ff.23 f. (LW 44, 25 f.)
    and 39II, 248,11. Also Althaus, The Theology of Martin
Luther, p. 450.

42 Ibid., p. 457.

43 From Luther's sermon on July 21, 1532. WA 36, 462,4 ff.

44 WA 2, 458,22 (LW 27, 172); 38, 198,15; 39II, 264,11; 40I, 285,22 f. (LW 26, 168); 57III, 169,12 f.

45 WA 10II, 73,16. LW 35, 132 (W. A. Lambert).

46 The Theology of Martin Luther, p. 79.

47 Ibid., p. 231.

48 See, for instance, WA 18, 692,20 ff. (Bondage, 180); and 40I, 91,28 (LW 26, 38).

49 The Church Teaches, trans. John F. Clarkson, et al. (St. Louis: B. Herder, 1955), p. 244.

50 Reflexive faith from its very origin involves a considerable amount of anthropocentrism. See note 29, above. It is significant that the anthropocentrism of some recent trends of decaying Catholicism, precisely as Protestantism has done before, rule out the primacy of love of God. This has at all times been the very heart of Catholic doctrine and ethics, but it is now as-serted that love of one's neighbor is the only form in which love of God can be practised.

51 WA 31II, 14,20-23; 25, 95,41 f.; 36, 363,10-23.

52 WA 11, 189,5.

53 WA 56, 389-392. Pauck, 260-264.

54 This and the following three paragraphs are a condensed summary of the last three chapters of my book, Das Ich im Glauben bei Martin Luther (Graz: Styria Verlag, 1966), pp. 204-323. With few exceptions, I have abstained from giving references and quotations, because these would have necessitated interpretations which would have expanded the present article beyond the limits accorded to it.

55 This experience seems to be reflected in several of Luther's writings of the years 1518-1520, and reminiscence of it is found in the famous preface he wrote to his Latin works in 1545. WA 54, 186-3-10. LW 34, 337.

56 On this, see Thomas Merton, New Seeds of Contemplation (New York: New Directions, 1961), p. 165: "If I think the most important thing in life is a feeling of interior peace, I will be all the more disturbed when I notice that I do not have it. And since I cannot directly produce that feeling in myself whenever I want to, the disturbance will increase with the failure of my ef-forts." Used by permission, copyright 1961, by the Abbey of Gethsemanie, Inc.

57 WA 5, 407,35 f.

58 Theologische Revue 64 (1968), 55. The earliest case of a secularization of Luther's interpretation of faith was per-

haps the epistemology of Descartes, who made truth ultimately dependent on self-reflection. In the introduction to my book, I hinted at "the problem of a pre-Cartesian, religious 'Cartesianism'" in Luther. Father Pesch, who has evidently overlooked the word "religious" in this expression, misunderstands me in saying that I place Luther's problem of salvation-certitude on a level with Descartes' problem of "philosophical-certitude" and interpret Luther's idea of certitude "after the pattern of theoretical certitude" (p. 53). But I think I have treated Luther's ideas as what they are, namely as religious ideas, and I have pointed to Descartes and other philosophers merely to show that what was originally a religious conception deviating from Scripture and Catholicism was later transposed into philosophy.

NOTES TO HARRY J. McSORLEY, C.S.P.
Erasmus versus Luther:
Compounding the Reformation Tragedy

1 This was the most neutral term Vatican II could find to
   describe the Protestant-Catholic separation. The Council
thus avoided giving a simple answer to the overly simple question: Did they leave or were they put out? See the Decree on Ecumenism, nn. 3 and 19.

2 Ibid.

3 Luthers Lehre vom unfreien Willen nach seiner Hauptschrift
   De servo arbitrio, in the series, Beiträge zur ökumenischen
Theologie, edited by H. Fries, Vol. 1 (Munich: Hueber, 1967).
The English version of this work has been released jointly by
Augsburg Publishing House of Minneapolis and Newman Press of
New York under the title, Luther: Right or Wrong? An Ecumenical-
Theological Study of Luther's Major Work, The Bondage of the
Will.

4 Cf. J. Lortz, The Reformation in Germany (New York: Herder
   and Herder, 1968), Vol. I, pp. 156 f., 195-200, 233 ff.; H.
Oberman, The Harvest of Medieval Theology (Cambridge, Mass.:
Harvard University Press, 1963), p. 426; and my essay, "Was
Gabriel Biel a Semipelagian?" in Wahrheit und Verkündigung: M.
Schmaus zum 70. Geburtstag, edited by L. Scheffczyk, W. Dett-
loff, and R. Heinzmann, Vol. II (Paderborn-Munich-Vienna: F.
Schöningh, 1967), pp. 1109-1120.

5 Cf. Denziger-Schönmetzer, Enchiridion Symbolorum, 33rd
   edition (Barcelona-Freiburg: Herder, 1965), n. 1492.

6 Denziger-Schönmetzer, n. 1486.

7 WA 1, 354,5 f. LW 31, 40.

8 We have traced this tradition in detail in our above-mentioned
   monograph in chapters two through seven.

9 WA 1, 359,35 ff. LW 31, 48 f. This is in opposition to the
   teaching of the Ockham-Biel school of theology which exaggerated the power of free will of the sinner. Cf. note 4, above.

10 That Luther's rejection of the Papacy was dependent on his
    conviction that the Pope did not teach the Gospel of grace
is seen long after his excommunication when he said in his Lectures
on Galatians (published 1535) that, if the Pope would only teach that
we are justified solely by the grace of Christ, he would not only
carry the Pope on his shoulders but would kiss his feet as well!
See WA 40I, 181,11 ff. (LW 26, 99).

11 Published December, 1520. Cf. WA 7, 94-151. A German

version appeared in March, 1521. A translation of the latter is found in LW 32, 3-100 (C. M. Jacobs and G. Forell).

12 WA 7, 148,14ff.: "In caeteris autem articulis, de Papatu, Conciliis, indulgentiis aliisque non necessariis nugis, ferenda est levitas et stultitia Papae et suorum, sed in hoc articulo, qui omnium optimus et rerum nostrarum summa est, dolendum ac flendum est, miseros sic insanire."

13 WA 7, 146,3-12: "Unde et hunc articulum necesse est revocare. Male enim dixi, quod liberum arbitrium ante gratiam sit res de solo titulo, sed simpliciter debui dicere 'liberum arbitrium est figmentum in rebus seu titulus sine re.' Quia nulli est in manu sua quippiam cogitare mali aut boni, sed omnia (ut Viglephi articulus constantiae damnatus recte docet) de necessitate absoluta eveniunt. Quod et Poeta voluit, quando dixit 'certa stant omnia lege.' Et Christus Matth. x 'Folium arboris non cadit in terram sine voluntate patris vestri . . .' Et Esa. xli eis insultat dicens 'Bene quoque aut male si potestis facite.'" This argument is not used in the German version of Luther's reply to Exsurge Domine.

14 WA 56, 385,19f. (Pauck, 252); 1, 365,33ff. (LW 31, 58); 18, 638,4-11, 662,7-11,752,7 (Bondage, 107, 137, 256); 40I, 293,29 (LW 26, 174).

15 In chapters eight and ten of our monograph we have argued that Luther ought not be called a determinist and have tried to show how a benign interpretation of such "hard sayings" of Luther is both possible and truthful. In the pre- or un-ecumenical climate of the 1520's, however, it was hardly likely that Catholics would be interested in interpreting Luther benignly!

16 We shall use as our text the edition of Johannes v. Walter, Quellenschriften zur Geschichte des Protestantismus, Heft 8 (Leipzig: A. Deichert, 1910) = Walter. Cf. Desiderii Erasmi de libero arbitrio diatribe sive collatio 1524, in Opera Omnia, ed. LeClerc, vol. IX (Leyden, 1706), pp. 1215-1247. A translation of extracts of Erasmus' De libero arbitrio and Luther's reply has been made by E. F. Winter and is available in paperback: Erasmus -Luther -- Discourse on Free Will (New York: Frederick Ungar, 1961).

17 Cf. K. Zickendraht, Der Streit zwischen Erasmus und Luther über die Willensfreiheit (Leipzig: Hinrichs, 1909), p. 11; G. Krodel, "Luther, Erasmus and Henry VIII," Archiv für Reformationsgeschichte, 53 (1962), p. 77.

18 Cf. Preserved Smith, Erasmus: A Study of His Life, Ideals and Place in History (new printing; New York: Harper, 1962).

19 *History of Dogma*, trans. N. Buchanan, Vol. VII (Boston:
    Little Brown, 1900), p. 203. See also P. Smith, *Erasmus*,
pp. 426 ff.

20 We have criticized this view, as well as Luther's charge
    that Erasmus was a skeptic, in our monograph in an ex-
cursus: "Was Erasmus a Skeptic, Uncommitted to the Christian
Faith?"

21 Walter, II a 12, p. 31, 8-13; II a 14, p. 32, 20 f.; II a 18,
    p. 38, 19-22; II b 1, p. 39, 3.7.10.24 and *passim*.

22 Wiclif held that God's grace necessitates our acts in some
    ways, but adds "*salva libertate arbitrii*." Cf. *De dominio
divino*, pp. 226 f.; cited by R. Seeberg, *Lehrbuch der Dogmengeschichte*, vol. III, 6th printing, of the 4th ed. (Basel: B. Schwabe,
1960), pp. 779. It is possible, but not evident, that Luther understood Wiclif's doctrine of necessity this way.

23 This is not to say that it was wrong for Erasmus to criticize
    Luther's necessitarian language and his assertion that "free
will" is merely a word without real content. On the contrary,
criticism was in order. But could not Erasmus have criticized
Luther while at the same time recognizing the correctness of
Luther's primary concern: to defend the absolute necessity of
grace for any act that is pleasing to God?

24 Walter, I b 10, p. 19, lines 7-10: "*Porro liberum arbitrium
    hoc loco sentimus vim humanae voluntatis, qua se possit
homo applicare ad ea, quae perducunt ad aeternam salutem, aut
ab iisdem avertere.*"

25 Compare his definition with that of Peter Lombard, for exam-
    ple: Free will "*est facultas rationis et voluntatis, qua bonum
eligitur, gratia assistente, vel malum ea desistente.*" *Sentences*,
lib. II, d. 24, cap. 3. -- Erasmus' definition is very similar to
the one found in Thomas Aquinas, *De Ver.*, q. 24, a. 1, arg. 6
except that Erasmus leaves out the words "*gratia assistente*"!

26 *The Reformation in England*, vol. I (London: Hollis & Carter,
    1948), p. 123.

27 This is acknowledged by such Protestant scholars as F.
    Kattenbusch, O. Scheel, F. W. Schmidt, J. MacKinnon and
J. von Walter. Walter, "Die neueste Beurteilung des Erasmus,"
*Jahresbericht der Schlesischen Gesellschaft für vaterländische
Kultur*, 89 (1911/12), pp. 16 f. likewise defends Erasmus against
the charge--for which Luther is ultimately responsible--that he
is a mere moralist.

28 *Conversion et Grâce chez Thomas d'Aquin* (Paris: Aubier,
    1944), pp. 94 f.; 97; 98-102; 114-121.

29 Cf. Denziger-Schönmetzer, n. 375.

30 Summa Theologiae I-II, q. 114, a. 5, ad 1. Bouillard, pp. 114 f., attributes this to the high authority Thomas ascribed to Augustine from whom Thomas learned of the doctrine of the necessity of prevenient grace for every salutary act.

31 Erasmus' dislike of Augustine--partly because Augustine was not proficient in Greek--has been documented by H. Humbertclaude, Érasme et Luther (Paris: Bloud et Cie, 1909), pp. 11-15.

32 Oberman, The Harvest, p. 426, calls Biel's doctrine of justification "at least semi-Pelagian."

33 Walter, II a. 9, p. 26, lines 15-27: ". . . homo nondum accepta gratia, quae peccatum abolet, naturae viribus exercere posset opera moraliter, ut vocant, bona, quibus non de condigno, sed de congruo promerantur gratiam gratum facientem . . ."

34 Walter, II a. 12, p. 30, lines 22-27: "qui longissime fugiunt a Pelagio, plurimum tribuunt gratiae, libero arbitrio pene nihil nec tamen in totum tollunt: negant hominem posse velle bonum sine gratia peculiari, negant posse incipere, negant posse progredi, negant posse perficere sine principali perpetuoque gratiae divinae praesidio."

35 Cf. Hyperaspistes, 1323 D. Abbreviated as Hyp.

36 Hyperaspistes, 1327 E: "Hanc opinionem quoniam Ecclesia, quod quidem sciam, nondum reiecit, ego nec defendo nec explodo." Ibid., 1330 D: "Quam sententiam non arbitror ab Ecclesia damnatam, . . ."; 1364 D; 1378 C and D.

37 Walter, II a 11, pp. 28, 21-29, 12. This gratia, says Erasmus, is the same as the "influxus naturalis."

38 Hyp. II, 1413 E: " . . . ut sunt iustitiae gradus, ita sunt et donorum, donec pervenias ad id quod mere naturale, atque hoc ipsum habet suam gratiam, cum auctor naturae sit Deus, ut frustra metuat Augustinus, ne initium gratiae dicatur ab homine proficisci." Cf. 1529 A; 1532 A.

39 Walter, I a 8, p. 6, 16: "totum ascribamus divinae benignitati." Cf. Augustine, De spiritu et littera 2, 4; 3, 5. -- Faustus of Riez, a leading representative of Semipelaginism, admitted that in the salvific event the very first beginning (initium inchoationis)--the vocation to salvation--comes from God. But this was not sufficient for the Second Council of Orange. It insisted that even the beginning of man's response was the work of the Holy Spirit, not the powers of nature. Cf. E. Amann, "Semi-Pélagiennes," Dictionnaire de Théologie Catholique, 14, 1835.

40 Hyp. II, 1528 E: "assentimur, quod certe possumus naturae
     viribus: de assensu loquor, non qui iustificat, sed qui
praeparat aliquo modo."

41 Denziger-Schönmetzer, n. 374.

42 Denziger-Schönmetzer, n. 1525 (Chapter 5 of the Decree on
     Justification). In contrast to Erasmus and his contempor-
aries Trent was able to draw upon the newly recovered decrees
of Orange II. Cf. H. Jedin, A History of the Council of Trent,
vol. II (St. Louis: B. Herder, 1961), pp. 142, n. 1 and 241.

43 Erasmus always maintained an attitude of obedience to the
     teaching office of the Church. "Whatever has been discussed
by us," he says toward the end of Hyperaspistes (1536 E and F),
"I submit to the Catholic Church, prepared to correct anything that
has departed from the truth."

44 It was published in Wittenberg in December, 1525. Seven
     other editions were published in 1526. Nearly twelve years
after its publication Luther wrote: "I consider none of my books
to be worthwhile, except perhaps De servo arbitrio and the Catechism," WABr 8, 99,7 f.; n. 3162.

45 WA 18, 786,26-31. Translation by J. Packer and O. Johnston,
     The Bondage of the Will (London: James Clarke, 1957), p.
319.

46 Walter, III b 8, p. 67, lines 10 f.

47 WA 18, 748-753. Bondage, 259-266.

48 Cf. Super Evangelium S. Ioannis Lectura (Marietti: Rome,
     1952), cap. XV, lectio 1, n. 1993: "These words close the
mouths of the proud, and especially of the Pelagians, who say that
they can do good works of virtue and of the law by themselves
without the help of God: in so doing, when they wish to affirm free
will they instead destroy it.

For the Lord says here that without him we are not only unable
to do great things, but insignificant things as well; in fact, we
can do nothing. . . . Our works are done either by the power of
nature or of divine grace. . . . No nature can move itself to do
anything without him . . . [nor] can any work be meritorious
without him."

49 Denziger-Schönmetzer, n. 377: "If anyone states that, by
     the power of nature we can think any good thought, choose
any good thing or consent to the salutary preaching of the gospel
. . . without the illumination and inspiration of the Holy Spirit
. . . he is deceived by a heretical spirit, not understanding the
word of God saying in the gospel: 'Without me you can do nothing
. . .'"

50 Cf. WA 18, 614-619 (Bondage, 79-84).

51 WA 18, 756-786 (Bondage, 271-318).

52 WA 18, 615, 13 ff.: ". . . Deus nihil praescit contingenter, sed quod omnia incommutabili et aeterna infallibilique voluntate et praevidet et proponit et facit. Hoc fulmine sternitur et conteritur penitus liberum arbitrium." Bondage, 80.

53 WA 18, 615, 31 ff.: "Ex quo sequitur irrefragibiliter, omnia quae facimus, omnia quae fiunt, etsi nobis videntur mutabiliter et contingenter fieri, revera tamen fiunt necessario et immutabiliter, si Dei voluntatem spectes." Bondage, ibid.

54 We have made such an effort in chapter ten of our monograph.

55 WA 18, 775. Bondage, 301.

56 WA 18, 634, 37--635, 17. Bondage, 103 f. In our volume on Luther we have devoted an excursus to this image on its historical origins and its use by Luther.

57 See our essay "Luther, Trent, Vatican I and II," McCormick Quarterly, 21 (1967), pp. 95-104.

58 He presents the biblical doctrine of the bondage of the will in WA 18, 756-786 (Bondage, 271-318). Here Luther's sustained exegetical incisiveness is remarkable. In this section it is mainly his speculative reflections on God's justice that cause us difficulty (WA 18, 784 ff.). Our only major criticism of his exegesis elsewhere in the book is his systematic refusal to allow that the biblical imperatives at least sometimes imply that the one commanded has the power of free choice. Here he stands alone in the history of exegesis.

NOTES TO PETER MANNS
Absolute and Incarnate Faith--Luther on Justification
in the Galatians' Commentary of 1531-1535

1 K. Holl, Gesammelte Aufsätze Vol. 1, Luther (Tübingen:
      Mohr, 4-51927). P. Althaus, The Theology of Martin Luther
(Philadelphia: Fortress, 1966); and Die lutherische Rectfertigungs-
lehre und ihre heutigen Kritiker (Berlin: Evang. Verlagsanstalt,
1951). W. Joest, Gesetz und Freiheit (Göttingen: Vandenhoeck und
Ruprecht, 1951). O. Modalsli, Das Gericht nach den Werken
(Göttingen: Vandenhoeck und Ruprecht, 1963).

2 For example, W. Stählin, Allein-Recht und Gefahr einer
      polemischen Formel (Stuttgart: Evangelisches Verlags-
werk, 1950), also in Symbolon (1958), pp. 190-211. Also, M.
Lackmann, Zur reformatorische Rechtfertigungslehre (Stuttgart:
Evangelisches Verlagswerk, 1953).

3 For example, E. Stakemeier, in Glaube und Rechtfertigung
      (Freiburg: Herder, 1937) and in "Trienter Lehrentscheidungen
und reformatorische Anliegen," in Das Weltkonzil von Trient, ed.
G. Schreiber (Freiburg: Herder, 1951), Vol. I, pp. 77-116. Also
W. H. van den Pol, Das Zeugnis der Reformation (Essen: Ludgerus,
1963).

4 For example, J. Lortz, in his contribution to this volume;
      H. Küng, Justification (New York: Nelson, 1964), pp. 236-
248; R. Grosche, "Simul peccator et iustus," in Pilgernde Kirche
(Freiburg: Herder, 1938), pp. 147-158.

5 H. Jedin, Papal Legate at the Council of Trent, transl. F. C.
      Eckhoff (St. Louis: B. Herder, 1947); Kardinal Contarini
als Kontroverstheologe (Münster: Aschendorff, 1949); and
History of the Council of Trent, Vols. I and II (St. Louis: B.
Herder, 1957 and 1961). Editor's Note: This essay originally
appeared in a Festschrift for H. Jedin.

6 "'And though I Had All Faith'--Luther's Interpretation of
      I Corinthians 13:2," and "Love and the Certainty of Salva-
tion--Luther's Interpretation of I John 4:17a," both in Althaus'
The Theology of Martin Luther, trans. Robert C. Schultz (Philadelphia: Fortress, 1966), pp. 429-458.

7 "Paulus und das luthersche Simul Iustus et Peccator," in
      Kerygma und Dogma 1 (1955), 269-320.

8 Glaube und Werk (Berlin-Hamburg: Lutherisches Verlagshaus,
      1962).

9 See, however, the excellent study by Karin Bornkamm,
      Luthers Auslegungen des Galaterbriefes von 1519 und 1531--

Ein Vergleich (Berlin: DeGruyter, 1963).

10 We will cite the printed version of the lectures, which was
    edited by G. Rörer from notes he had taken at the lectures
and published in 1535 (now in WA 40I and 40II). Luther wrote a
preface and introduction (WA 40I, 33,2 ff.), giving his approval
to the work Rörer had done. For treatment of the textual questions, see the Introduction by A. Freitag, WA 40I, 1-14.

11 See K. Bornkamm's *Luthers Auslegungen* des *Galater-*
    briefes, pp. 89-153 and 316-358. It is furthermore im-
portant to know that, according to Miss Bornkamm's intensive
comparative study, the lectures of 1531 do not break with the
framework of thought Luther established in his 1519 lectures on
the same epistle. This is in spite of additions to the topics treated
and a shift of emphasis toward more stress on factors giving objective reassurance, such as ministerial office, the scripture
principle, doctrine, the Church, and the sacraments. See Bornkamm, p. 382 ff. She points out Luther's massive concentration
on this aspect of the work of Christ (pp. 165-176).

12 WA 40I, 48,28 f. LW 26, 9.

13 Ibid., 49,26 f. LW 26, 10.

14 Ibid., 181,11 ff. LW 26, 99 (J. Pelikan).

15 Ibid., 36,35 ff. See also 11. 30 ff. for Luther's moving
    complaint over the sects arising in his own camp.

16 Ibid., 474,32 f. LW 26, 305.

17 Ibid., 36,21 f. LW 27, 149.

18 "Thus we see today that because of the persecution and
    blasphemy of our opponents and the contempt and ingratitude
of the world many evils follow upon the preaching of the Gospel.
This bothers us so much that we often think, according to the flesh,
that it would have been better if the teaching of godliness had never
circulated . . ." Ibid., 678,18 ff. LW 26, 452 (J. Pelikan). See also
the moving testimony at 475,27 ff. (LW 26, 306).

19 At table in 1531, in the time of these lectures, he spoke of the
    Epistle to the Galatians as "mea Ketha de Bora." WA 40I, 2.

20 Yves Congar rightfully maintained this view in *Vraie et fausse*
    Reform dans *l'Eglise* (Paris: du Cerf, 1950), p. 382. Congar
speaks here (see n. 53) of his plan to demonstrate how Protestantism
is "a onesidedly developed Galatisme" with some basis in the Pauline
text, since Galatians is itself the most onesided of Paul's letters. I
would register a hesitation about this "Galatisme," as Congar understands it, although I would also admit that the difficulties Luther
presents in Congar's field of ecclesiology are greater than the problem
we are persuing.

21 With Paul Luther proclaims a doctrine, which although
related to the Church he has not learned from the
Apostles but received from God: WA 40I, 144, 20-29; 145, 18 ff.
(LW 26, 75). With Paul Luther opposes Peter to his face: 193, 15 ff.
(LW 26, 107). He stands alone as Paul did against a greater power or even against "the Church": 55, 16 f.; 130, 32 ff. (LW 26,
15.65). Just as the Apostle he appears as a heretic: 267, 25 f. (LW
26, 156). See also 134, 20 f.; 137, 15 f.; 212, 31 f.; 644, 14 f.; 645,
28 f.; 675, 29 ff.; 678, 34 (LW 26, 67 f. 70. 119. 425 f. 427. 450. 452 f.).

22 WA 40I, 1.

23 Ibid.

24 Wherever Luther polemicizes directly against the works of
the Law and against the "opinio iustitiae" or against the
scholastic doctrine of charity, he is attacking self-justification
through works, and not good works in themselves or the actions
of a Christian. This is a wide-ranging thesis, but I am so convinced of its truth that I feel no need to give an extensive and
complex documentation of it at present, especially since this
study contains a vast number of probative texts.

25 "For between these two kinds of righteousness, the active
righteousness of the law and the passive righteousness of
Christ, there is no middle ground." WA 40I, 48, 30. LW 26, 9
(J. Pelikan).

26 See ibid., 114, 12 (LW 26, 54); 209, 12 (LW 26, 116);
263, 24 (LW 26, 152 f.).

27 Ibid., 458, 13 ff. (LW 26, 294 f.), cited above, p. 32. See
also 459, 11 ff. (LW 26, 295).

28 See, for instance, the controversy O. Modalsli carries on
with Karl Holl (Das Gericht nach den Werken, pp. 27-34)
over the question whether for Luther charity and the good works
in which faith is fruitful belong--as Holl maintained--within the
doctrine of justification itself. The controversy is even more
indicative, since both scholars agree that Luther taught a real
and not merely imputed justification.

29 Understandibly, the Protestant investigator of Luther faces
this danger in a special manner. Abrecht Peters sees in
Luther a "contradiction" which expresses the existential experience of the dialectic found even in Scripture (Glaube und Werk,
p. 13). He is further convinced that Luther thought through the
question of justification as no theologian before or after him
(p. 14). Then, while admitting the impossibility of an easy and
obvious systematization (p. 22), Peters still ends with a systematic interpretation that sees in Luther the historical turning-

point to a new, existential mode of theology (p. 258 f.). Here, a contradiction has unintentionally become a basic principle of a systematization that does not even exclude the logically contradictory (p. 21). A. Brandenburg is a Catholic researcher who sought to demonstrate a similar existential interpretation (in the Bultmannian sense) in Luther's first Lectures on the Psalms (Gericht und Evangelium [Paderborn: Bonifacius, 1960]). Yves Congar tends to systematize Luther in another fashion. See "Considerations and Reflections on the Christology of Luther, " in Dialogue between Christians, transl. P. Loretz (Westminster: Newman Press, 1966), p. 399 ff. In Vraie et fausse Reform, p. 379, Congar also warns against the dangers entailed in such a deductive treatment of Luther.

    30 "Considerations and Reflections, " p. 379 ff. and 384 ff.

        Congar speaks of Luther's Commentary on Galatians on p. 382 ff. See also Congar's excellent little book Christ, Our Lady, and the Church, trans. H. St. John, O.P. (Westminster, Md.: Newman, 1957), pp. 25-30.

    31 Das Gericht nach den Werken, p. 39 ff. Since Modalsli interprets "incarnate faith" wholly according to Luther, he does not see the christological problematic drawn out by Congar.

    32 "We also distinguish faith in this way, that sometimes faith is understood apart from the work and sometimes with the work. For just as a craftsman speaks about his material in different ways. . ., so the Holy Spirit speaks about faith in different ways in Scripture: sometimes, if I may speak this way, about an abstract or an absolute faith and sometimes about a concrete, composite, or incarnate faith. Thus if Christ is looked at on the basis of outward appearance, He seems to be mere man. And yet Scripture sometimes speaks of Christ as God, and sometimes it speaks of Him as composite and incarnate." WA 40I, 414,24 ff. LW 26, 264 (J. Pelikan).

    33 Ibid., 417,27. LW 26, 266.

    34 Ibid., 417,29-33. LW 26, 267.

    35 Ibid., 416,22. LW 26, 266.

    36 Ibid., 417,34. LW 26, 267.

    37 Ibid., 415,31. LW 26, 265.

    38 Ibid.,

    39 Ibid., 416,9. LW 26,265.

    40 Ibid., 416,16. LW 26,265.

    41 "ita tribuitur etiam iustificatio fidei incarnatae seu fideli facere." Ibid., 416,25. LW 26,266. Modalsli mistakenly

saw Luther coming here very near to teaching justification through works. Das Gericht nach den Werken, p. 40.

42 WA 40I, 416,17. LW 26, 265.

43 Ibid., 417,13 f. LW 26,266.

44 Ibid., 1. 15 f.

45 Ibid., 1. 25 ff. LW 26, 266 f.

46 For instance, ibid., 273,17 ff. (LW 26,159 f.); 433,26 ff. (LW 26, 277) 451,14 f.: "He attached Himself to those who were accursed, assuming their flesh and blood; and thus He interposed Himself as the Mediator between God and men." (LW 26, 289). Also 546,18 f.; 290,32 f.; 297,33 f.; 299,25 f.; 389,11 f.; 423,27 f.; 443,29 f.; 564,11 f. (LW 26, 357.172.177.178 f.246 f. 270.283 f.369).

47 "That Mediator is Jesus Christ. He does not change the sound of the Law, as Moses did. . . . But He sets Himself against the wrath of the Law and abolishes it; in his own body and by Himself He satisfies the Law." Ibid., 503,19. LW 26, 325. (J. Pelikan). Also 566,15 ff., 535,24 f.; 339,2 f. (LW 26, 370 f.349. 210).

48 Congar, "Considerations and Reflections," p. 381 f.

49 Ibid., p. 467, n. 36.

50 "But by the true definition Christ is not a lawgiver; He is a Propitiator and a Savior. Faith takes hold of this and believes without doubting that He has performed a superabundance of works and merits of congruity and condignity." WA 40I, 232,29 f. LW 26, 132 (J. Pelikan). Luther also speaks of the merit of Christ at 264,21 ff. and 265,13 f. (LW 26, 153 f.).

51 Ibid., 301,31 ff.; 303,21 ff.; 589,18 f. (LW 26, 180. 181 f. 387).

52 Ibid., 417,33 f. LW 26, 267 (J. Pelikan).

53 "'By faith they worked righteousness. . .' [Heb 11] thus faith embodies and informs the 'doing'. . . . For reason should first be illumined by faith before it works. Once a true idea and knowledge of God is held as right reason, then the work is incarnated and incorporated into it." Ibid., 418,25 ff. LW 26, 267 f. (J. Pelikan). At first glance this text undoubtedly supports Congar's thesis ("Considerations and Reflections," p. 400 f.). Luther appears to understand the relation of faith and work in terms of flesh being divinized, that is, instead of faith becoming incarnate in works, works are turned into faith. This would be a monophysite reversal of the Incarnation. But Luther's obvious confusion of the ideas of incarnation and information arises against this. What Luther is trying to bring out with the unhappy

image of works being incarnated in faith, is basically nothing else but the often repeated principle that grace precedes salvific actions and that a man must first become a believer in Christ before he can bring forth the true fruits of his new life. See especially the texts cited in note 55, below.

54 WA 40I, 427,11 ff. LW 26, 272 (J. Pelikan). Note how Luther worked out the Christological parallel to this in the lines that follow immediately. His intention is clearly ortho- dox, even though here as well he does not maintain the distinction between person and nature with complete clarity. The hypostatic union of the distinct natures is not brought out with complete un- ambiguity.

55 Ibid., 402,15 f. LW 26, 255 (J. Pelikan). A slight variation on this analogy connects the tree with the person: "But once the tree has been planted, that is, once there is the person or doer who comes into being through faith in Christ, then works follow." Ibid., 1. 19f. We will take up Luther's use of this model below.

56 In the third section of this article, on the relation of faith and charity, we will take up this point in detail.

57 WA 40II, 37,15 f. LW 27, 30 (J. Pelikan).

58 "Considerations and Reflections," pp. 400-402, and p. 380, n. 28. Here one can see how extensively Congar's inter- pretation of Luther is influenced by the work of A. Nygren.

59 WA 40II, 27,20 f. LW 27, 23. On the problem taken up in this and the following section, see the valuable investigation by R. Schwarz, Fides, spes, und caritas beim jungen Luther (Berlin: DeGruyter, 1962). '

60 WA 40II, 25,27 f. LW 27, 22 (J. Pelikan).

61 WA 40I, 21,22.

62 Ibid.

63 Ibid., 1. 33 ff.

64 Ibid., 1. 22.

65 WA 40II, 23,18 ff. LW 27, 20.

66 "Through the Spirit, by faith, we wait for righteousness with hope and longing; that is, we are justified, and still we are not yet justified, because our righteousness is still sus- pended in hope, as Romans 8:24 says: 'In hope we were saved.' For as long as we live, sin still clings to our flesh; there remains a law in our flesh and members at war with the law of our mind and making us captive in the service of sin (Romans 7:23). While these passions of the flesh are raging and we, by the Spirit, are struggling against them, we have occasion to hope for righteousness.

We have indeed begun to be justified by faith, by which we have also received the first fruits of the Spirit; and the mortification of our flesh has begun. But we are not yet perfectly just. Perfect justification lies ahead, and this we expect in hope." Ibid., 24, 13 ff. ET by the Editor. This text shows well the importance of an eschatological viewpoint in rightly understanding Luther's idea of iustitia. The nondum of the hidden future consummation in no way abolishes the sumus justificati which already holds good for faith.

67 Ibid., 24,21. LW 27, 21 (J. Pelikan).

68 For example, A. Brandenburg, Gericht und Evangelium, p. 97 ff. However, Brandenburg did not take into account that the word on which our hope is based speaks not so much of future salvation as of the future revelation of God's gifts which have been given but for now remain hidden.

69 WA 40II, 24,25 f. LW 27, 21.

70 Ibid., 1. 23.

71 Ibid., 1. 27 ff. LW 27, 21 (J. Pelikan).

72 We will take this up in our final section on faith and charity. Let it suffice here to note that Luther is speaking of a "sin" that coexists simul with justice. This, however, is something Luther would never say about an consciously willed and intended sinful deed or omission.

73 WA 40II, 30,26 f. LW 27, 25.

74 Ibid., 31,18 ff. LW 27, 26. Compare Luther's important remarks on Galatians 3:13, where he stresses so emphatically Christ's overcoming of sin in men of faith. WA 40I, 445, 19 ff. LW 26, 285 f. However, his emphasis should not make us fail to notice that he is speaking in strict and proper terms only of the remnants of sin, which still remain in the saints. The true victory therefore is a hidden reality, which we grasp in faith.

75 W. Joest, in Gesetz und Freiheit, pp. 82 ff., treats Luther's simul iustus et peccator in two ways: there is a hidden forensic justice by which one is wholly just quoad Christum and wholly a sinner quoad nos; and an empirical, visible justice which is partial, coexisting with the roots of sin. Joest, however, does not bring out clearly enough that the progressive manifestation of the latter justice is in fact making visible the former hidden justice of Christ. The first justice is no less real for being of the Spirit and hidden beneath its contrary, as Luther's "theology of the cross" leads him to say.

76 WA 40I, 21,20 f.

77 It is instructive how Luther emphasizes the fides quae

when he is distinguishing faith from hope. This is documented in
his lecture notes (WA 40I, 21, 15 ff.), in terms that came up in
both the oral and printed versions of the lectures: the "subject"
of faith is the intellect; its task is teaching, directing, and giving
knowledge; it fights errors and heresies, and judges spirits and
doctrines; it pertains to doctrine, dialectics, wisdom, and pre-
dence.

78 See note 73, above. Also WA 40II, 31, 31 f.: "you should
    look patiently with hope for the righteousness that you
have now by faith, though only in an incipient and imperfect
form." ET by the Editor. Also 33, 29 f.: "They know that they
have eternal righteousness, laid up in heaven, when they are
most aware of the terrors of sin and death." LW 27, 27 (J.
Pelikan).

79 See note 74, above.

80 "Therefore when I take hold of Christ as I have been taught
    by faith in the Word of God, and when I believe in Him
with the full confidence of my heart. . . then I am righteous
through this knowledge." WA 40II, 27, 14 f. LW 27, 23 (J. Pelikan).

81 "This is the true faith of Christ and in Christ, through
    which we become members of His body, of His flesh and
of His bones. Therefore in Him we live and move and have our
being. Hence the speculation of the sectarians is in vain when
they imagine that Christ is present in us 'spiritually,' that is
speculatively, but is present really in heaven. Christ and faith
must be completely joined . . . Christ must be, live, and work
in us. But he lives and works in us, not speculatively but really,
with presence and with power (praesentissime et efficacissime)."
WA 40I, 546, 21 ff. LW 26, 357 (J. Pelikan).

82 Ibid., 21, 20 ff.

83 WA 40II, 27, 18 ff. LW 27, 23 (J. Pelikan).

84 Ibid., 24, 19 ff. LW 27, 21.

85 ". . . I am righteous here with an incipient righteousness;
    and . . . in this hope I am strengthened against sin and
look for the consummation of perfect righteousness in heaven."
Ibid., 25, 24 f. LW 27, 22 (J. Pelikan).

86 Ibid., 29, 12. LW 27, 24.

87 Ibid., 1. 20.

88 Ibid., 26, 18 f. LW 27, 22.

89 Ibid., 30, 10. LW 27, 25.

90 ". . . faith is prior to hope; for it is the beginning of life
    and begins before any tribulation, since it learns about
Christ and grasps Him without having to bear a cross. Never-

theless, cross and conflict follow immediately upon the knowledge of Christ. When this happens, the mind should be encouraged to find the fortitude of the Spirit." Ibid., 29,29 ff. LW 27, 25.

91 Explicitly at ibid., 27,18 ff.29 f. (LW 27, 23). Implicitly at ibid., 26,18 f.; 28,25 ff.; 31,25 f. (LW 27, 22.23 f.26). This victory is naturally not definitive, but turns one to a daily struggle in following Christ. Hope wins this victory only in alliance with faith.

92 Ibid., 27,29. LW 27, 24.

93 It is indicative for Luther's theological method that he does not determine the relation between the two virtues speculatively, but describes what this is in life and experience: "Haec tum recte intelliguntur, cum ad usum transferuntur." Ibid., 25,26.

94 For instance at ibid., 33,27 ff. LW 27, 27.

95 Ibid., 31,25 ff. LW 27, 26.

96 "'But I am not yet conscious of having righteousness, or at least I am only dimly conscious of it!' You are not to be conscious of having righteousness; you are to believe it." Ibid., 32,16. LW 27, 26. Even though here the fundamental reversal is the work of faith alone, still one cannot deny that the experience of faith strengthened for battle in hope is the real experience by which the greater power of the sensus peccati is broken. See also ibid., 33,19 (LW 27, 27) on hope making the spark of faith into an all-consuming fire.

97 See ibid., 30,20 ff. LW 27, 26.

98 "So these three abide: faith teaches the truth and defends it against errors and heresies; hope endures and conquers all evils, physical and spiritual; love does everything good." Ibid., 30,12 ff. LW 27, 25 (J. Pelikan).

99 Ibid., 30,14 ff. LW 27, 25 (J. Pelikan).

100 See Luther's initial remark on Galatians 5:6: WA 40II, 34,10 f. LW 27, 28.

101 See note 104, below, regarding Luther's weak attempt to differentiate between branches of scholastic theology.

102 WA 40I, 228,27 f. LW 26, 129 (J. Pelikan).

103 R. Schwarz, Fides, spes, und charitas, p. 431 f., has listed the basic secondary studies. In addition, one should consult the bibliography of the excellent article, "Charité," in Dictionnaire de Spiritualité Vol. II/I (1953), Col. 507-691. Important works on the Catholic idea of agape would also include these: M. C. D'Arcy, The Mind and Heart of Love (London: Faber and Faber, 1945); V. Warnach, Agape, Die Liebe als

Grundmotiv der neutestamentlichen Theologie (Düsseldorf: Patmos, 1951); G. Gilleman, The Primacy of Charity in Moral Theology, trans. W. F. Ryan (Westminster, Md.: Newman, 1957). For a comparison with Luther, study of the monastic theology of the 12th century and of early scholasticism (both neglected by R. Schwarz) will be fruitful. On Bernard of Clairvaux, see Bibliographie Bernardine 1891-1957 (Paris: Lethielleux, 1958). On late scholasticism: H. Oberman, The Harvest of Medieval Theology (Cambridge, Mass.: Harvard, 1963).

104 For example, WA 40I, 226, 18 f. (LW 26, 128), where Luther distinguishes the doctrine of high scholasticism from Scotus and Ockham. We should not be deceived by Luther's knowledge of the different schools, nor even less by his ability to express himself more scholastico. In reality, there is an impassible abyss between the theological mentalities of Luther and the scholastics. They battle each other with global condemnations, since they do not understand each other, even when they speak the same language and use the same terminology. Because of this, our methodological choice to omit a detailed investigation of scholastic doctrine is quite justified. For it is questionable if any basis can be found for comparing Luther and the scholastics, as R. Schwarz and R. Weijenborg ("La charité dans la première théologie de Luther," Revue de Histoire Ecclesiastique 45 [1950], 617-669) have attempted. The results of such investigations are destined from the very beginning to be negative. The method of S. Pfürtner, Luther and Thomas on Salvation (New York: Sheed and Ward, 1964), seems far better, since Pfürtner has out of his understanding of the two positions supplied the mediating interpretation necessary for dialogue.

105 For example, WA 40I, 226, 22 ff. and 227, 11 ff. LW 26, 128 f. On the Ockhamist doctrine, see R. Schwarz, Fides, spes und caritas, pp. 358 ff. and 388 ff. Also, E. Iserloh, Gnade und Eucharistie in der philosophischen Theologie des Wilhelm von Ockham (Wiesbaden: F. Steiner, 1956), pp. 104 ff. and 126 f.

106 WA 40I, 422, 18 f. LW 26, 269.

107 Ibid., 1. 28 f. LW 26, 270 (J. Pelikan).

108 Ibid., 1. 31 ff.

109 Ibid., 226, 13 ff. LW 26, 127 f. See also 303, 20 ff. and 436, 27 ff. (LW 26, 181 and 279).

110 Ibid., 424, 12 ff. LW 26, 270.

111 "In this way Paul clearly refutes the gloss made up by the sophists about a 'formed faith,' and, putting the law aside, he speaks only about faith. Once the Law has been put aside, love

is also put aside, as well as everything that belongs to the Law;
all that is kept is faith, which justifies and makes alive." Ibid.,
1.16 ff. LW 26, 270 f. (J. Pelikan).

112 Ibid., 425,21 f. LW 26, 271.

113 Ibid., 141,22 f. LW 26, 73 (J. Pelikan).

114 Ibid., 1. 21.

115 Ibid., 1. 23 f.

116 Ibid., 240,29 ff. LW 26, 137 (J. Pelikan). Again: ibid.,
446,26 (LW 26, 286). A. Nygren has interpreted these
texts onesidedly (Agape and Eros, trans. P. S. Watson [London:
SPCK, 1957], p. 720 f.), by failing to notice that Luther is attacking a love and activity that would take Christ's place, and
not the activity that is made possible for us in our union with
Christ.

117 WA 40I, 164,18 f. LW 26, 88 (J. Pelikan). Therefore, insofar as the doctrine of "formed faith" denies a faith that
grasps Christ and replaces Christ's redemption by our own works,
the attack against this doctrine becomes the pivotal Reformation
challenge. Only then is its denial the articulus stantis et cadentis
ecclesiae (so ibid., 167, 18-27 [LW 26, 90 f.]).

118 Ibid., 240,21 ff. LW 26, 137. Also 436,24 ff.; 237,25 ff.;
249,12 ff.; 252,29 ff.; 253,15 ff.; 301,31 ff.; 436,24 ff.;
606,10 ff.; and 40II, 19,25 ff. LW 26, 279.135.143.144 f.145.
180.279.398 and LW 27, 17.

119 "By faith we are in Him, and He is in us (John 6:58). This
Bridegroom, Christ, must be alone with His bride in His
private chamber, and all the family and household must be shunted
away. But later on, when the Bridegroom opens the door and comes
out, then let the servants return to take care of them and serve
them food and drink. Then let works and love begin." WA 40I,
241,11 ff. LW 26, 137 f. (J. Pelikan).

120 For example, ibid., 402,15 ff. (LW 26, 255).

121 This has been emphasized by W. Joest, Gesetz und Freiheit, p. 32 f.

122 WA 40II, 70,18 ff. LW 27, 56 (J. Pelikan). Admittedly,
by "leges" Luther could here mean ceremonial or ecclesiastical prescriptions, to which the Christian can freely submit
out of consideration for others. But Galatians 5:14 speaks of "the
whole law," which Luther said (WA 40I, 302,17 ff.) includes the
decalogue as well. A few lines after the text cited, Luther explained, making no reservations: "But above all persevere in the
doctrine of faith, which you have received from me. Afterwards,
if you want to do good works, I will show you in one word the

highest and greatest works, and the way to keep all the laws
. . ." WA 40II, 74,20 ff. LW 27, 59 (J. Pelikan).

123 WA 40I, 182,11 ff. LW 26, 99 (J. Pelikan). See also
167,20 f. LW 26, 90.

124 Ibid., 182,15 ff. LW 26, 100 (J. Pelikan). See also
213,11 ff. LW 26, 119.

125 Agape and Eros, pp. 726-733. On p. 733, Nygren speaks
of the Christian as "the channel of God's down-pouring
love."

126 Congar sees Nygren's explanation as best corresponding
to Luther's thought. "Considerations and Reflections,"
p. 379 ff., esp. p. 380, n. 28, and Christ, Our Lady and the
Church, p. 28 f. It is noteworthy that in spite of growing criticism
of Nygren, his theses on Luther have found greater acceptance
among Catholics than among Protestants. A Catholic critic of
Nygren is V. Warnach, Agape, see esp. his index, s.v. "Nygren."
Neither Joest nor Peters cite the Swedish theologian, although
their conceptions remain true to his pattern of descending divine
love.

127 WA 40II, 37,26 ff. LW 27, 30 (J. Pelikan).

128 Ibid., 62,14 ff. LW 27, 49 (J. Pelikan). See also 59,34 f.;
60,13 ff.; 144,15 f. LW 27, 48 and 113.

129 On the removal of sins: "This is grasped by faith alone,
not by love, which nevertheless must follow faith as a
kind of gratitude." WA 40I, 241,21. LW 26, 138 (J. Pelikan).

130 WA 40II, 38,9 f. LW 27, 30.

131 "Thus faith is universally the divinity in the work, the
person, and the members of the body, as the one and
only cause of justification; afterwards this is attributed to the
matter on account of the form, to the work on account of the faith."
WA 40I, 417,26 ff. LW 26, 266 (J. Pelikan). Thus, Luther feels
he has avenged the alleged degradation of faith in scholasticism.
See, for example, 422,29 ff. (LW 26, 269).

132 Ibid., 239,23 ff. and 240,14 ff. LW 26, 136 f. See Paul
Althaus' two essays on Luther's theology of charity,
given in the Appendix to his Theology of Martin Luther.

133 WA 40II, 37,26 ff. LW 27, 30.

134 Ibid., 38,5 f. LW 27, 30 (J. Pelikan).

135 At ibid., 72,13 f., Luther speaks of having treated the
commandment of love at greater length elsewhere (LW
27, 57). What he does say about it here (on Gal 5:14) contains
surprisingly traditional turns of phrase, such as these: ". . .
nor can there be a nobler or more profound attitude of the mind

than love," (ibid., 1. 16 f.) or, "love is the highest virtue. It is
ready to be of service not only with its tongue, its hands, its
money, and its abilities but with its body and its very life. It is
neither called forth by anything that one deserves nor deterred
by what is undeserving and ungrateful." Ibid., 1. 27 ff. LW 27,
58 (J. Pelikan). The ground Luther gives brings out the Protestant
conception of agape.

136 For instance, WA 40I, 253, 18 f.; 263, 28 ff.; 265, 29 ff.;
266, 15 ff.; 275, 13 f.; 287, 19 ff.; 352, 14 ff.; 573, 21 f.
LW 26, 145.153.155.161.169.220.376.

137 Ibid., 234, 19 f.; 275, 13 f.; 405, 11 ff.; 428, 17 ff.; 431, 11 ff.;
508, 34 ff.; WA 40II, 95, 11 f.; 81, 11 ff. LW 26, 133.161.
257.274.275.329; LW 27, 76.65.

138 WA 40I, 428, 17 f.; 508, 34 ff.; 529, 29 f.; WA 40II, 80, 31f.
LW 26, 273 f.329.345f. LW 27, 65.

139 This is primarily true of love of neighbor: WA 40II, 64,
25 ff.; 144, 15 ff. (LW 27, 51.113). But it also holds for
heartfelt devotion to God, in which faith takes love's place (as
we will show below).

140 WA 40II, 81, 31 ff. LW 27, 64 f. (J. Pelikan).

141 "Therefore faith is our righteousness in this present life.
In the life to come, when we shall be thoroughly cleansed
and shall be completely free of all sin and fleshly desire, we shall
have no further need of faith and hope." Ibid., 1. 13 ff. LW 27,
64 (J. Pelikan). See also WA 40I, 428, 29 ff. and 429, 12 f. (LW
26, 274).

142 We give only a few select references from Luther's
Lectures on Romans, found in WA 56. The Law's ultimate
demand is the love of God and of man (197, 7 [Pauck, 45]). Thus
works do not fulfil the Law, but only a devoted will (200, 22;
201, 3 f.; 253, 21 ff.; 255, 4 ff. [Pauck, 49.50.106.108]) or the
"voluntary" man (191, 22; 208, 10; 237, 16 [Pauck, 40.58.59]).
His love must be pure of selfseeking, as he acts gratuito or
gratuiter (241, 23; 308, 7 [Pauck, 93.163]). Thus, the real question is whether we have acted out of a pure love of God (235, 23;
236, 20; 248, 14; 258, 12; 306, 28; 357, 20 [Pauck, 86.88.101.112.
162.220]). Luther sees even more demanded from this love,
where he speaks of observing the Law "liberrima voluntate"
(338, 10; 358, 4 [Pauck, 198.221]), or "suaviter in gaudio et amore
plenissimaque voluntate" (257, 23 [Pauck, 111]), or "hilari voluntate"
(205, 21; 235, 7.23; 241, 23; 257, 23.27; 291, 11; 236, 14 [Pauck,
55.86.93.111.144 f.87]), or where the issue is "facilitas" (341, 31;
343, 1 [Pauck, 203 f.]). Luther's exposition of the demand of love

climaxes in his words on the devotion that rushes toward God "liberrime, purissime, et laetissime (341,32 [Pauck, 203]), and which would totally transform sinful concupiscence. I have treated this in my Afterword to Fénelon, Geistliche Werke (Düsseldorf: Patmos, 1961), pp. 374-387.

143 WA 40I, 431,13 ff.27 ff. LW 26, 275 f.

144 Ibid., 508,34 ff. LW 26,329.

145 Ibid., 529,29 f. LW 26, 345.

146 Ibid., 496,24 ff. LW 26, 320.

147 Ibid., 524,21 ff. LW 26, 340 f.

148 Thus understood, A. Nygren's investigation of the basic motif, and motif-research as a method, retains great significance. The special merit of Nygren's work is to have pointed out the central place of agape in Luther's thought. More recent research has to its own detriment taken very little account of and often completely neglected this insight.

149 WA 40II, 80,13 f. LW 27, 65.

150 On Galatians 5:22, Luther commented: "It would have suf-ficed to list only love, for this expands into all the fruits of the spirit. . . . Nevertheless, he wanted to list it among the fruits of the Spirit and put it in first place. Thus he wanted to exhort Christians that above all they should love one another, through love out-do one another in showing honor. . .--all this on account of the indwelling of Christ and the Holy Spirit, and on account of the Word, Baptism, and the other divine gifts which Christians have." Ibid., 117,15 ff. LW 27, 93 (J. Pelikan).

151 WA 40I, 428,20 ff. LW 26, 274 (J. Pelikan).

152 "It [faith] always justifies alone. But it is incarnate and becomes man; that is, it neither is nor remains idle or without love." Ibid., 427,13 f. LW 26, 272 (J. Pelikan).

153 WA 40II, 90,24 ff. LW 27, 72 (J. Pelikan). This state-ment gives the conclusion following from this: "But we declare it as a certainty that Christ is our principal, complete, and perfect righteousness. If there is nothing on which we can depend, still, as Paul says, these three abide: faith, hope, love." Ibid.

154 WA 40II, 37,26 ff., cited on p. 142, above.

155 Ibid., 65,17 ff. LW 27, 52.

156 Luther's fixation can be understood in the context of his polemical situation. His stress upon works and mutual love fends off the charge of idle quietism and at the same time shifts this charge to an attack on scholasticism. The exclusively

downward movement of active love serves to protect the gratuity of grace, which Luther instinctively sees endangered whenever the Law is actually fulfilled.

157 WA 40II, 94,28ff. LW 27, 75.

158 Ibid., 95,11f. LW 27, 75 (J. Pelikan).

159 Ibid., 1. 13ff.

160 Ibid., 91,21ff. LW 27, 72.

161 Ibid., 93,20f. LW 27, 74 (J. Pelikan).

162 See W. Joest, Gesetz und Freiheit, pp. 57ff. and 65ff.

163 WA 40II, 93,19f. LW 27, 74. Here the commentary on Galatians agrees essentially with Luther's exposition of Romans 7. The will now agrees with the law (WA 56, 341,20f. [Pauck, 202]); in fact for Luther its velle is the "promptitudo spiritus, quae ex charitate est" (344,24 [Pauck, 206]), but accomplishing (perficere) the law is prevented by the resistance of the flesh (342,14 [Pauck, 203]).

164 "Whoever keeps the whole law but fails in one point has become guilty of all of it." Luther cited this, his favorite verse in the despised Epistle of James, in commenting on Galatians 5:9. WA 40II, 47,15f. LW 27, 38.

165 "Therefore it is a great error to attribute justification to a love that does not exist or, if it does, is not great enough to placate God." Ibid., 80,16f. LW 27, 64 (J. Pelikan). Thus, when the fulfillment of the Law is taken into account, the contradiction disappears between the affirmations of total righteousness and partial righteousness.

166 WA 40I, 228,27. LW 26, 129.

167 See the texts given in note 118, above.

168 See, for instance, WA 40II, 79,25ff. and 80,19ff. (LW 27, 64). Also 95,16ff. (LW 27, 75). In these texts the faith that grasps Christ makes up for an imperfect love. Luther can speak as well of an imperfect faith, which, while being formal righteousness, still is weak and flawed because of the flesh. These failings though are not imputed and so they do not prevent salvation (WA 40I, 364,12-28 [LW 26, 229f.]). Similarly: 365,30ff.; 408,11ff. (LW 26, 231.260). Therefore, what Luther says about love can be affirmed in the same way about faith. This total exchange of predicates would be impossible and utterly confusing unless the two subjects were related to each other in a special manner.

169 Ibid., 535,23ff. LW 26, 349 (J. Pelikan). Similarly: 261,25f.; 262,28f.; 599,18ff. (LW 26, 151.152.393). Then, in Luther's final comment on Galatians 5:23: "Spontaneous-

ly they do what the Law requires; if not by means of perfectly holy works, then at least by means of the forgiveness of sins by faith --for Christ is the consummation of the Law for righteousness to everyone who has faith . . ." WA 40II, 121,19ff. LW 27, 96 (J. Pelikan).

170 WA 40I, 578,17ff.; 579,14f.; 598,25-30. LW 26, 379. 380.393.

171 Ibid., 275,12ff. LW 26, 161.

172 With this in mind we can fully understand Luther's battle against the idea of "unformed faith." See ibid., 422,14-30 (LW 26, 269).

173 "The good will is present, as it should be--it is, of course, the Spirit resisting the flesh--and it would rather do good, fulfill the Law, love God and the neighbor, etc. But the flesh does not obey this will but resists it." WA 40II, 95,13ff. LW 27, 75 (J. Pelikan).

174 Ibid., 79, 30. LW 27, 64.

175 Ibid., 91,22-30. LW 27, 72. See also 100,35ff. (LW 27, 80).

176 For with entry into the future life, faith and hope are at their goal and perfect justice is revealed.

177 This formulation retains, however, its practical, pastoral significance. One notes, though, that such formulations are very seldom found in the commentary on Galatians.

178 Luther's exaggerated expressions of the power of the flesh, e.g., "ut incipiamus diligere, sed valde tenuiter (WA 40II, 80,34f. [LW, 27, 65]), take nothing away from the good will and spontaneity (and the non-accomplishment) he also asserted. On the power of self-love, see ibid., 79,31f., and 85,15-25 (LW 27, 64.67f.), but also on the power of the Spirit, 98,25ff. and 99,31ff. (LW 27, 77f.79).

179 Ibid., 24,19ff. and 80,33f. LW 27, 20f.65.

180 See WA 40I, 283,26ff.; 285,24ff. (LW 26, 167.168). Also 540,17ff.: "to put on Christ according to the Gospel is a matter, not of imitation but of a new birth and a new creation." LW 26, 352. Further: 541,34f. and 546,21-38 (LW 26, 353.357).

181 See WA 40II, 95,13ff., cited above in note 173.

182 Ibid., 1. 21.

183 "Such people do not minimize sin; they emphasize it, because they know that it cannot be washed away by any such satisfactions, works, or righteousness." Ibid., 1. 22ff. LW 27, 75 (J. Pelikan).

184 Ibid., 93,20f. and 98,25ff. LW 27, 74.77.

185 For instance, 95,26 ff. (LW 27, 76), where Luther crudely
    qualifies the remaining sin as "mortal." He spoke this
way in his early works as well, but on the whole the significance
of this sin is less emphasized in the Commentary on Galatians.
The straining tension of Luther's simul is less, and thereby he
emphasizes far less the faith by why we "become sinners" in our
own eyes (as in WA 56, 231,6 ff. and 233,5 ff. [Pauck, 81.83]).

186 WA 40II, 86,14 ff. LW 27, 68.

187 The fact that Luther's deepest intention needs to be ex-
    plicated and interpreted does not weigh as an argument
against our thesis. For Protestant researchers find themselves
in the same situation. A. Peters comes to admit this: "The
tragedy of the Reformation is probably to be seen in the fact that
Luther did not fully grasp the specific character of his own point
of departure." Glaube und Werk, p. 259, n. 6. We are in a comparatively better position to interpret Luther than, say, A.
Peters and W. Joest, since we do not attempt to defend a system
built upon logically contradictory elements (see Peters, ibid.,
p. 21).

188 See WA 40I, 568 ff. (LW 26, 372 ff.) and 40II, 80,15 ff.;
    85,20 ff. (LW 27, 64.68).

189 And when these conditions are fulfilled, Luther does not
    even raise a protest against merits and rewards: "It is
no wonder, then, if merits and rewards are promised to this
incarnate faith, that is, to this working faith, such as the faith
of Abel, or to faithful works." WA 40I, 415,25 ff. LW 26, 265.

190 Gesetz und Freiheit, pp. 32 ff. and 118 ff.

191 Here we are of course not speaking of the conversion of
    Law into Gospel, nor of any blending of the two. Luther's
strong polemic against these is clear.

192 Gesetz und Freiheit, pp. 196 ff. See also p. 132.

193 Ibid., 192 ff. Also p. 52.

194 This remark sounds ironical, but is not so intended.
    Rather we are filled with both envy and admiration for
Lutheran theologians like W. Joest and A. Peters, who, while
not being exegetes, are able to undergird their complex and
subtle findings in Luther with even more subtle exegetical ex-
curses. Independently of our methodological reservations about
such an approach, our admiration turns to consternation and to
a theological opposition when the exegetical investigation of
Pauline theology finds "an intellectually insoluable contradiction."
(Joest, Gesetz und Freiheit, p. 76). Our opposition grows when
A. Peters interprets Joest's results and concludes that "the

logically contradictory becomes intelligible, in Paul and in the whole New Testament, when one seeks himself to live out the obedience of faith." (Glaube und Werk, p. 21). This is distressing, and we hesitate not to imitate Luther, not in opposing the biblical testimonies to good works, but in having recourse to the Lord of Scripture as against Scripture's interpreters. WA 40I, 458,13f. LW 26, 295. Surely Luther experienced the "contradiction" entailed in the objective dialectic posed by Scripture. But precisely because of this, he was not certain about the logical antinomy that so disturbs us in Luther's interpreters. Actually, we are facing a limit that for the sake of faith itself we are unable to cross. We feel confident that Luther as well would have taken a strong stand here. Only in holding to the paradox of the cross, not to the "logically contradictory," can we say in Luther's name that we have encountered the truth and unity of God's Word as we set out in obedience with Christ. In this sense we would want to understand W. Joest's position (e.g., Gezetz und Freiheit, p. 180). On the question of paradox, see H. Schröer, Die Denkform der Paradoxalität als theologisches Problem (Göttingen: Vandenhoeck und Ruprecht, 1960), pp. 36f. and 194ff., who refers to the simul iustus et peccator as Joest treated it in Kerygma und Dogma 1 (1955), pp. 269-320.

195 WA 40II, 80,32f. LW 27, 64f. (J. Pelikan).

196 Ibid., l. 33f. The following statement in the same context shows how unprecisely Luther can speak when the issue is charity: "Indeed, one who loved God truly and perfectly would not be able to live very long but would soon be devoured by his love." Ibid., 81,15f. LW 27, 65 (J. Pelikan).

197 Following from the previous citation: "But human nature now is so submerged in sin that it cannot think or feel anything correct about God. It does not love God; it hates Him violently." Ibid., l. 16ff.

198 Luther speaks of the monstrous "opinio iustitiae" at WA 40I, 482,22 (LW 26, 310), and then describes why God is so opposed to it: "For He is the almighty Creator, who makes everything out of nothing. In the performance of this, His natural and proper work, He does not allow himself to be interfered with by that dangerous pest, the presumption of righteousness (opinio justitiae), which refuses to be sinful, impure, miserable . . ." 488,19ff. (LW 26, 314 [J. Pelikan]). See also 499,18ff. and 517,27ff. LW 26, 322.335.

199 See the texts given in note 118, above.

200 "But once the tree has been planted, that is, once there

is the person or doer who comes into being through faith in Christ, then works follow." WA 40I, 402,19f. LW 26, 255 (J. Pelikan).

201 Ibid.

202 See the texts given in note 180, above.

203 Thus we see the positive core of the "si vultis addere." See G. Ebeling, Luther--Einführung in sein Denken (Tübingen, 1964), p. 157 ff.

204 For instance: WA 40I, 402,15f.20; 404,17; 234,21f.; 265,29ff.; 330,26f.; 351,36ff.; 352,15f. LW 26, 255f. 257.133.155.204.220.221.

205 "They want to prescribe a work before the good will, although in philosophy it is necessary for the person to be justified morally before the work. Thus the tree is prior to the fruit, both in essence and in nature. They themselves admit this and teach that in nature being precedes working and that in ethics a good will is required before the work. Only in theology do they reverse this and put a work ahead of right reason." Ibid., 410, 18ff. LW 26, 261 (J. Pelikan). See also 407,14ff. (LW 26, 259) on the hypocrisy that refuses God's blessing but strives to work out justification on its own.

206 So in explaining Galatians 5:6: ". . . that is, a faith that is neither imaginary nor hypocritical but true and living. This is what arouses and motivates good works through love. This is the equivalent of saying: 'He who wants to be a true Christian or to belong to the kingdom of Christ. But he does not truly believe if works of love do not follow his faith.'" WA 40II, 37,15f. LW 27, 30 (J. Pelikan). See also 40I, 266, 15ff. on faith without works being worthless (LW 26, 155). Therefore, according to these two texts Luther asserts that faith justifies, not because of good works, but not without the works of love that flow from truly justifying faith. As a fact, although not expressly, Luther makes Matthew 7:19 his own!

207 So Joest, Gesetz und Freiheit, p. 199.

208 WA 40II, 79,16ff. LW 27, 63.

INDEX

228